Love is the Reason for it All

The Shirley Booth Story

By Jim Manago
with Special Research by
Donna Manago

Love is the Reason for it All: The Shirley Booth Story
© 2008 Jim Manago. All Rights Reserved.

All illustrations are copyright of their respective owners, and are also reproduced here in the spirit of publicity. Whilst we have made every effort to acknowledge specific credits whenever possible, we apologize for any omissions, and will undertake every effort to make any appropriate changes in future editions of this book if necessary.

No part of this book may be reproduced in any form or by any means, electronic, mechanical, digital, photocopying or recording, except for the inclusion in a review, without permission in writing from the publisher.

Published in the USA by:
BearManor Media
P O Box 71426
Albany, Georgia 31708
www.bearmanormedia.com

ISBN 1-59393-146-8

Printed in the United States of America.

Book and cover design by Darlene Swanson of Van-garde Imagery, Inc.

Table of Contents:

Foreword by Ted Key	5
Introduction	11
Stage-Struck Kid The 1900s - early 1920s	17
Broadway Thespian, Next A Star! The mid-1920s -1930s	31
Hello, Miss Duffy The 1940s	53
Glowing With Success! The 1950s	83
Everyone's Favorite Maid The 1960s	167
Mrs. Claus' Spirit Till The End The 1970s - 1990s	221
References	245
Credits	247
Index	269

Foreword: How Hazel Came to Life

by Ted Key

It was a Thursday night, September 28, 1961. I, my wife and two friends sat in the living room of my home in Valley Forge, Pennsylvania and watched a 21-inch screen. We were looking at the first *Hazel* television show.

What goes on in the mind of a cartoonist who sees his creation come to life on TV? And not animated, but with real, flesh-and-blood characters?

It had been 19 years since the first *Hazel* cartoon appeared in *The Saturday Evening Post*. *Hazel* was not conceived as a feature. She was just one of 15 weekly cartoons that I submitted regularly to the magazine. This one was bought. A thin, round-shouldered, bleary-eyed, lumpy-nosed maid stood in the living room and addressed her employers, who had just returned home from the movies, presumably Dish Night. "A Mr. Marmon - or Harmon - called and you're to meet him tomorrow morning on the corner of Elm and South - or was it North Street - about 8 - or did he say 9 o'clock - and if you can't make it you're to phone Sycamore 8-5-7-something -4, - as it's very important."

That was November 1942. It was the first of the "Hazel's," although then she was nameless. The gag would not have sold today; it's not the way Hazel operates. Hazel today would not only get the message straight but would have gone ahead and straighten out that Harmon fellow.

Magazine cartoonists, unlike newspaper strip cartoonists, do not draw for the public. They draw for editors, and what sells. When that first maid cartoon sold, I began submitting five Hazel cartoons a week to a board of four editors. Within six months the callous-stupidity theme was shed, the name Hazel crept into one of the captions, and a responsive, spirited woman emerged. She wore a girdle. And took charge.

Now here, years later, she was being portrayed by Shirley Booth. I had never met Miss Booth until the making of the pilot film, and that occurred in February 1961, on the Columbia Pictures lot in Hollywood. Screen Gems was the production company. But I had seen and heard Miss Booth on innumerable occasions, on the stage, on the screen, on TV and radio. The scope of her talent had amazed me. She had played the wisecracking Ruth in the original stage version of *My Sister Eileen* and the poignant Leona in *The Time of the Cuckoo*. Whether it was high-mannered drawing-room comedy or a boisterous farcical musical, the melancholy, tragic Lola of *Come Back, Little Sheba*, or a TV Perle Mesta, Shirley Booth never played herself. I could think of no other actress with this dimension or versatility. I had thought, for years, that she is the greatest actress in the world. I think so now.

So how did a famous actress become interested in a cartoon character? It was simple. Bill Dozier, the production chief at Screen Gems, had shown her the script for the series' test film. And she had liked it.

She was familiar with a Hazel play I had written with a colleague, Bob Cenedella, years ago. We were radio writers on the staff of the J. Walter Thompson advertising agency in New York before World War II.

Following my discharge from the Army, I commuted to Manhattan from my Pennsylvania home for six months. The result was a three-act Hazel comedy, much too episodic in structure to be produced on Broadway but enticing enough to interest Max Gordon the producer. He said he would stage it if it were rewritten. Shirley Booth, my choice to play the role, agreed with his viewpoint: She liked the character but not the play. But I couldn't take six more months of commuting three times a week. Many years later, though Miss Booth remembered.

Alas, Bill Dozier and I were the only ones at that Columbia Pictures production meeting in Hollywood who were rooting for Shirley. She was relatively "unknown" then. The director, casting director, producer, and everyone else suggested actresses they admired to play the role. We compromised, and decided to have four screen tests made of the four chosen Hazels: Agnes Moorehead, Bibi Osterwald, Betty Field, and my Shirley.

Bill Dozier flew to Manhattan to seek out Shirley's manager, Bill McCaffrey. Dozier asked Bill to allow him to see Shirley; he had a great TV role for her. Bill said no. Shirley wasn't interested in any TV shows. None. Those were her instructions. Dozier begged. "I've come all the way across the country just to see her. If she says no, I'll leave. At least phone her." McCaffrey reluctantly got on the phone: "Bill Dozier, from Screen Gems, is here to see you, Shirley. He says he has a magnificent role for you in a TV project." It's made for you," Bill told Shirley. "What's it called?" she asked. Bill glanced at Dozier. "What's it called?" "*Hazel*," replied Dozier. "*Hazel*," Bill told Shirley. "I'll do it," she said. That was all there was to it.

So I was having an opening night after all. The stage I was now viewing, to be sure, wasn't Broadway. It was measured in inches, not yards. And no one in the audience wore a black tie. But there were millions watching, not dozens. And the artistry of a superb actress was creating the maid as I drew her and saw her. She wasn't Shirley Booth. She was Hazel. I was moved and shaken.

A cartoon character is most difficult to translate into reality for TV, stage or screen. Normally, in a play, the actress need concern herself only about the opinions of a few - the playwright, the director, the producer and, of course, herself. But a play based upon a cartoon character is something else. In Hazel's case, millions of *Post* readers were familiar with her. Each had his own opinion of what she was really like. Each had subjectively cast the part and brought to this viewing a bias. And, of course, I was bringing mine.

And there is a particularly irksome problem that confronts not only the actors in the show but the producers, the writers, the director and all those involved in making cartoon people come alive. That is, what interpretation do you give the cartoon? Is it to be a literal presentation? Are the people to look exactly like the cartoon people, nose for nose? Or is one to seek the essence, the spirit of the characters? We could go either way. With *Li'l Abner*, the musical legend leaned toward a literal treatment. We chose another course.

For instance, the way I drew George Baxter, the father in my cartoon, he is heavy set, not tall, and rather round. He wears glasses and a lot of his hair has vanished. Don DeFore, who portrays the role brilliantly, is tall, handsome, not thin but certainly not round. He has all his hair and he doesn't wear glasses. Unlike my cartoon in many ways. Yet I would swear, in watching him now on TV, that he is exactly the person I drew in the *Post*. The man's an artist. He aims for the heart of the matter, Baxter's character.

And it's this same quality, too, that Whitney Blake maintains in the role of the mother.

For many years I had drawn a maid who had never lost a battle. She was designed that way; that was the "joke." I tried to make her real and believable. But the last line always had to be hers. This placed a special burden on the producers and writers. No human being could continually top others, line after line, for almost 30 minutes and be made to appear sympathetic and credible. Invincibility had to be maintained and yet it had to be tempered.

Harry Ackerman, executive producer, and Jim Fonda, producer, wrestled with this one. A team of highly inventive writers, Bill Cowley and Peggy Chantler, was brought in to write the script. And an able director, Bill Russell. I had written a 20-page briefing of do's and don'ts, my understanding of Hazel and her family, their milieu, behavior, antecedents, characteristics, quirks and idiosyncrasies. It was mimeographed and distributed to anyone who would have a hand in the production - producers, writers, director, cameraman, casting director, set designer, hair dresser, etc. Each then studied the cartoon from his point of view and set in motion his own interpretation. But without good writing this would have been meaningless. Someone had to make Hazel walk and talk, and to invent language, style and a speech pattern for a cartoon family that had seldom, if ever, talked at all - the Baxters. Remember, since the panel's inception, it was always Hazel who'd had the lines. A magazine cartoon panel, single captioned, doesn't have the give-and-take dialogue of a newspaper comic strip. And all this had to make sense in a sympathetic storyline with Hazel, not her employers, dominating the plot. It wasn't easy. Good writers just make it seem easy. And we had them in Cowley and Chantler.

So now 19 years had passed. I remembered those who had

shown interest in *Hazel* during that long span, some as a vehicle, others as a "property": Mary Pickford, Marilyn Monroe, Thelma Ritter, David Susskind, George Gobel, 20th Century-Fox, General Electric, MCA, Four Star.

In 1945, Mary Pickford formed a film production unit with Ralph Cohn of Columbia Pictures. She wanted *Hazel* - to produce, not to star in. We never could agree on price. Ralph Cohn left Hollywood to start a TV company in New York. He called it Screen Gems.

In 1954, there was a lunch with Thelma Ritter. She wanted to play Hazel on TV. Marilyn Monroe's company would finance the production. But rights to the character weren't available. More inquiries about Hazel's rights to the character weren't available. More inquiries about Hazel's availability for TV came from 20th Century-Fox, General Electric and others. Curtis Publishing controlled the rights. Not until 1959 did Curtis permit the cartoon character to appear on television.

Then David Susskind's Talent Associates, Gobel's Gomalco Company and Screen Gems all submitted plans for a half-hour situation comedy. Others wanted it. Talent Associates thought Audrey Meadows would make an ideal Hazel. Gomalco had Ann Davis in mind. Both companies would make pilot films. Screen Gems would commit itself only to a pilot script; then a pilot film, if the script problem could be licked. To us, this made sense. We joined forces and we were on our way.

It has been a very pleasant journey.

Introduction

Sometimes the best things in life seem to come by accident. However, as I've seen many times in my life, there are few accidents.

It seems I discovered the impressive diversity and acting skill of Shirley Booth quite by accident. My familiarity with Booth came from viewing reruns of *Hazel* in the late 1960s on a New York local television station (perhaps it was WPIX Channel 11). Along with *The Munsters, I Love Lucy*, The Three Stooges, Abbott and Costello, Laurel & Hardy, and a dozen or so other television programs, my after school viewing habits included watching a funny maid named Hazel.

Hazel stood out from every other show I watched. She amused me as that smart, sassy take-charge woman that seemed to always get her way. By comparison, Lucy always compromised somehow or got her comeuppance for trying to upstage or outsmart Ricky. Things did not always work out for Lucy. However, Hazel stood her ground and won out. I admired her unique common sense wisdom. Hazel's way of doing something may have seemed quirky to Mr. Baxter or Missy, but she had common-sense wisdom that changed things for the better. In short, I quickly came to love the self-assured character of Hazel.

What seemed to be an accident one day, perhaps when I was about fourteen years old, I saw a television listing for a Shirley Booth movie called *Come Back, Little Sheba*. I watched it - expecting the Hazel character and realizing quickly how different the character of Lola was. Lola opened up to me another aspect to Shirley Booth that I was completely unaware of. To my amazement, I learned from one of my film books that this *Sheba* actually celebrated on film Booth's first love and real home; namely, the theater. This other side to Shirley Booth captivated me. I wanted to see more of her non-*Hazel* roles.

After viewing Booth playing Lola, I learned of the incredible range of this gifted actress. Unfortunately, to my dismay, Booth's Broadway or stock theater performances were not filmed as far as I could determine. So the closest I could ever come to understanding the critics' considerable esteem for her is the audio from a few cast albums that were made.

Just a sample of Booth's delightful singing on the cast album for *A Tree Grows in Brooklyn* is enough to wish there was a time machine so that I could have been there in the audience of that and so many of her other Broadway shows.

Although I completed a Master's degree in Cinema Studies, and had written dozens of articles and columns on movies, and studied the careers of many in the business, the thought that someday I would be Shirley Booth's biographer never came to mind. That too seemed to come by accident.

At the 2004 Friends of Old Time Radio Convention in Newark, New Jersey, I met up with publisher Ben Ohmart. A conversation developed as Ben showed me a list of upcoming books his company intended to publish. I responded to the name of Shirley Booth on his list by asking, "Who's writing that? He replied, "Why, are you interested?" From that moment on, my involvement quickly grew . . . Inevitably, I agreed to do Shirley's biography.

My fascination with Daniel Defoe's novel *Robinson Crusoe*, and the notion of divine providence suggested therein, entails that seeming accidents may not be accidents at all, but divinely chosen events. This is a matter of faith. I'm certain that Shirley Booth's life was no accident. She was meant to be. And thank heaven for that! Regrettably, I did not have the opportunity to meet her in person. With this project, I have learned much about Shirley Booth by reading hundreds of pages of interviews, reviews, and articles. This has made me appreciate her phenomenal natural talent so much more.

In my research, I discovered that Shirley's own scrapbooks reside in the Museum of the City of New York's Theater Collection. Thanks to the Museum for conserving these materials. Unfortunately, their reproduction and permission charges to publish letters and photographs made their one-of-a-kind items impossible for me to include here. In short, I had to do without the aesthetic enhancement those items would have provided. That made my labor of love even more challenging.

However, I do wish to thank those that did not stifle this project, but generously assisted me. Thanks to the staff at the Billy Rose Theater Collection and the New York Public Library, The Paley Center for Media (formerly The Museum of Television and Radio), Randy Bonneville for reviewing and updating the television credits, Bob Burchett and Gary Mercer for the radio shows, Charles Stumpf, Martin Grams, Jr., Prof. Barbara Appleby (St. John's University, NY), Franklin Baer from CreativeQuotations.com, and all those individuals that interviewed Shirley Booth in published excerpts herein.

Special thanks to Kevin Minton for his permission to reprint many valuable interviews he conducted with those who knew Booth, most now no longer with us. As a youngster living in Starke, Florida, Kevin had the courage to first contact Booth by phone in 1973 by looking her up with the help of directory assistance under her married name of Mrs. W. H. Baker or Shirley B. Baker in LaQuinta, California. Kevin's fondness for Miss Booth deserves particular admiration.

And a BIG thanks to Thomas J. Watson for providing many of the photos, a last minute, unexpected surprise!

Ann Jillian, Joyce Van Patten, her brother Dick Van Patten, and Martha Randall all provided wonderful assistance. I offer a very special thanks to Elizabeth Wilson for her interest and support. Unfortunately, Julie Harris' physical condition precluded her from offering a detailed interview. However, her statement is greatly appreciated. Many thanks!

I owe much gratitude to Ted Key, the creator of *Hazel*, for elucidating his character in material provided so thoroughly that my chapter on the show is largely his own words.

With only several weeks before submission of this manuscript, my computer burned out. To my rescue came a real friend, Sandy Bernstein, business manager for *The Wave*, a paper I worked at as an editorial assistant several years back. My thanks to Susan Locke, the publisher, for giving me her computer to finish this project.

And with only three days before the manuscript was officially due, my apartment was burglarized. A copy of the manuscript was stolen. More importantly, all the artwork assembled over the past two years (stills, theatre programs and clippings), some of it on loan, was taken. So began the search for more artwork.

Through all of this, there is one person who could not be overlooked since he has offered so much more than normal assistance to this project. For over 20 years, he has provided positive energy to me both professionally and personally. A very special thanks to Joe Franklin for his extraordinary interest and friendship.

While working on this project with me, my darling wife Donna came to one very important realization: "Shirley Booth did not allow her personal sorrows to overshadow her performances." How true that is! I thank Donna for her research assistance and love throughout this project.

And last but not least, my thanks to my mother Marie and to my late father Joseph for cultivating my interest in the movies at a very young age.

When asked to define herself, Booth responded, "Well, I would say that I was an enigma." This book is a fervent attempt to unravel some of Booth's enigma. However, many of those that knew her personally or who worked with her are deceased. Some of the few survivors, perhaps due to their advanced age, poor health, and/or disinterest, have not been willing to participate at all in this biography. Thus, I quickly learned the immense difficulty and problems inherent in trying to fairly capture and summarize 94 years of living into the confines of a 200-page book, especially with the limitations of obtaining, verifying, and selecting information. Nonetheless, whatever life this book takes on, my intention has always been to be as accurate as humanly possible and stay true to the essence of Shirley Booth's impressive life. I have never been a fan of tell-all scandal sheet biographies, which actively seek out sensational anecdotes and rumors to shock readers as well as to taint, wreck or destroy a person's good name. Much of the time, such biographies are geared to increasing the sale of books. I have sought a higher ground by balancing the need and right for the public to know the truth with a reasonable scale of verification to substantiate information and be fair to the deceased. As a result, I believe I have honored and respected Shirley Booth.

Anyone with further information regarding Shirley Booth is welcome to contact me in care of the publisher for future publications. The ultimate tribute will be when Shirley Booth's story is depicted on Broadway where she devoted so much of her time and energy. Until then, it is hoped this biography will serve her memory well.

Shirley Booth once said, "I feel sorry for people that don't have the pleasure of acting because I think it's a great release." I experienced that pleasure whenever my cousin Joseph Nizzari would visit my family in Richmond Hill, New York. He encouraged and indulged my interest in acting and cinematography by recreating Abbott & Costello routines, gangster movie skits, and so forth. I wish he could have lived to see this book in print. With much sadness, I dedicate this book in memory of him.

I learned many things while researching this book, one message in particular: Despite the numerous difficulties engendered on the bumpy road of life, there is always the possibility that success and good results from a life lived with passion and love. Shirley Booth's life is such a story. . . .

May this book inspire both young and old. May this book reawaken warm and joyful memories for some that lived during her heyday. Finally, may this book significantly memorialize the ever-popular and always charming Shirley Booth - a real trouper with her own unique contribution to the world of entertainment.

Jim Manago

Stage-Struck Kid
The 1900s – early 1920s

The Hollywood Walk of Fame has a star for her at 6840 Hollywood Boulevard. If not for that, she might be unknown or forgotten by most people. The caption on a drawing by Robert Greenhalgh said: "SHIRLEY BOOTH - in a puzzling, uncertain modern world, she personifies a warm-hearted, open creature we can trust." Indeed, she had a glow and sincerity all her own.

Yet, Shirley Booth's life was troubled and full of disappointments. As a child, her father's harsh personality crushed her spirit. Shy and alone, her imagination helped to fill the void. She played pretend games with her sister. Booth acted like she was "such unusual objects such as a clock, a cat, a bedspread or anything else that needed imagining or animation."*

Booth: "Nothing has ever come easy for me anyway. From the very beginning my parents were set against my going on the stage and what coaching I got had to be kept from their ears."

As an adult, if she did not spend her time acting, she spent most of it alone despite two marriages - divorced by her first husband, widowed by the sudden death of her beloved second husband.

---
*Jessyca Russell Gaver.

For over fifty years, starting as a teenager, she had a passionate love affair with audiences everywhere. Always living for and loving applause, she never really stopped performing. Producer George Abbott asked, "How can there be any better when she's perfect?"

On Broadway for over two hundred and fifty times in 1951, she exuberantly sang "Love Is the Reason For It All." This delightful song humorously recognizes the reality of love; if it says anything, it tells of the trouble love causes. If something could explain why Shirley Booth went through all the troubles of her life, and why she gave so much of herself as a performer, then this might be it. Audiences loved her, and this resulted from her intense love for audiences. Her need for love and her wish to give love is truly the reason for her whole career.

Shirley Booth's appearance seemed quite ordinary. She stood merely five feet three and one half inches, had brown eyes and brunette hair. Her gabby characters spoke with an amusing twang; "her funny, cracked voice," as one critic called it. However, the truth is that Shirley Booth stood above the ordinary. To theater, radio, movie, and television audiences everywhere, Booth had an exceptional gift to entertain, especially to make people laugh.

The personality traits common to many of the characters Booth excelled at included being sassy, salty, wisecracking, plucky, forthright, lively, exuberant, and easygoing. Although she never went to a school to study acting, Booth succeeded as a consummate and dedicated professional, expertly handling drama, light comedy, and musical comedy equally well. She excelled in most anything she did. Most importantly, she became critically acclaimed as the finest actress in the theater.

If Booth gets any mention in theater literature, it is primarily for playing the "slovenly" wife Lola in her tour de force of acting, *Come Back, Little Sheba*. Her other great achievement playing the title character on the television show *Hazel*, draws the rest of the attention.

But the endearing Shirley Booth accomplished so much more. She appeared in over thirty Broadway shows creating distinctive and vastly different characters, toured the country performing thousands of times in over 600 stock theatre productions. She made dozens of radio show appearances, including a regular role for three seasons as the sassy and nitwitted Miss Duffy in *Duffy's Tavern*. She starred in four movies and made an appearance in another. Booth made numerous television appearances.

But if she had done nothing else other than playing the title character in the television series *Hazel*, Booth provided a lasting impression on millions of people during the first half of the 1960s. In addition, her voice work included the memorable voice of Mrs. Santa Claus in the delightful Rankin-Bass classic that still airs regularly each holiday season.

At her peak, Booth earned acclaim, winning every major acting award, including an Oscar, three Tonys, two Emmys and numerous other awards. All of this accomplished without ever receiving any formal dramatic training or schooling.

As an "actor's actor," she once said, "Actors should be overheard, not listened to, and the audience is 50 percent of the performance."*

If anything, this indicates Booth's unwillingness to take all the credit for her great success. This is so typical of Shirley Booth.

The *New York Times* critic Brooks Atkinson's review of the Broadway show *By the Beautiful Sea* could have applied to any of her shows: "The stage begins to glow the moment she steps on it and the audience melts, like a crowd of children whose imagination has been captured by someone they trust."

---

*News summary, December 13, 1954, recorded in *Simpson's Contemporary Quotations* (1988).

She continually worked as a character actress by doing her all to satisfy audiences. Booth's acting involved the audience. She told Earl Wilson: "Sometimes you do so much the audience has nothing to do. The actress should stimulate the audience to use its imagination. When I play a drunk scene, I try to underplay it and let the audience sense the turmoil the woman is in."

Audience response was basic to Booth. She told the *Philadelphia Inquirer Magazine* at the height of her success in 1951: "When you come on stage, you must throw out your antenna to the audience because an audience is the best monitor in the world." In short, Booth took seriously the dictum: "Know Your Audience."

Booth: "I'm lucky. I play characters, not types. I don't care what the part is as long as it's a person I'm interested in, someone I want to introduce to people." Once she worked the role out, Booth would not change her performance for the sake of either the audience or the other actors. "First, if it's finally right, there's no point in changing it," Booth told Jon Whitcomb. "And I have a duty to the audience to give them the performance they've read reviews about. Moreover, it's only fair to the other actors to play it the way we've rehearsed it. You can't have a horse race with only one horse."

To understand how this truly revered, versatile and energetic actress and star of stage, screen, radio and television, did it all with an inimitable zest and energy is to know passion. It was a long and arduous road before she would reach her rainbow. Shirley Booth labored diligently for many years in the resident stock theater and then for many years on the Broadway stage. She shined even in all the shows that were "turkeys." It took years of demanding work before she became the endearing, award-winning actress and star. What she had more than anything was a great passion for acting throughout her life, starting when she was still a child. For as long as she can remember, Booth always wanted to be an actress.

Although her success made it possible for Booth to indulge herself with material things, this ultimately did not motivate her. Even after winning awards for stage and screen, and poised to make millions of dollars as television's maid Hazel, Shirley said in an interview, "Jewels and other physical possessions are meaningless to me." In short, the love of acting apparently filled and fulfilled her immensely.

No stranger to disappointments in her career, Shirley appeared in shows that ultimately failed or ended too quickly. She chose not to remember: "That's why I'm so happy. I forget my failures." However, Shirley rarely could be faulted. Mediocre writing or other factors could be blamed. Booth's stage acting got high marks from most critics and audiences throughout her long career. Walter Kerr, *New York Herald Tribune* critic, expressed the problem as such: "What I really long for, in my secret heart, is the day I can write a review saying that the play was wonderful but Shirley Booth was terrible. I know it's a silly dream, but how are we to go on this way - endless Valentines for the girl we all love, and endless outrage for all the lulus in which she appears?"

Although it took about thirty years before she had her first huge success, it did not seem to matter much to Booth. It was always only about acting, even from the beginning. Booth worked through the many lean years and she had the patience to keep at it. She told the International News Service: "I am a girl who believes that anything I can't get for myself, I can do without."

Booth told *The Theater's* Morris Gelman: "I have the average woman appeal. I'm not terribly different. I symbolize the average woman with the same frailties; the audience can identify with me."

Information about Shirley Booth's birth name is confusing. Despite the database searches showing a "Thelma Marjorie Ford," and biographies offering Booth's original name as "Thelma Marjorie Ford" or "Thelma Booth Ford," the actual birth certificate record is of a "Marjory Ford."

Marjory was born on August 30, 1898, to Albert James Ford, age 26, and the former Virginia Wright, age 23, at 305 West 118 Street in the Morningside Heights section of upper Manhattan, in New York City. Her parents baptized her at Trinity Church in Manhattan.

In addition, throughout her career, Booth's birth date is often incorrectly given as 1907. Apparently, she changed her age early in her career to make herself nine years younger. Thus, magazine articles will wrongly note that Shirley Booth made her debut on Broadway at not yet eighteen years old. In actuality, she involved herself in stock theater at that time. When she made movies in Hollywood in the 1950s, Booth apparently got even younger; she was now born in 1911 - thirteen years later than her actual birth.

Different accounts have been given regarding Booth's first public performance. Booth revealed that her first public performance was singing the song "In the Good Old Summertime" at Sunday School. **Booth:** "I was just two years old and was the star of the church entertainment in Flatbush." Interestingly, she later sang this melody again on Broadway in *By the Beautiful Sea*, one of her musical successes.

Another account contends that Booth's first appearance occurred later while attending P.S. 152 in the Flatbush section of Brooklyn. There she read in class her Thanksgiving composition entitled, "The Autobiography of a Thanksgiving Turkey." Booth delighted her classmates with impersonations and recitations.

The middle-class family moved to five different homes during Shirley's childhood. They lived in the Flatbush section of Brooklyn, New York early on. Booth said that when she was seven years old she lived in a hotel in downtown Philadelphia while the Fords searched for a house.

Booth told the *Philadelphia Inquirer*: " . . . We shared our table in the dining room with another man. When I found out he was an actor, I began asking him a hundred questions. But my parents quickly interrupted, explaining that I was just another stage-struck kid."

Then her father's work as a district manager for International Business Machines Corp. (I.B.M.) entailed a move to Hartford, Connecticut by the time she was twelve. Shirley's relationship to her father apparently was a strained one. She was at odds with him from early in life. Albert Ford has been described as an austere, cold-hearted, and reserved businessman, quite different from her tender, loving, and expressive mother.

Booth: "He was the kind of man you'd run up to breathless and happy . . . and he'd say, 'Don't touch me, your hands are dirty.'" He supposedly ridiculed her stutter. In addition, her parents' marriage was fraught with difficulties, which eventually led to their separation when Booth was a teenager.

She explained her relationship as follows: "Well, I had a divided allegiance to my father and mother. I was an only child until I was 12 years old and I think you're pretty well set in your mode of thinking by that time. And I had definitely lined myself up with my mother against my father." When asked why she did that, Booth replied, "I had plenty of instances but I don't want this to be a soap opera particularly."

Later on, even when famous, Shirley still would never speak to him. The Fords had a second daughter named Jean Valentine Ford. After her parents' divorce, Booth's father remarried. Shirley's sister Jean and her stepmother Rita tried to reconcile Shirley to her father to no avail. Nevertheless, it did not change a thing. The pain of those early years, especially the alleged mistreatment by her father toward her mom and herself, left an indelible space between them.

Shirley's sister (the late Mrs. Jean F. Coe) reluctantly shared just two memories about her sister Shirley to Kevin Minton: "Shirley always had a passion for changing the furniture in rooms. One day when Mother was downtown, she moved all the furniture (including the baby grand piano) from the living room across the hall to the dining room and the dining room over to the living room. When Mother came home, she thought she was in the wrong house and walked out."

Coe continued: "One more comes to mind. One day when Shirley was about five or six, she was dressing up with a long train flowing out behind her. Mother asked her who she was supposed to be. When Shirley said, 'A king,' Mother said, 'Kings don't wear trains.' To which Shirley replied, 'This king does!' As you can see, even at an early age, she always led, never followed the crowd."

Her upbringing included the perspective that children should be seen and not heard. In her senior years, Booth may have seen something positive amidst the negativity of her early years: "Well this is the way I was trained. Not many children were trained this way but I had an English father who did not believe in children monopolizing the conversation at the table. I think he was right. I think all discipline is good for children."

It is at the time she lived in Philadelphia that Booth remembers meeting up with a family friend. One Sunday, Mr. J. Hammond Daly, who happened to be a stock company actor, and his actress wife, visited the Booths. "I let the Dalys finish their soup before I began bombarding them with questions that time." An eager young Shirley managed to get her parents to agree to allow her to get involved in the stock theater.

Mr. Daly arranged Booth's debut. Apparently, Booth's mother gave consent for Shirley to contact the casting director for the Sylvester Poli's Stock Theater Company. The Poli Players, also known as Poli Repertory's Players, had operated in Hartford, Connecticut. Here Booth learned to read plays and to perform some small children's parts in the company's matinee shows.

In 1881, at the age of 23, Sylvester Z. Poli arrived in America from Italy. Poli, as a resident of New Haven, Connecticut, started the theater company around 1907. His business consisted of a huge chain of theaters in which stock theater performances were offered to the public. Poli's string of theaters were located in cities such as Hartford, Connecticut; Springfield, Massachusetts; Scranton, Pennsylvania; Washington, D.C., etc. In 1927, Poli sold the theater chain to Fox Enterprises for 30 million dollars.

With Mr. Daly's help, Booth's first appearance occurred in the stock company's production of *Mother Carey's Chickens* when she stepped on the stage at the tender age of 12 years old.

Mr. Ford did not appreciate Shirley's theatrical aspirations at all. He certainly did not want his daughter to be on stage and act. However, Booth quit school at age twelve and started acting. Another account has her dropping out of high school at around 14 years old against her father's wishes.

In addition, her father did not want her to use her family name. No, he did not want his name associated at all with the theatre. One night he did appear at the company's dressing room. Booth expected that he would force her to return home. **Booth:** "All right, I'll pack up and go home." Instead, Booth's father said, "Oh, no you won't. You're staying here till you're fed up with acting."

Nat Dorfman later would tell it this way: "With her mother's secret consent she sought out the casting director for the Poli circuit and after many tries he finally agreed to cast her in a few tiny parts in the Hartford stock company. Her father stamped his paternal foot and swore that he'd never speak to her again and Shirley was resigned to a horror of being disowned. However, several months later she did some careful detective work and discovered that he had been sneaking into the theatre several times a week, with various business friends, to see his daughter perform. When he was confronted with this, he admitted the truth and the air was cleared for future theatrical conquests."

Later on, Booth would declare, "It takes courage and fortitude. And maybe a family that's dead set against the stage as a career so there can be no turning back if only to prove them wrong." Because of her harsh upbringing, Booth developed the determination to succeed no matter how difficult acting proved to be at times.

Marjory Ford, so as not to embarrass her family, changed her name to Shirley Booth. The problem is Booth said this name change happened when she graduated high school in Brooklyn, and thence she went to Hartford to work as an actress for a stock company.

Booth claimed in an interview that she got the name "Shirley" from the character of Shirley Rossmore in *The Lion and the Mouse*. *

Some press releases from Booth's agent, Barry Hyams, offered more confusion, noting that Shirley was "daughter of Ford and Shirley (Wright) Booth, christened Thelma Booth."

Nat Dorfman's press release from around December 1940 indicated that the name Shirley came from "one of the wispy ingénues she played in stock called 'Shirley Rossmore.'" Supposedly,

---

*A movie version with that character appeared in 1919, which starred Alice Joyce. Known as "The Madonna of the Screen," Joyce became a leading lady during the silent era, reaching her peak in 1920s feature films. She started out doing shorts for the Kalem Studios, later purchased by Vitagraph Studios.

Joyce played Shirley Rossmore, a Federal judge's daughter, who tries to prove her father is innocent of alleged conflict of interests in one of his rulings. Since Booth's name change occurred earlier than this 1919 film, it could not have been that Booth took it from the film.

Later, May McAvoy, standing only 4 feet 11 inches, did a remake of *The Lion and the Mouse* in 1928. The daughter's name in this remake changed to Shirley Ross.

she tried several names before calling herself "Shirley Booth." Dorfman claimed "Selma Ford" was her real name, and "Booth" a middle name.

Booth's statement on the origin of her name includes the claim that she effected her name change after high school. Yet the information circulating says she quit high school to work for Poli's Stock Company between 1912 and 1914. Dorfman noted that the family returned to New York so Booth could attend Erasmus Hall High School. Erasmus' prize dramatic pupil, notes Dorfman, was none other than Shirley Booth! She graduated in 1916, according to school records. However, it seems to make sense that she must have taken "Shirley" from a stage production as the Dorfman press release says.

Although Booth herself said, in that same interview, that her real name was 'Thelma Booth Ford," birth records do confirm a ""Marjory Ford." Hollywood columnist Myrtle Gebhart reported once that the "Booth" came from Shirley's godmother. This means that Booth used her christened name when referring to her original name, and not her birth certificate name of "Marjory Ford."

Nonetheless, as far as her year of birth, this same columnist mistakenly gave it as 1911 - a full 13 years after her real birth year.

Shirley got her first work as an actress with a stock company. The stock company consisted of an essentially permanent group of actors performing various plays for a limited time. In the beginning, they had ensembles of players held in high regard. However, by the time Booth entered this world of stock theatre, the practice of open casting allowed beginners and mediocre actors to act in shows performed by the best theatres from past seasons. The Wallack family launched the stock theatre ensembles in America during the 1850s. Later, Booth's first work on Broadway was at Wallack's NY theatre.

Mrs. Ford went against her husband's wishes and sent Shirley to New York when she was 14 to stay with an aunt who suggested she work for $35 a week with the Poli's Stock Company's acting troupe unit in New Haven. In other words, Booth left Hartford to go to New York to find a job. The job she got was in New Haven - not that far from Hartford.

Booth's two-week tryout in New Haven as an ingénue became a 35-week job. Accordingly, Booth came to be the only actor staying that long with the company. Then she returned to New York to start another job, but it failed to materialize. After several weeks, she left to do more stock work. Booth toured through many small East Coast towns with Poli's Stock Company in Poli's chain of theaters. She traveled to cities such as Rochester, Syracuse, Albany, Springfield, Louisville, Toronto, Portland, Milwaukee, Kansas City, and Cincinnati - all except New York.

Ultimately, Booth would play stock all over, including in the West and Southwest United States, and Canada.

Booth: "The critics haven't always been kind to me. When I was doing stock in Toronto, a Canadian critic really panned my performance."

Some of her stock theater stage credits included *Scandal*, in which Booth played Beatrice Vanderdyke, the bride in *La La Lucille*, and as Patricia O'Day in *Little Old New York*. In the musical *Pitter Patter*, an Albany reviewer indicated, "Miss Booth proved to be the Caruso and Melba of the organization." The Rochester critic noted, "Miss Booth has wonderful judgment of finesse. Her work is so natural that she makes you forget she is acting." In short, Booth impressed the critics and seemed to excel as an actress from the start of her career.

Later theater cast credits in 1940s revealed that Booth had played a 74-year-old woman in a Hartford stock company production when she was fourteen.

Booth: "At sixteen, I was working hard at the profession I had chosen, and have never swerved from. I started at twelve, with only one idea in mind, and this idea has grown into a career that never, at any time, has failed to hold my interest and enthusiasm. This is because I have given most of my love, all of my time, and 80 percent of my vitality to it. Mine is a profession which must be your work and play combined, because if you really expect to succeed you must give it every waking moment. But it's worth it."

Booth told Earl Wilson about her mother, Virginia Wright Ford: "She used to say there was no such thing as standing still . . . you're either going forward or backward." Her mother also taught her: "Don't show your emotions in public," according to an interview with *TV Guide*.

Although she had been acting for several years now, sometime between 1921 and 1923, Booth had what was billed as her "first role or formal debut as a professional actress" in the thriller *The Cat and The Canary* in a Hartford, Connecticut production. She played the frightened heroine. She stayed in New Haven through 1922, playing in stock theater. [Broadway had a production of this show in 1922.]

Dorfman noted that "Shirley Booth devoted her time exclusively to stock engagements, with the result that she became one of the most widely traveled young woman in the theatre. Still, she was reluctant to try her luck in New York - mainly because she was known on the road and was used to good parts and hated starting afresh in Manhattan in a small part."

Her appearance in small stock roles continued to give her invaluable experience until a fortuitous opportunity came along.

After Booth substituted for one of the leads that took ill, she got more featured parts. From 1921 to 1925 Booth worked the stock theatre circuit. Inevitably, a New York agent caught her in a summer performance, liked Booth, and signed her.

Years later, when she became a known star, Booth would reveal her understanding of the training an actor must undergo. Shirley Booth wrote in a bylined article: "Whenever a young aspiring actress or actor comes to me for advice, I always tell them the best way I know to thoroughly learn the profession is to study people.

"It is very important to know the technique of acting, to master the intricacies of speech, posture and movement, but you must also learn about people, absorb their characteristics and know what it is that makes them tick. Remember, you may be cast to portray just such a character as you've studied in real life. And what a head start you've got, thanks to your being observant!

"I try to keep a mental notebook of the mannerisms, odd inflections, appealing facial expressions not only of friends, but of strangers, as well. It's these tell-tale details, such as a slight twitch of the mouth, a rubbing of the chin, the shifting of the feet, the fumbling of the hands, that I recall, select and often use in rounding out a character I am about to play.

"A successful actor or actress is always in class. But it's a classroom not bound by four walls. It can be any place. The street, the seashore, a restaurant, a crowded theater lobby between acts, or a noisy cocktail party. Knowing people doesn't come solely from books, but also from close observance of people and their individual characteristics."

Broadway Thespian, Next a Star
The mid-1920s – 1930s

Booth's stock theatre touring eventually led her to Broadway. Her career here consisted of 31 shows; five of them were musicals, most of the rest were comedies. At the high point of her career in the 1950s, Booth expressed the view that "the challenge to talent is much greater in comedy than drama. Nothing can kill a tear if the play is worth it; but anything, even a cough in the audience, can spoil a laugh."

Little is known about many of Booth's early appearances on Broadway. Whatever is known comes from the limited mention of her name in theater reviews of the period. Although many of the shows ended briefly, Booth reached a point in the late 1930s when she seemed to select parts in successful shows, which offered long runs.

Herman Gantvoort found her work impressive enough, based on notices from his hometown of Cincinnati, to sign Booth for her first Broadway production. She made her Broadway debut on January 26, 1925 in an original play called *Hell's Bells*, written by Barry Conners. Booth played Nan Winchester, one of two unconcerned sisters, going through an about face when they believe their adventurer brother is now prosperous. This supporting role presented Booth as a slim ingénue cast opposite her love interest; namely, the character of Jimmy Todhunter, played by, the then unknown, Humphrey Bogart. Interestingly, Booth commented over twenty-five years later, "I especially ducked when Bogie tried to kiss me. Don't ask me why. There was just something about the man."

Hell's Bells ran for only four months with 120 performances at the Wallack's Theatre. *The New York Times* reviewer noted that although many found it quite funny on opening night, it is "much funnier in the imagination.... The piece is of the stage, stagey. Its situations are artificial... Humphrey Bogart, Shirley Booth and Olive May did their best with stock roles."

Drama critic John Mason Brown acknowledged that Booth "followed *Hell's Bells* in a series of plays, many of which closed so swiftly that only the more agile theatergoers got to see her." Actually, the fact is that, with the exception of her next play, Booth appeared in eight more shows running for 40 or less performances, except one play with 80 performances.

Booth once said that nine of her shows "closed before theatergoers got to see me." This claim could not be substantiated. Even though she did get second lead in the shows that followed *Hell's Bells*, Booth continued to go on the road acting in every possible role in stock theater productions. Thus, she alternated between starring roles in stock theater with supporting player parts in Broadway shows over the next ten years, until around 1935.

Though the theatrical parts to follow were by no means substantial, Booth could still rejoice that she finally was appearing in Broadway productions.

Her next show, *Laff That Off*, presented by Earl Carroll, opened on November 2, 1925 at the Wallack's Theatre before moving to the 39th Street Theatre in December. Don Mullally wrote this enjoyable comedy with not much of a plot about three bachelors and a girl. Act One takes place in the living room of a bachelor apartment occupied by three boys during mid-September, 1916. Act Two takes place eight months later. Act Three occurs on Christmas Eve, 1918. Booth played a waif named Peggy Bryant in love with Leo Mitchell (Alan Bunce).

Although the *World* critic considered the play's acting to be "uneven" and "At times all the cast seemed terrible . . . Shirley Booth, as the girl befriended by the triumvirate of friends, carries off the honors because she is consistent and her performance is even."

"The best work was done by Shirley Booth as the nice little thing whom we all loved," according to Alan Dale. "She played with discretion and charm."

Laff That Off ran for 263 performances, and closed on January 2, 1926. Booth's next Broadway role was *Buy, Buy, Baby*, which opened at the Princess Theatre on October 7, 1926. The show told of three couples that have a chance at a big fortune, provided an heir is born. Although *The New York Times* gave the cast of this farce a favorable review, the show closed after a meager dozen performances.

At this point, she even went on the road to Kansas City.

Back at the Wallack's Theatre on Broadway almost a year later, another farce, *High Gear*, did not do much better with twenty shows. Chaos ensues for a wife who misleads her uncle that she is affluent. When he visits, she has to fake her status. At least this time, Booth is mentioned in *The New York Times* review. "As the fluttery and wide-eyed young wife, Shirley Booth contributes a acceptable performance in a role that easily might be made to seem more silly than it is."

Walter Winchell called *High Gear* "an incoherent tale at times and probably fashioned for the adolescents . . . It is strictly Grade B minus entertainment, and only the performance of Miss Booth is worthwhile."

On September 24, 1928, the National Theatre opened *The War Song*. Despite the title, this show was mostly a comedy about a Jewish draftee Eddie Rosen in World War I France played by George Jessel, who also co-wrote the production. Booth played the expectant mother Emily Rosen, Eddie's unwedded sister.

Albert Lewis and Sam H. Harris produced *The War Song* in three acts. Act One took place in the home of the Rosens' in New York City in September of 1917. Act Two began seven weeks later in the orderly room of Camp Upton in Yaphank, Long Island. Act Three had three scenes; an entertainment hut in the back of the lines somewhere in France six months later, a shell hole two days later, and the officers' quarters inside the German lines about three hours later.

Although Booth is not mentioned, comments by an unknown writer in an unpublished note from the Shubert Archives offered a brief assessment of the production: "The program states that this is a comedy-drama. It is but from that standpoint only a fair one. There is comedy. There is pathos, and there is near tragedy. The authors push a little realism in also. The only trouble is that instead of having the above-mentioned qualities evenly divided, each has its own scene, a rather poor arrangement.

"The producers are to be commended for having the German officers speak only in German, except through an interpreter. This however caused a great deal of restlessness in the audience. This German dialogue should be cut to a minimum. The shell-hole scene is very well done. As a whole the play is good for all Jessel admirers. It does not compare to *The Jazz Singer*.'"

The War Song lasted until December 1, 1928 with 80 performances.

Booth supposedly met a wisecracking salesman named Edward Poggenberg (also spelled Peggenburg) at a theatre director's home around this time. Born June 29, 1901, in Astoria, New York, Ed had worked in many capacities, including briefly as a fight manager, and a pianist. As a salesman he sold practically everything, including miniature golf courses, paint, pianos, and typewriters. He changed his last name to Gardner, and become involved in the theatre, apparently, at Shirley's urging. Booth married Gardner after the opening of *Claire Adams* on November 23, 1929. Then Gardner got into directing for the WPA Federal Theatre Project.

Apparently, their marriage started with Ed's infidelity. As told in his autobiography *So Far, So Funny*, screenwriter Hal Kanter revealed: "On their first night at sea, Shirley caught Ed stealing out of another woman's stateroom. 'Now you know the truth,' he said. 'I'm an international jewel thief.'" Kanter later worked on *About Mrs. Leslie*, one of Booth's films.

Her next Broadway show, *School for Virtue*, produced by Edward Casey, survived seven performances in April 1931 at the Longacre Theatre. *The New York Times* called it a "vague and nasty little comedy." Information about the performers is limited, except that the cast, including Booth as Marg, "did what they could for the play in their acting. And, not unnaturally, their contribution resembled some such gesture of complete futility as might be achieved by tossing a glass of water into the Atlantic Ocean."

Six months later, Booth appeared in *The Camels Are Coming* at the President Theatre. Donn Mullally produced, directed and wrote this light comedy, which revolved around the woes that tormented genius, Terry Tracy (J. Anthony Hughes), must go through to get his work produced. Rich businessman Milton Markowitz (Joseph Greenwald) will produce Terry's play if Terry will take

Milton's ideas about people and camels and write a great Jewish epic for him. Milton will advance Terry $2,500, and offer another $2,500 upon completion, but Terry must not claim authorship.

Despite the fact that Terry would rather drink than write, Milton, Terry, and Terry's friends argue about the play. Of course, *The Camel's Are Coming* is about the theatre "angel" and his money trying to control the artist. In short, Milton is paying, and he thus must have a play with his sixty camels in it for atmosphere.

Booth portrayed the playwright's girlfriend who believes in the sober Terry. Reviews say little of Booth. Some just mention her in the cast. *The American* notes that the play opens with hung-over Terry "confronted by an angry fiancée (Shirley Booth)." Another states, "Miss Shirley Booth makes a good start as Bobby Marchante, the pie-eyed playwright's clear-eyed fiancée . . . " *The News'* Burns Mantle sums it up: "The camels are coming. The camels are going. The camels are here. Who cares?"

The Camels Are Coming opened at the President Theatre on October 2, 1931, and it closed after a mere 11 performances.

On November 30, 1931, *Coastwise* opened at the Provincetown Playhouse. Ed Gardner, Booth's husband, produced this drama. Donn Mullally directed and co-wrote with H. A. Archibald.

Booth played a prostitute, Annie Duval, also known as "Coastwise Annie," working on the ships off the coast of British Columbia. She marries and reforms a drunkard named Alan Farquhar (Richard Stevenson). After Alan goes off to the war, Annie figures that she will return to her trade. However, Alan returns from the war and wants Annie to go back to England with him. Annie refuses and stays behind.

The Post critic said, "Shirley Booth was simple and strong as the long-suffering heroine." *The New York Telegram* thought Booth "plays with understanding and restraint." *The Herald Tri-*

bune found Booth's performance "sound and moving, if slightly too much in one key."

The Mirror pointed to the show's flaws: "Tragedy and Broadway melodrama blend like oil and water in *Coastwise*, the story of a girl who loved above her station, which was played last night on the cramped stage of the Provincetown Theatre . . . The playing, especially that of Miss Shirley Booth, Richard Stevenson, Priscilla Knowles and Thomas McQuillan, has a professional finish worthy of more honest drama."

"What makes the drama a discouraging topic is its childlike innocence. It prattles away brightly about the old dilemmas of its battered, paper dolls," said *The New York Times*. Coastwise closed after 37 shows.

Among the ongoing stock theatre productions that she alternated with Broadway shows, Booth performed in *Death Takes a Holiday* with the Nashville Civic Repertoire Comedy in Nashville, Tennessee. A review in December of 1932 explained, "Lovely Shirley Booth played the part of Grazia with perfection . . . " W. Somerset Maugham wrote Booth's next Broadway show, *The Mask and the Face*, a comedy translated from the Italian of Luigi Chiarelli. Brock Pemberton offered an earlier rendition in 1924 on Broadway. The esteemed Theater Guild presented a cast that included Humphrey Bogart as Luciano Spina, Judith Anderson (later famous as the sinister housekeeper in Alfred Hitchcock's *Rebecca*), and Leo G. Carroll (better known from TV's *Topper*) as Cirillo Zanotti.

The Mask and the Face opened on May 6, 1933 and ran for 40 performances at the Guild Theatre (later renamed the Virginia Theatre). Booth plays Elisa Zanotti in this story about a Count Pacia Grazia (Stanley Ridges), his unfaithful wife Savina Grazia (Judith Anderson), and how he avoids ridicule and saves face with a cynic. Before the infidelity occurred, the Count had told the cynic that his answer to infidelity is homicide.

A critic later observed, "This adaptation was not among the Guild's more memorable products, but it added to Miss Booth's prestige and whetted her ambition to a finer edge."

Booth's husband, Ed Gardner, directed her tenth Broadway show, *After Such Pleasures*. Gardner adapted the series of comedy sketches from a book by Dorothy Parker. It opened on February 7, 1934 at the Bijou Theatre. Although it ran for just 23 performances, Gardner received praise for expertly adapting Parker's acid wit, and Booth was considered particularly good as a bride.

Of the eight vignettes presented in *After Such Pleasures*, Booth appeared in four. She played the returned traveler in "A Young Lady from Paris," the bride in "Here We Are," the fan in "Glory in the Daytime," and a character named Bubbles in "The Mantle of Whistler."

At this time, Playbill gave her a very brief cast biography: "Shirley Booth is a native Gothamite who started her stage career in stock companies at the age of 15. The productions in which she has appeared include *The Cat and the Canary*, *Laff That Off*, and *The Mask and the Face* with Judith Anderson."

Booth started bartering for hotel room and food. This she did by performing Dorothy Parker skits at the Barbizon-Plaza Hotel. One account says Gardner rented the hotel's theatre so that Booth could perform in *Sunday Nights at Nine*. The New Yorker critic Robert Benchley aptly predicted, "Miss Booth is a comedienne who ought to be playing on Broadway six nights a week instead of one, and probably soon will be."

Just several months later, she would achieve such stardom.

A turning point in her career now arrived. Supposedly, George Abbott noticed Booth's performance in the Barbizon-Plaza Ho-

A young Shirley, 1937.

tel shows. This is why he cast her in *Three Men on a Horse*. As an important milestone in her early career and her longest running show to date, this role gave Booth a substantial part and real star billing in lights on Broadway. It began at the Playhouse Theatre on January 30, 1935, and moved to the Fulton Theatre in October of the following year, running for a stupendous 835 performances.

George Abbott co-wrote (with John Cecil Holm) and staged, and Alex Yokel produced, this comedy farce about unlucky gamblers who meet up with a timid greeting card verse writer Erwin Trowbridge (William Lynn) who has a knack for picking winners. The show opens in the living room of the Trowbridge House in Ozone Heights, New Jersey. The funny thing is Erwin is inspired only when riding buses. Therefore, off he goes with gangsters in tow until he fails them.

Booth had a substantial role as Mabel; the luscious ex-Follies girl-turned-gun moll. William Lynn, Teddy Hart, Sam Levene, and Edith Van Cleve co-starred. Abbott observed: "I have worked with more actresses than I can count, and to me Shirley is easily tops."

"There are lively performances by Millard Mitchell and Shirley Booth," said Brooks Atkinson, *The New York Times*.

Robert Benchley characterized *Three Men on a Horse* as "distinctly low in tone, broad in method, and ostensibly mad in design, but there is an underlying comic truth running through it, even in minor roles, which made it consistently funny to me, and sometimes more than funny."

One performance had the accidental on-stage appearance of Booth's puppy during a hotel scene. This caused Booth to be unnerved. Gardner let go of the leash backstage. As recounted in *Theatre Arts* 23 years later: "Miss Booth, gracious as always, smiled at the animal, patted him once or twice, and then watched helplessly as the play went out the window. Not so, Sam Levene. Never one to upstage a fellow artist, but still not the man to be pushed around - especially by a dog - Levene stepped forward, picked up the little fellow and carried him to the edge of the stage . . ."

Gardner went away with the dog, only to be chased down by assistant stage manager Garson Kanin. The latter realized the audience stopped laughing; waiting for what became of the dog taken into what they thought was part of the hotel bathroom. Kanin got the dog back. Levene went back through the door carrying the dog. This got the audience's attention back on the actors and they laughed again.

Booth: "Don't weep for me! I say this to the various people who ask the same question constantly: 'Doesn't it get to be very boring, this playing the same part for two years?' So I want to reassure all and sundry that I love it, and who wouldn't?

"I started my career in that now almost obsolete branch of the theatre, 'stock,' and by that I don't mean the summer flings that one indulges in now just for fun. I mean hard, grueling work that goes on not for a few weeks during the summer but week after week all the year round. As the seasons tick off and the various parts you have played are tucked under your mental belt for future reference you find you've had your fill of variety, and when at last you've reached the heights of New York you thank your stars for a part that has a chance to grow and become a close relative - not a guest for the week.

"The first few plays I did in New York were lucky enough to please the audiences for months. Then came a series of breathtaking, soul-shaking failures - one month, one week and finally one day. But before I was completely submerged, to the rescue 'came the marines' in the form of Alex Yokel and *Three Men on a Horse*."

Booth is credited with helping at least one person pursue acting as a profession. She encouraged the diminutive shoe salesman Billy Curtis to take part in a stage production as a midget. He met Booth and explained to her how much he wanted to act. The 4'2" Curtis eventually became a professional actor, appearing in stage roles and in films such as *The Terror of Tiny Town*, *Superman and the Mole Men*, *The Incredible Shrinking Man*, *High Plains Drifter*, etc. His best-known role is as Mayor of Munchkin City in *The Wizard of Oz*.

Victor Wolfson's *Excursion* followed *Three Men on a Horse*. This fantasy comedy is about a skipper on the final voyage of the *S.S. Happiness*, a Coney Island steamboat. In the hope that he can give the passengers a real excursion and some genuine happiness on their return trip from Coney, the skipper takes his passengers to the Caribbean instead. Booth played a prominent role as Mrs. Loscavio, described by Playbill as "forlorn and frustrated."

Excursion opened on April 9, 1937, and it ran for a sizeable 118 performances at the Vanderbilt Theatre. Though *The New York Times* critic Brooks Atkinson does not single Booth out, he does call the show "refreshing" and notes: "In the long cast, they are all good actors. . . . There is, unfortunately, no time left to bestow a boutonnière on the many actors who contribute gayety, wonder and anguish to Mr. Wolfson's fable. And that is a pity, for they perform well together . . . "

"Long identified with edged and comic roles, Miss Booth in *Excursion* demonstrates that her gamut is not narrow," observed one critic, "for here she is a wracked and embittered woman, tragic, resentful and seeking escape from the life which crushes her."

On November 15, 1937, the comedy *Too Many Heroes* opened at the Hudson Theatre. Garson Kanin (later playwright and director) staged and Dore Schary made his debut on Broadway as a writer. Although *Too Many Heroes* dealt with the lynching of kidnappers for the murder of a girl, it focused on character and avoided depicting the hanging. The cast included the later voice of Mr. Magoo, Jim Backus, billed here as James Backus.

The New York Times critic Brooks Atkinson declares: "As the wife of one of the lynch victims, Shirley Booth gives the most lucid performance in the cast, catching all the anguish of the character in the dull hatred of her acting." Atkinson acknowledged the other characters' good performances. "In fact, they are sturdier than *Too Many Heroes*, which never recovers from the outbreak of violence at the close of the first act."

Too Many Heroes closed after just 16 performances. Gardner got an offer to direct a radio show called *Ripley's Believe It or Not* on the West Coast. They moved to Hollywood in 1938, and Booth took a sabbatical from acting for about a year.

Booth gave this account some fifteen years later: "The first time I saw Hollywood was when I was married to Edward Gardner. We had moved to California when Ed was headquartered there as a radio director. I gave up my acting career because I thought it important to be a good wife and follow my husband. I soon became so engrossed in running the house we had rented on a hill that I never came down to the lowlands to see what was going on and who was there."

Ed had first appeared on radio when he substituted on a CBS Sunday night revue called *This Is New York*. Gardner directed the show, and Booth appeared on the series in episode five, broadcast on January 8, 1938. From this opportunity, Gardner went on to write for a show called *First Line*, and then direct radio programs such as *Burns and Allen* and *The Texaco Star Theater*, among others.

Wearing her beau's fraternity pin, Miss Duffy (the Irish soprano who bloodshots smiling eyes) says to Vera, her girl-friend: "What, you didn't pick up that sailor? You just happened to be swimming past a battleship?"

"Lousy hours," says Archie, "but consider the pay—$15 a week." Not long ago, Gardner thought $15 a week was pretty good, too. Everything's different now. In addition to radio, he's making a movie, "Duffy's Tavern."

END

Ed and Shirley on *Duffy's Tavern*.

Shirley would appear on a quiz show in 1939 sponsored by Philip Morris. Whether she had a recurring role cannot be determined. A promotion for the show noted: "Shirley Booth is the winsome young lady who helps with the quizzing on *Guess Where?* The popular series, aired over WLW from Mutual each Friday at 7 p.m., EST, also features Budd Hulick and Charlie Cantor. The idea is for the contestant to guess, by means of both broad and subtle clues, where he is supposed to be."

In this retirement while in Hollywood, Booth became very absorbed in her home. "Once I went to the races at Santa Anita and that was about the extent of my getting around. Ed used to bring the news home to me. After a year we returned east, Ed to sell his idea for *Duffy's Tavern* and I subsequently to work again in the theatre."

Ed and Shirley returned to the East Coast in 1939. Of course, in the rush to go back East, Booth did not notify the post office to forward her mail. A friend revealed to Booth that for weeks the Theater Guild had been trying to wire her in California.

Booth began starring in a series of long-running hit shows. A distinguished cast comprised of Katharine Hepburn, Joseph Cotten, and Van Heflin all starred with Booth in her next Broadway show, *The Philadelphia Story*. Phillip Barry wrote that familiar comedy of manners.

Booth plays Elizabeth Imbrie, a sardonic society photographer/magazine writer for *Destiny* magazine. Elizabeth tries to get the scoop on the expected second marriage of society goddess Miss Tracy Lord (Hepburn) to straitlaced George Kitteredge (Frank Fenton) at the latter's upper-class estate. Complexities arise when the first husband, C. K. Dexter Haven (Cotten), enters the scene.

Although Booth and the rest of the cast were given good credit for doing their part, reviewers gave Hepburn much of the praise. Richard Watts, Jr., *New York Herald Tribune*, observed: "Van Heflin and Shirley Booth portray the investigators from *Destiny* humorously and sanely . . . " Richard Lockridge, *New York Sun*: " . . . Forrest Orr, Shirley Booth, Frank Fenton and Vera Allen brighten the scene." The aforementioned "help to round out a joyful evening," according to Brooks Atkinson, *The New York Times*.

As one might expect, the marriage ceremony never happens, thanks to several developments, including a drunken swim with another man (Van Heflin). Tracy is back in the arms of her first husband by the denouement.

Playbill noted that since *Hell's Bells*, Booth "has been constantly in demand, as the long list of plays in which she has appeared will attest."

The Philadelphia Story opened on March 28, 1939 and closed on March 30, 1940, for a substantial 417 performances at the Shubert Theatre. Although critics thought Barry had written better material, the quite successful Theatre Guild production offered a welcome respite to a company financially strapped due to failed productions.

At this time, Booth wanted to go to Hollywood to make a picture. But she had some reluctance. Of course, she dragged her feet. However, this gave her the opportunity to perform in one of her biggest hits.

The Philadelphia Story had two screen adaptations. Katharine Hepburn, Cary Grant, and Jimmy Stewart did the 1940 screwball comedy version. Booth chose not to be in this movie production. (Her part was played by Ruth Hussey.) Later in 1956, a musical rendition, *High Society*, had Grace Kelly, Bing Crosby, Frank Sinatra, and John Lund. Celeste Holm played Shirley's stage role.

Booth: "The day I was to catch my train for Hollywood, I left my apartment to do some last-minute errands. While I was out, a burglar broke into my apartment and stole a new mink coat. I was sad, but in a way I was glad, for it gave me an excuse to postpone my trip to Hollywood. So I cancelled my train tickets and remained in New York to help catch the thief. While I was waiting for reports from the detectives, I got a telephone call asking me to read for a role in *My Sister Eileen*."

That phone call gave Booth another job - one that lasted for over two years.

My Sister Eileen, Booth's next Broadway show, was also adapted for the screen two times; the first in 1942, with Rosalind Russell (playing Ruth Sherwood) and Janet Blair as Eileen Sherwood (her younger sister), the second was a 1955 musical with Betty Garrett (Ruth) and Janet Leigh (Eileen). Again, Booth did not participate in the movie versions.

Max Gordon produced and George S. Kaufman staged the successful and hysterically funny *My Sister Eileen*. Booth played the older sister Ruth Sherwood, an aspiring writer with an acid tongue who wants to get the "Manhatter" magazine editor Robert Baker (William Post, Jr.) to accept her work. Broadway newcomer Jo Ann Sayers played Eileen Sherwood, hopeful theater actress.

Burns Mantle, *New York Daily News*: "Shirley Booth plays the level-headed, wise-cracking Ruth, and plays her well." Said Brooks Atkinson, of *The New York Times*, "As Sister Ruth, Shirley Booth gives an admirably timed portrait of comic skepticism." Later in her career, Playbill acknowledged that this show "definitely established her as one of the foremost comediennes of the American theatre."

Based on Ruth McKenney's sketches in *The New Yorker*, *My Sister Eileen* tells of two Midwestern sisters who come to Greenwich Village in New York. Joseph A. Fields and Jerome Chodorov wrote this humorous comedy of incidents focusing on the anarchy and eccentricities of the Village inhabitants invading Eileen and Ruth's basement apartment.

Brooks Atkinson explains: "And quite a variety of madmen trickles through their door - a drug-store counterman with bohemian notions, a vagrant newspaper writer, a prostitute who once did business at the same address and, finally, six cadets from the romantic Brazilian Navy." The Navy cadets come by because Ruth had a newspaper assignment with an arriving ship.

Richard Watts, Jr., *New York Herald Tribune*: Booth "is both briskly amusing and warmly agreeable as the steady Ruth . . . " Sidney B. Whipple, *New York World-Telegram*: "Shirley Booth is as perfect as can be as Ruth . . . She is extremely effective in her handling of the crackling wit that comes in part from Miss McKenney's foundation and in part from the Fields-Chodorov." Richard Lockridge, *New York Sun*: "Miss Booth's Ruth is a brisk delight." John Mason Brown, *New York Post*: "As Ruth, Shirley Booth once again demonstrates her superlative skill. She is warm, human, resilient, hopeful. There is no other actress on our stage - including the dazzling Jean Dixon - who can excel her when it comes to the precise firing of a Kaufman line."

Of course, by the finale of *My Sister Eileen*, Eileen finds a job as an actress after she appears in the newspaper for punching a police officer. Predictably, love conquers all for Ruth and Robert Baker.

A tragic automobile accident killed the real Eileen heading to see the opening night performance of her sister Ruth's play. *My Sister Eileen* opened on December 26, 1940 at the Biltmore Theatre.

Booth: "I never have been nervous on an opening night. Never. As a matter of fact, George Kaufman paid me a very great compliment one time when we were opening in *My Sister Eileen*. He was pacing up and down backstage, and I said what are you doing, 'Mr. Kaufman, are you nervous?' And he said, 'yes aren't you?' And he said, 'no, you wouldn't be, you're an actor's actor.' This was a very nice compliment which I cherish very highly."

On March 2, 1942, after 500 performances, the show's cast assembled at the Village Barn in Greenwich Village to do a benefit for the American Theater Wing called *Strictly for Laughs*. The show's guest stars included Keenan Wynn and Benny Baker.

Max Showalter played the drugstore clerk Frank Lippencott in *My Sister Eileen*. He recalled to Kevin Minton: "I first became aware of Shirley Booth when I read glowing reviews she received by performing vignettes written by Dorothy Parker at the Barbizon Hotel. It was later that I met her during rehearsals of *My Sister Eileen*. Max Gordon, the producer, and George Kaufman, the director, had cast her as the older sister, Ruth Sherwood. My roommate, Richard Quine (who later became a successful film director) was cast as the drugstore clerk, Frank Lippencott. The comedy was a huge hit and garnered more superlative reviews for Shirley. Two road companies were formed: one for Chicago and the West, and one to tour the East. Fortunately, I was cast as Frank Lippencott in the eastern company headed by Betty Furness. While we were appearing at the Colonial Theater in Boston, Joseph Chodorov and Joseph Fields (the authors) attended a performance and insisted that I was to be transferred to the New York company. I was elated over the prospect and the opportunity to act with Shirley Booth.

"My expectations were more than fulfilled. Never before, or since, have I ever acted with anyone who gave more to her fellow actors and taught them miraculous tricks of comedy timing. What a thrill and joy each performance generated . . . It was a difficult time for Shirley. She had been married to Ed Gardner and had been such an integral part of their radio show *Duffy's Tavern*. In fact, once Shirley left the show, it was no longer the success it had been, and Ed was constantly inundating her with accusing and blasphemous phone calls and letters. She would arrive at the theater tense and shaken. I recognized this difficult situation and offered to massage her neck and back with my strong piano-playing hands. It became a ritual before every performance, and she never forgot it.

"While Shirley and I were in New York in *Eileen*, she'd grab me several nights a week after our show and insist we go to a late movie. She would make a point of going to the movie that had the worst reviews and had the worst actors. We'd sit there with our popcorn and laugh our heads off. It was her way of totally relaxing after a night's work.

"My final performance in *Eileen* I'll never forget. After the bows, the entire company was on stage. Shirley stepped forward to speak to the audience. 'Ladies and gentlemen, tonight we are saying farewell to one of our *Eileen* family members. He goes into the army tomorrow morning, and we want to wish him well and tell him how much we'll miss him. Max, please come down here.' A cast member gave her a wrapped parcel. 'We want you to have this from all of us.' I opened it (a toilet kit). 'Something you'll use every day and maybe think of us because we'll be with you wherever you go, literally.' She put her arms around me, hugged me, and whispered, 'I love you.' There were tears in my eyes as I thanked them from my heart. The audience cheered and applauded as the curtain came down, and I was sent to Camp Kilmer, point of demarcation in New Brunswick, New Jersey."

Showalter's assessment of Booth: "She was so honest in her approach to acting. She became the character, and the character became her. She had the unique ability to touch your heart and make you cry and the next moment make you laugh hysterically. She had no use for the Method of the Actors' Studio and the teachings of Lee Strasberg. She had the innate sense to read a script and know the whole character immediately. No time was wasted on extraneous symbols or problems. It was all right to the point and brilliantly so."

In an article entitled "Shirley Booth is Stubborn," appearing on the March 2, 1942 of the *New York World-Telegram*, Booth revealed some things about her marriage to Ed Gardner: "I used to freeze and refuse to argue, until I was married." The author noted that Ed liked to bicker. She added: "My husband says that I am anti-social, but that is not the case. The fact is, I'm not a graceful hostess. I worry about people. I'm afraid they are bored or uncomfortable. I see every movement. For me the curtain is always up. Ed, however, is the perfect guest in his own home. When we have people around you will find him in the best chair, talking to the most interesting person in the room. But he likes people and doesn't want to be alone for a moment."

Booth describes a present she bought for Ed: "It was this lovely encyclopedia I gave my husband. It was a marvelous thing, leather and beautifully bound. It was our 12th wedding anniversary and I knew he would appreciate it more than anything I could have found." Ed did not appreciate it, so Booth returned it.

Marriage, Booth says, has made her "a nicer person.... Marriage has been good for Ed, too. He was a pretty wild hairpin, except that he will never admit it."

In addition, the newspaper article disclosed that Booth talks loud into the telephone; she straightens pictures when visiting strangers' homes, Ed keeps her from getting fat because of his dislike of fat woman, and as for cocktail parties Booth has never tossed one in her twelve years of marriage.

Booth decided to leave *My Sister Eileen* before it ended its run. She told Earl Wilson the reason: "Because it was moving to a bigger theatre where I would have gone against all the things I think are important in the theatre. I would have had to play very broadly, do mugging and make faces for the bigger house. The trouble with me is I love the theatre. I'm stage struck. And that's the trouble with the critics - they're not stage struck. . . . It annoys me to hear people say, 'I'm going to see the Barrymore play or the Hayes play' because it's not healthy. They should just be going to see a play." Booth repeated that she's simply stage struck.

My Sister Eileen* moved production three times (Martin Beck, Ritz, and Broadway Theatres) during the last six months of its run, before closing January 16, 1943 after 864 performances.

A press release from Nat Dorfman at the time observed: "Although Shirley Booth will always have a soft spot in her heart for the road she feels that the rest of her theatrical life will transpire in New York. As a matter of fact she doesn't care if she never sees the countryside again. As urban a young woman as you could find hereabouts, she has no yen for a shack in the woods near a babbling brook. Just give her an apartment in Manhattan close to the theatres, a fat role in a good play, like the part of 'Ruth' in *My Sister Eileen* and she'll unpack her trunks for keeps."

---

*With Betty Comden and Adolph Green writing the lyrics, and Leonard Bernstein composing the music, Rosalind Russell starred in the 1953 Broadway musical version of McKenney's stories called *Wonderful Town*.

Hello, Miss Duffy
The 1940s

Booth now had achieved recognition as a comedienne. She explained the problems to newspaper columnist Marion Kelley: "The chief difficulty encountered by a comedienne is when the audience laughs at the wrong time. That is most disconcerting. It's worse than that, it is just plain terrible, and you cannot let them get out of hand.

"There are certain lines in most comedies that hold a depth of feeling that should go much deeper than a surface laugh. When the audience does not get it, then I think it is the actor's fault. When it happens to me the first time I consider it an accident, but if it occurs twice then I know I am not putting it across properly. Many times, I just will my audience to be quiet or laugh as the case may be-you know-thought waves. You would be surprised how often this works."

Shirley Booth's voice is unmistakable. There was a baby-voiced quality to it, similar to Fannie Brice's Baby Snooks, but not exactly. As Miss Duffy on the radio show, *Duffy's Tavern*, Booth's delivery in that "Brooklyn twang" accounts for plenty of the audience satisfaction. Where or when she developed that "Brooklyn twang" is anyone's guess. It might have developed in part when the Fords lived in Flatbush, a section of Brooklyn, New York.

Booth said to a magazine interviewer in 1951 that she developed her voice as such: "I rode the New York subways and eavesdropped on as many conversations between girls as I could." She continued, "But I'm afraid many of them aren't printable."

For three seasons, two on CBS Radio for the years of 1941 and 1942, and one on the NBC-Blue Radio network from 1942-1943, Booth lent her Brooklynese voice to the irrepressibly funny and light-hearted Miss Duffy, the cashier daughter of the owner of the tavern on *Duffy's Tavern*. Many listeners loved her Miss Duffy characterization with all of the mutilated talk, but hardly any knew Booth's name.

Booth: "The audience loved Miss Duffy. Every time I had a personal victory on the show they had one. It's true that not many people knew I played Miss Duffy but that was the way I wanted it. I wanted them to remember the fictional character. In fact, I believe that all applause for actors at the end of a play should be eliminated. The play should end with them in character. The curtain should come down and the audience is carried away with the play."

Booth had this regularly recurring role on the radio show at the same time she was acting in *My Sister Eileen* on Broadway. The theatre permitted a Sunday performance to allow her to do her radio show on Monday night from 8:00 to 8:30 p.m.

Ed Gardner wore many hats. In *Duffy's Tavern* he, not only played the bartender Archie, the main character, but also produced, directed, and wrote the radio program.

Duffy's Tavern opened every week: "Hello, Duffy's Tavern, where the elite meet to eat, Archie da manager speakin,' Duffy ain't here ... Oh Hello, Duffy." The theme song "When Irish Eyes Are Smiling" played.

It has been commonly believed that no shows with Booth survived. The earliest surviving episode is the pilot episode (without

Booth) from 1940. In addition, the shows starting in the fall of 1943 (without Booth) exist. However, two episodes with Booth have been found. One show, dated March 23, 1943, has Susan Hayward and Frank Buck as the guest stars. The other existing show with Booth has Clifton Fadiman as guest star. The following part of an exchange from the latter show, broadcast June 15, 1943, is typical of the lunatic and wisecracking Miss Duffy; however, it suffers here without Booth's superb comedic delivery.

Miss Duffy: Archie, did you see my Dostoyevsky?

Archie: Your what?

Miss Duffy: My Dostoyevsky.

Archie: Is it an animal, vegetable or mineral?

Miss Duffy: No, it's a book.

Archie: Miss Duffy, what would you be doing with a book?

Miss Duffy: Well, Clifton Fadiman is coming down here and I don't want him to catch me not reading.

Archie: Well, naturally.

Miss Duffy: You see, if everybody stopped reading, authors would stop writing. And if authors stopped writing because nobody was reading, Mr. Fadiman being a critic couldn't read what authors were writing and that would put an end to his writing about reading and the poor man would be out of a job.

Archie: Mmm, yeah, I see what you mean.

Miss Duffy: Or to put it in another way, if author's write and people don't read . . .

Archie: Oh please, Miss Duffy, I don't think I care to go around again.

Booth started *Duffy's Tavern* with the episode broadcast March 1, 1941. Her last appearance occurred on June 29, 1943. Later, when the opportunity came to play Miss Duffy in the movies and on television, Booth told columnist Earl Wilson, "I feel I'm too old now for the part."

When Booth left the role of Miss Duffy, Gardner had a slew of replacements, including Florence Halop, the sister of Dead End Kid Billy Halop. For the fourth season of the show, Halop did a remarkably good impression of Booth's Miss Duffy.

Years later when Booth had received awards and accolades, she recalled a conversation she had with Ed. "Ed said: 'Shirley, people envy me my success, but they all hope you'll make it to the top one of these days. They say, good ol' Shirley. She's been pluggin' away a long time.'" Booth explained: "The difference was that Ed, who's really a very talented man, rose to the top so very fast."

By now, Booth became very active on radio. In fact, during the 1940s, she kept quite busy doing radio shows.

One of the earliest credited appearances of Booth on a radio show occurred on December 17, 1936 with *The Royal Gelatin Hour* starring Rudy Vallee and the Connecticut Yankees. Booth and Douglass Montgomery appear in *Three Diamond Bid*, possibly a parody of *Three Men on a Horse*.

She appeared in several episodes of *Columbia Workshop*. The earliest appearance occurred on October 24, 1937 with an episode entitled "I've Got the Tune." This tells of the search by Mr. Musiker and assistant Beetzie for lyrics to fit the tune.

While performing on Broadway in *The Philadelphia Story*, Booth joined the cast of *The Goldbergs* on CBS in July of 1939. Gertrude

Berg, who wrote the serial and starred as Molly, selected Booth over others auditioning for the part. Booth played a character named Ana, whom the Goldbergs picked up in their trailer while touring the U.S. and Canada. The show ran Mondays through Fridays from 1:00 p.m. to 1:15 p.m. EDST.

Husband Ed Gardner appeared with Booth on *The Texaco Star Theater*, starring Fred Allen broadcast on February 11, 1942.

Booth tried mystery radio with *The Adventures of Ellery Queen* in an episode broadcast on the East Coast on May 2, 1942 entitled "The Living Corpse."

On November 15, 1942, she made her first appearance on *Hallmark Reader's Digest*, also known as *Radio Reader's Digest*, in the episode "They Called Her Mouse"/"The Clock Strikes."

She appeared on an episode of *Stage Door Canteen*, with guest star Yehudi Menuhin on March 4, 1943.

Back in 1942, Ed Gardner had asked Booth for a divorce because he loved another woman. Their marriage undoubtedly had its share of problems. Certainly, it did not help that Ed liked to hang out and drink and Booth liked staying home. Gardner would go on to marry Simone Hegeman in 1943. He would die on August 17, 1963 in Hollywood, California.

Years later Booth would reflect (to *TV Guide's* Robert Musel), "I gave up the stage in the early days of our marriage. I thought it more important to be a good wife than a good actress. I took good care of him. I saw that he didn't drink too much and that he husbanded his strength. Maybe I took too good care of him. The concentration you need for acting . . . it isn't always good in private life. Having been alone part of the time, you dedicate yourself to marriage. You get sold on the idea so much you want to be with them more than they want to be with you."

Without knowing much about the actual details of their

doomed relationship, Booth and Gardner's living preferences as far as East Coast or West Coast location had some influence. These preferences resulted from a difference in personalities. Booth loved the East because of Broadway, and Gardner felt most comfortable on the West Coast with Hollywood and radio production.

As recounted in the April 1960 issue of *The Theatre*, Booth told a *Herald Tribune* reporter: "I've never mentioned this before but there was a time after my divorce when I came closest to having a nervous breakdown. I guess I just lost my confidence . . . that's all. Suddenly I was afraid to face an audience. I can't describe how horrible it was to go out in front of a thousand people and I feel my insides jerking, sweat pouring out of my palms, completely unsure for the first and last time in my life. I fought it. I went to all kinds of doctors, but the only medicine that seemed to work was the hardest to take - just keep going out there."

The divorce occurred in August of 1943. Not too long after that, Booth met a noncommissioned army officer, Corporal William Hogg Baker, Jr. Several months later, Corporal Baker, son of the late Mr. and Mrs. William H. Baker, married Shirley Booth. Rev. Norris L. Tibbetts, from the Riverside Church, performed the ceremony at the home of William's aunt, Mrs. Franklin Baker, Jr. Baker had received a four-day furlough from the 100th division located in Fort Jackson, South Carolina.

Booth's love of interior design led to her frequent redecorating. As for her townhouse apartment in 1943 on East 61 Street in New York City, Booth told Earl Wilson that she: " . . . made the bedrooms very frivolous and very frou-frou - pink." Then, "I couldn't stand to live in pink anymore so now I'm doing it all over again with white walls, yet low bedspread and maybe green and white chairs."

With World War II in full fury, the American Theater Wing

organized the Stage Door Canteen in the basement of a 44th Street Theatre to entertain servicemen. The Canteen had started a year earlier, in March of 1942. Booth volunteered as a nightly hostess. Of course, she still maintained her aversion to alcohol. Booth told Earl Wilson: "I'm the girl that's always afraid somebody's going to ask her to take a drink." Booth often jitterbugged with the famous Coast Guard sailor known as "Killer Joe." He became known for tossing the women over his head. At 116 pounds, Booth found that it kept her hips in shape.

Max Showalter recalled to Kevin Minton: "World War II had begun, and Shirley was the most energetic star helping out at the Stage Door Canteen. Her jitterbugging with Killer Joe was always a show stopper, and her laugh could be heard above all others. Whenever we had free time from *Eileen*, Shirley and I were escorted to and from every camp and fort in the country to perform. I played the piano and sang. She sang. We sang together. One of the boys' favorites was her high-pitched 'nasal' rendition of 'Tangerine.' They'd shriek with laughter, and the next moment she would reduce them to tears with her low sensitive vocal of 'Joe Never Brings Me Pretty Flowers.'"

With an investment broker background, Baker became Booth's manager. Booth, for the second time, retired to focus on being a wife. With their savings the couple bought Windrace, a 64-acre dairy farm in Buck's County, Pennsylvania, complete with cows, sheep and chickens.

Bill Baker painted and so Booth took up the activity, becoming quite adept at it. Years later, Booth remembered it as being in Upstate New York: "I'm a farm girl to start with, you know. When my husband was alive, we used to have a farm of our own in upstate New York. We raised cows. We'd go to bed at nine in the evening and get up a dawn."

Her two farm mascots were the red-brown cocker spaniel named "Baker's Candy," and a boxer named "Sugar." Referring to "Baker's Candy," Booth later reflected: "I became a painter when my husband did that portrait of our dog. But he painted him with his tail drooping. I took the brushes and repainted the tail so it is standing defiantly up in the air. Since then I've been a determined artist."

Booth noted in 1954: "I love painting - painting ceilings and the kitchen walls. Also oil painting. I do oils. It's the most absorbing occupation one could have. You can say this about an oil painting - it somehow never gets done. There's always one more touch you discover you can add."

Later on, Booth talked about her other dogs: her two female miniature poodles. She had Prego, a white toy poodle with shiny black button eyes, and Grazia. Booth told Jon Whitcomb how she traveled by train since airlines like to put animals in the cargo section. There was the story of a party Booth went to where the wife of an airline president said, "Why don't you do what I do and just tuck them into the sleeves of your mink coat?" Booth replied, "You'll notice that they're not terribly chic. I like to be comfortable at home and my dogs to be the same."

Another offer to go to Hollywood had been made. Booth: "I am an actress, a stage actress. I am in a play that is providing merriment, thought and entertainment. I would be a quitter if I should walk out on the play just because I could make a great deal more money in Hollywood."

Three plays were offered to Booth. She selected the one that passed her exacting tests for choosing a role. The play had to have entertainment value; it had to be something someone wanted to see. In addition, it had to be done for more than just a salary. The role needed to be one that she would do even for a low pay because of its importance and entertainment value. By thinking in this fashion, Booth put audiences above her own interests. Often Booth managed to select hit shows with this method.

Her next starring role on Broadway exhibited Booth's non-comedic talents. By now, Broadway audiences were quite familiar with Booth's ability to portray the "wise-cracking, hard-boiled comedienne." Even though she appeared in dramatic roles before, with *Tomorrow, the World*, Booth proved her superb dramatic skill.

Booth: "I was never in a dramatic school in my life but I watch people always - how they look and talk and behave. When the time comes and with theatrical license, of course, I draw on that stock . . . . The audience guides me. I try to establish my contact the minute I step on the stage. All I can do is suggest to them the character I am playing. They fill in the rest. And that's the reason I have never had stage fright. The people out front come prepared to like you. They grab any thought you send out."

Just as rehearsals for *Tomorrow, the World* began, Booth had her marriage to Ed falling apart. Later *TV Guide* would report that her friends said she became so engrossed with her personal troubles that she walked into walls.

Beginning its Broadway appearance on April 14, 1943, *Tomorrow, the World* told the stirring and shocking narrative of a 12-year-old German youth Emil Bruckner (Skippy Homeier) brought to a Midwestern town to live with Professor Michael Frame's (Ralph Bellamy) family. Chaos ensues for the family as the youth quickly exhibits his menacing Nazi-indoctrinated tendencies. Professor Frame's fiancée is the schoolteacher Leona Richards. Booth played the brown-eyed, red-headed Richards, who offers more than a glimmer of hope for the boy's reclamation in the finale.

Written by James Gow and Arnaud d'Usseau, and under the

direction of Eliot Nugent, *Tomorrow, the World* was a huge success partly due to its timely subject matter of the Nazi menace. One 1943 magazine offered a photograph of a scene of Emil falling back after Leona disciplines with the following caption: "Slapped across the face by Leona (Shirley Booth), Emil shrinks away. When she tries to reason with him about his fiendish misdeeds, he calls her 'a Jewish whore.'"

Booth received critical praise for her acting. John Anderson, *New York Journal American* called Booth "excellent." Ward Morehouse, *New York Sun*, noted: "Shirley Booth is a natural and enormously able young actress. She gives another of her convincing performances as the Leona of this play." Howard Barnes, *New York Herald Tribune*: "Shirley Booth is excellent as the embattled Jewish school teacher ... "

Louis Kronenberger, *New York Newspaper PM*: "Shirley Booth plays the Jewish teacher, whom the boy detests, with remarkable naturalness and understanding." In reference to Ralph Bellamy and Shirley Booth, *New York World-Telegram's* Burton Rascoe observed: " . . . they both turn in warmly human, utterly convincing characterizations and endear themselves to the theater audience."

"Shirley Booth as the fiancée who helps wrestle with the Nazi problem child, turns in what is probably the best performance of her career in a role that, in other hands, might have let down the play rather badly," noted Wilella Waldorf of *The New York Post*.

The New York Times reviewer Brooks Atkinson singled out "Another good young player," namely, Joyce Van Patten (sister of Dick Van Patten). Joyce played the Professor's 10-year-old daughter, alternating the role with Nancy Nugent.

As the understudy for the role given to director Eliot Nugent's daughter, Van Patten recalled that sometime when *Tomorrow, the*

World appeared in New Haven and Boston, Nancy Nugent, was fired from the show. Van Patten would do all appearances on Broadway, with the exception of the Wednesday and Saturday matinees, which Nancy would still get to do.

Although the play and cast got a good rating, there were flaws. Brooks Atkinson: "The early part of the play is on the slow side, and during the course of the action the central figure is made so despicable that his sudden reformation may appear as just another of his tricks to divide and conquer."

For a couple of months (April - June 1943), until she bowed out of doing *Duffy's Tavern*, Booth had to do her radio show on Tuesday nights for East Coast audiences at 8:30 p.m. Her curtain call for *Tomorrow, the World* was at 8:55 p.m. Then she needed to go back to the radio studio after the play to do Miss Duffy for West Coast audiences.

The hectic schedule balancing her time between radio studio and theater stage is explained by Booth: "I sneak out of the N.B.C studio, jump into a taxi, and pray that the traffic lights won't stop me. There's a studio rehearsal every Monday afternoon, and at 7:30 that night we give a preview. On Tuesdays we work from 3 'till 7:30, when I rush here to the theater to make up and dress for the play. Before 8:30 I'm at the studio again, ready to go on the air. The worst of all, though, is getting back there after the play for the west coast broadcast, which starts at 11:30."

She stayed true to playing the part as scripted without fitting it to her own personality, or confusing her personality with the character she's acting. Those actors that tamper with the part, "begin playing themselves, instead of the characters the author intended ... I leave the character with the costume," explained Booth.

Booth: "At the performances I like to work with audiences and feel them being carried along by the story. No two audiences are quite alike. When Mrs. Roosevelt came one evening lately, we thought the house would divide its attention between her and us - which always makes a difficult crowd to play to. But it didn't turn out that way; the house seemed absorbed in the play.

"The next night, for no reason we could discover, we had one of those audiences that you can't get hold of. They elude you. The worst example of this I ever saw was one night during *My Sister Eileen*, when three picture stars were out in front. The audience was so busy watching them that it was only semi-conscious of what was happening on stage."

Booth told Earl Wilson: "I'm not in this business to make money. I'm in it because I like acting . . . I was offered $25,000 to do a movie. It would take about nine weeks, which would bring my salary up to about $3,000 a week. That's more money than I will get in years and years. I turned it down because the part was Mrs. Duffy in *Duffy's Tavern*, and I didn't want to establish myself as that character. I turned down $3,000 a week and am very happy getting a great deal less in *Tomorrow, the World*."

When asked how much she did make, Booth replied $600 a week. She explained: "I told you I'm not in this to make money. Salaries are the producers' way of showing their respect for you, but actors and actresses don't need a lot of money. A good part is what you go for, rather than money."

Booth: "I've played the part so long that Miss Duffy will own me if I don't break away. I invented her. She's really another incarnation of Mabel in *Three Men on a Horse*, and I've got to get out of her clutches before it's too late. In radio, with millions of listeners, the public identifies you with the part you play. It's now or never for me."

Of course, Booth had divorced recently, so any mention of *Duffy's Tavern* could only remind her of her failed marriage. She did not want to be identified with the part of Miss Duffy any longer.

Once Gardner asked ex-wife Booth to be the star in a Charles O'Neill play called *Praise House*. Press reports noted he took an option on it and wanted her to play "the starring role of a colored woman, wearing corp make-up, as Ethel Barrymore once did in *Scarlet Sister Mary*." Booth refused.

Tomorrow, the World ran for 500 performances at the Ethel Barrymore Theatre, before closing on June 17, 1944. The riveting drama was adapted for the screen with Fredric March, Betty Field and Agnes Moorehead.

Playbill made it clear that Booth, unlike most actresses, stayed with the New York stage despite some alluring movie offers. "Radio provides the outlet for her excess energy."

During the run of *Tomorrow, the World* Booth continued to make radio appearances. Booth appeared on July 19, 1943 in a fifteen-minute episode of *Treasury Star Parade* called "I Am an Army Nurse." Booth contributed to NBC's *Cavalcade of America* in a show entitled "Check Your Heart at Home," broadcast on December 13, 1943.

On May 10, 1944, Booth reprised her part as the society photographer/ writer from the stage hit *The Philadelphia Story* in an episode of *Arthur Hopkins Presents*.

For almost a full year after *Tomorrow, the World* closed, Booth was free to concentrate on radio.

On July 9, 1944 and July 23, 1944, Booth did two episodes of *The Silver Theater*, entitled "Adventure for Two" and "Long Engagement."

Booth returned to *Cavalcade of America* on the evening of August 14, 1944 when she played Jo Sullivan, wife of Corporal Bill Sullivan, in "The Gals They Left Behind." Her co-star Helen Claire played Cathy Smith, wife of Private Hank Smith.

This home front story, adapted from a book, tells of two soldiers' wives who bravely fight the loneliness and keep busy doing the ordinary farmhouse chores until the day when their men will return from the war.

It opens as the two New York City women arrive in Horsetrot, Maine, to take over the Perkins farmhouse. Although they are surprised at the condition of the place, they decide to fix it up. Jo keeps Bill's pipe in her bed as a talisman to remember him. One of their first challenges is dealing with the dead muskrat in the well. From then on, Jo and Cathy dedicate their time to caring for the 12 egg-laying hens, Amy - a deaf dog, Rosie - a brown and white cow who gives birth to twins in their parlor, and Eloise - a little 9-year-old girl with Mommy and Daddy both overseas and whose favorite author is Edgar Allen Poe. Eloise helps in feeding the chickens and scrubbing the house.

The three lonely women deal with the cold temperatures of 30 and 40 degrees below zero. Jo writes letters to Bill throughout the story. Cathy plays the harmonica but looks to run away to escape the cold, demanding farm life. Jo (Booth) tries to keep things together as she tells Cathy she suffers from "a cracked morale." The women stick together as the story concludes with talk of painting the farmhouse in the spring.

"The Gals They Left Behind" is a salute to the other army; those women who the host called "an army of occupation because they are truly occupied with waiting, working, praying for their sons and husbands."

Several months later, Booth appeared on the game show *It Pays to Be Ignorant* on November 3, 1944.

Booth did the radio version of *Bachelor Mother* on CBS' *Theater of Romance* show of November 21, 1944. This show offered listeners a half-hour of classic romances with the obligatory happy conclusion.

Bachelor Mother is the story of Polly Parish (Booth), who is terminated from her job at John B. Merlin & Son's Department Store on Christmas Eve. She finds a baby on her apartment steps. Everyone thinks that it's Polly's baby. This leads Merlin Jr. to reinstate Polly with a $5 increase. Tired of arguing that the baby is not hers, Polly makes up a story about an abusive husband. However, Merlin Sr. believes his son is responsible for the baby. By the finale, Merlin Jr. realizes he loves Polly, and he asks her to marry him so he can be a father to the baby.

Booth returned to the *Theater of Romance* program broadcast on January 25, 1945 to do the screwball comedy *Ball of Fire**. In this show, Booth plays Sugarpuss O'Shea. An English Professor Bertram Potts thinks Sugarpuss is a perfect example for observation for his research project. She rejects him at first, but then agrees to live with him because she sees the project as a safe haven from a pursuing hood. The professor sees no progress, and, in fact becomes attracted to Sugarpuss, even though he believes that cannot happen. She encourages him and becomes engaged to him. Her hood boyfriend tries to take advantage of this situation but she tells him to get lost. She loves Professor Potts.

In another regularly recurring role, Booth appeared on NBC's *Eddie Bracken Show* in the role of Betty Mahoney. Bracken played his usual bumbling persona on this situation comedy that ran for eighteen weeks on Sunday's from January 28 to May 27, 1945. It hopped over to CBS from for an additional 26 weeks from September 29, 1946 to March 23, 1947. Whether she was on beyond the first season is not clear. It is presumed this role provided Booth another chance at her famous "Mahoney" character she did on so many radio variety shows, including on Fred Allen's programs.

---

*Gary Cooper and Barbara Stanwyck had appeared in the movie version of *Ball of Fire* in 1941.

There were several appearances by Booth on Kate Smith's radio show. On the episode broadcast September 29, 1944, she offered listeners her Dottie Mahoney character that lived at 1741 Gowanus Avenue in the gritty Gowanus section of Brooklyn, New York. Accordingly, the ditzy girl is unable to get someone to take her out on a date.

She then reads from her memory book, *The Gowanus Canal Diary*. She tells Kate Smith about the big party she gave: "The biggest party since O'Malley's block party to celebrate their older son's parole." There were 16 girls and five fellows: "Every girl had approximately one-third of a fellow for herself." In the confusing manner reminiscent of Gracie Allen, Dottie describes one of the party games the guests played.

At her Halloween party, Dottie describes the decorations: orange and black streamers, a big skeleton, and a piece of mistletoe from the chandelier. When Smith tells Dottie that mistletoe only goes with Christmas celebrations, Dottie responds: "At my house mistletoe is standard equipment." Finally, Dottie asks Smith if she will see her next week. Smith adds, "Unless you have a date?" Dottie sadly replies, "I'll see you next Sunday night."

On Kate Smith's February 18, 1945 program, Booth did a comedy routine and sang "When Irish Eyes Are Smiling." She returned two weeks later on March 4, 1945. Booth sang "It Could Happen to You." She did another one of her routines on March 18, 1945. The following week, March 25, 1945, Booth gave her rendition of "Let Me Call You Sweetheart." For several weeks during April of 1945 Booth sang "I'm in The Mood for Love." Booth's first appearance on Kate Smith may have been on December 11, 1942 in an episode called "The Waltz."

"I am not what you'd call a really happy woman," Booth told the International News Service in May of 1945. "But I am a contented woman, and what more could I ask? Fortunately there have never been a few moments when I have been ecstatically happy. They never lasted more than a minute but who could bear being ecstatically happy for longer?"

She continued: "And this is an unfortunate commentary on my thinking. I can remember the sadness in detail, but I can't remember the ecstatically happy moments. Perhaps that's because I am sadder when I am sad than I am happy when I'm happy."

On May 31, 1945, Booth made her first musical comedy appearance on Broadway in the failed *Hollywood Pinafore (Or the Lad Who Loved a Salary)*. This Max Gordon production at the Alvin Theatre, now called the Neil Simon Theatre, originated from Gilbert & Sullivan's *Pinafore*. Playbill notes: "Book and Lyrics revised by George S. Kaufman, with the deepest apologies to W. S. Gilbert." The opera *Pinafore* provides the music, with additional music by Sir Arthur Sullivan.

Hollywood Pinafore takes place at Pinafore Studios in this reworking. It is the story of a screen star's dilemma of picking a husband. Among the cast is Victor Moore as the dumb studio head, William Gaxton as agent Dick Live-Eye, Ralph Rackstraw as writer Gilbert Russell, and Mary Wickes as a sardonic secretary.

Booth played the exuberant gossip columnist Louhedda Hopsons, which combined the names of real-life Louella Parsons and Hedda Hopper. Brooks Atkinson: "Shirley Booth is funny as a columnist called Louhedda Hopsons ("Little Miss Butter-Up")."

She told *The Philadelphia Inquirer*: "I was supposed to be a cross between Louella Parsons and Hedda Hopper. I wore a dress emphasizing a very full bosom and a fantastic hat with doves on it. On opening night they were the most active doves I had ever seen. The play didn't last long in New York."

Though the singing and cast are given generally good rating,

The New York Times reviewer seemed dissatisfied since the musical: *Hollywood Pinafore* "shows zest only once in a while; it is one of those musicals which never seem to get fully under way." The show closed on July 14, 1945 after 52 performances (53 according to Playbill).

Back on radio, Booth reprised her role of Ruth in *My Sister Eileen* for *Theater of Romance* audiences on August 7, 1945. Judy Holliday co-starred. The September 9, 1945 episode of *The RCA Show*, also known as the AFRS program *The Tommy Dorsey Show*, featured Booth as a guest in a malapropian version of *Hamlet*.

Booth did her Dottie Mahoney characterization in a show called *The Raleigh Room*, broadcast on October 2, 1945. She also satirized *To Have and To Have Not* with Stu Erwin. The AFRS version of the show called it *Hildegarde's Radio Room*.

On November 25, 1945, Booth appeared with Stu Erwin in an episode of ABC's *Theater Guild on the Air*, called "Morning's at Seven." This highly praised series offered actors from the celebrated Theater Guild the opportunity to bring Broadway dramas to radio listeners. This Paul Osborn play takes its title from a poem by Robert Browning. It tells of the issues that arise and affect a family of four sisters, three of them have husbands.

Also on November 25, she did a take-off of her Broadway musical *Hollywood Pinafore* in an episode of Fred Allen called "Brooklyn Pinafore." Booth often appeared on the *Fred Allen Show** during the 1940s.

Two weeks later, on December 9, Booth returned to *Theater

---

*Booth shared the microphone with Billy White on at least four of the following ten Fred Allen shows: February 9, 1947 (with Leo Durocher), October 12, 1947 (with The Harmonaires), January 11, 1948, February 29, 1948, April 4, 1948 (with The Harmonaires), June 13, 1948, December 12, 1948, March 13, 1949, April 10, 1949, and June 9, 1949. Since these episodes are all lost, little is known, except that she apparently played her Dottie Mahoney character.

Guild on the Air, along with Richard Conte and Diana Lynn, in an episode called "Ned McCobb's Daughter." Booth reprised her role of Mabel from her Broadway hit *Three Men on a Horse* on January 6, 1946, with co-stars Stu Erwin, Sam Levene, and David Wayne. Booth did *Three Men on a Horse* again on June 1, 1947. She did a version of *Broadway* with co-star James Dunn on December 29, 1946. On April 21, 1949, she offered her rendition of *Hamlet* with Mary Jane Walsh, Phil Silvers, and Laurence Olivier, and on December 11, 1949, she appeared in *Street Scene* with Richard Conte and Diana Lynn.

Booth sang and did her Dottie Mahoney routine on *The Vaughn Monroe Show*, once in 1946 and twice in 1947. The Veterans Administration syndicated the 1947 appearances as *Here's to Veterans*.

She guest starred on the February 16, 1946 episode of *Celebrity Club* with Art Carney.

Booth's next Broadway show opened at the end of the year on December 11. This drama, *Land's End*, based its story on a romance novel, *Dawn in Lyonesse*, by Mary Ellen Chase (produced by Paul Feigay in association with George Somnes). *Land's End* is about an imaginative betrothed bride moved by her reading of the legendary romance of *Tristan and Isolde*. Booth starred as bride Susan Pengilly in love with Derek Tregonny (Walter Coy) whose been engaged for years to Ellen Pascoe (Helen Craig).

The tragic suicide of Derek is connected to the locale, as explained by John Chapman, *Daily News*: "Land's End, in Cornwall, is the jumping-off place of England - an area of spooky folk-tales and mysterious carved stones." Chapman notes that Craig and Booth provided "some nice performances." Howard Barnes, *New York Herald Tribune*: "The girls take on something more than two-dimensional shape as they are interpreted by the Misses Craig and Booth."

Barnes continued: "Miss Booth is correctly wanton as the second Isolde of the legend . . . " Ward Morehouse, *The Sun*, called them "capable actresses . . . and both are moving at times - Miss Craig particularly." William Hawkins, *New York World Telegram*: "Shirley Booth does a job of infinite expertness as Susan."

However, critical response to the woefully inadequate script by Thomas Job accounted for *Land's End* shutting its doors at the Playhouse Theatre after a measly five performances, closing on December 14, 1946.

Robert Garland, *New York Journal American*, characterized the actors in *Land's End* as "a truly distinguished cast." Thus, the actors are not to be faulted. The undeveloped script weakened the production considerably. Brooks Atkinson: "Since the actors are doing, not what comes naturally, but what they have been told to do, they must not be held to account for trying to deliver more than the script contains."

Arthur Laurents' *Heartsong* appeared briefly at the Walnut Theatre during March of 1947. Booth played a chatty neighbor named Malloy. The show had a three-week pre-Broadway engagement, but never made it to Broadway. Linton Martin: "Although *Heartsong* was a flop on Broadway, it was given whatever appeal it possessed by Miss Booth's individual acting assets in a brief and limited character part."

The role lasted only several weeks, but Booth told an interviewer in November 1949: "The part I enjoyed most in my entire career I believe was playing the role of a dipsomaniac in *Heartsong*. The show was a dismal failure but my part was a distinct personal success. I do not drink liquor and dislike people who cannot handle it gracefully, so I played the part of a drunk with all the vehemence I could muster. Maybe I helped close the show by making the role too dominant. I certainly gave it all I had."

She again appeared on *Hallmark's Reader's Digest Radio*. The NBC broadcast on May 8, 1947 of "Uncle By's Two Wives" is the story of Paulina (Booth). Before this story of one woman's love and devotion opens, the master of ceremonies, Broadway actor and producer Richard Kollmar, introduces Booth in the following exchange:

Kollmar: Thank you, Tom Shirley, and Good Evening Ladies and Gentlemen. Tonight we bring you the story of a marriage. A story set in the granite hills of Vermont where people take a rugged pride in concealing what is deepest in their hearts. Tonight you will meet an extraordinary woman. To play her part the makers of Hallmark Greeting Cards have chosen an extraordinary actress, known for her vivid characterizations, her humor, and her fine dramatic talent. She has been seen on Broadway as Ruth in *My Sister Eileen*, Elizabeth in *The Philadelphia Story* and the lead in *Tomorrow, the World*. Incidentally, she happens to be one of my favorite stars, Shirley Booth.

Booth: Thank you, Dick. It's nice of you.

Kollmar: ... Shirley, I couldn't say anything about your talent the public doesn't know.

Booth: Dick, do you by any chance write those nice messages on the Hallmark Greeting Cards?

Kollmar: Well, no, why do you ask?

Booth: You always say the correct and appropriate things.

Kollmar: Lady, I am susceptible to flattery.

Booth: That's what I counted on. But, Dick, it's good to be here.

And I'm enchanted with the part of Paulina. She reminds me of something I read not long ago in the *Reader's Digest*.

Kollmar: What was that?

Booth: A little bit of wisdom by Oscar Wilde. It really sums up our story, he said: "Men always want to be a woman's first love, but women have more subtle instincts - they like to be a man's last romance."

Kollmar: That's right on target for tonight. Ladies & Gentlemen the makers of Hallmark Greeting Cards take pleasure in presenting on the *Reader's Digest Radio* edition, Shirley Booth in the story of one woman's love, "Uncle By's Two Wives.'"

Everett Sloane played Uncle By. Karl Swenson narrates the story and plays the nephew. Swenson is better known as Lorenzo Jones on radio and later as Lars Hanson on TV's *Little House on the Prairie*.

She returned to *Hallmark Reader's Digest* show for an episode called "The Bradlock Chest" on October 23, 1947.

With Booth's next Broadway show, things could not get any worse. *The Men We Marry* opened on January 16, 1948, and it closed the following day after only three performances. This botched comedy, written by Elizabeth Cobb and Herschel Williams, told a story about some sophisticates.

There's a "good cast," including Shirley Booth (as a character named Maggie Welch), Margaret Hamilton, and John Hudson, "But the direction is so inept and the parts so monotonous that there does not seem to be much point in discussing the actors," observed Brooks Atkinson.

Another appearance on *Hallmark Reader's Digest* offered a show called "The Woman Detective and the Stolen Jewels," broadcast February 26, 1948 on CBS. This episode is based on the true story entitled "Almost a Perfect Detective," written by Anthony Abbott. Booth plays Amy Bundy, a librarian who quits her job when she acts on an impulse to do detective work. Amy tries to convince a famous detective that she should be his assistant. He says no; that is, until a rich society woman, who happens to be a suffragette, has her jewels stolen - and doesn't want to deal with policemen. Amy pursues her intuition, despite the detective's disagreement.

At the conclusion of this appearance on *Hallmark Reader's Digest*, Booth said, "I liked the spirit and I liked playing in a true story. That's what I like about the Hallmark Program - the stories are so unusual and so varied."

The first audition show of *Our Miss Brooks*, broadcast on April 9, 1948, had Booth in the schoolteacher role made successful by Eve Arden.

Three days later, Booth made another appearance on *Cavalcade of America*, entitled "The Man Who Took the Freedom Train." Her co-star was Eddie Albert.

Booth reprised her role from her stage hit *My Sister Eileen*, again; this time it was for the *Ford Theater* audiences on June 13, 1948. Sponsored by the Ford Motor Company, *Ford Theater* offered famous plays and novels featuring Hollywood and Broadway stars. This short-lived, hour-long weekly series started on NBC and then moved to CBS after the first season.

After a string of theatrical failures since 1943, Booth finally approached her pinnacle of success. The comedy *Goodbye, My Fancy* received high marks, and it gave Booth her first major award.

Under the direction of Sam Wanamaker (who also acted), produced by Michael Kanin, and written by Fay Kanin, *Goodbye, My Fancy* opened on November 17, 1948, and it ran until Christmas Eve, 1949 for 446 performances (Morosco, Fulton, Martin Beck, and John Golden Theatres).

Madeleine Carroll starred as Agatha Reed, a liberal Congresswoman who returns for an honorary degree at the Good Hope College for Woman. Expelled years earlier because of an affair with a professor, Agatha comes to realize that her former love is now the school president (played by Conrad Nagel), and he is not the upright educator she remembered and loved. Rather, he lacks the integrity that she believed he had years earlier. By the conclusion, a news photographer (Sam Wanamaker), she had an affair with during the war, becomes her husband.

Booth played Grace Woods, Agatha's intelligent and straight-faced secretary, called acidulous by some. *The Daily Mirror* observed: "Shirley Booth, given a plethora of salty and amusing lines as the secretary, capitalizes them into some of the season's heartiest and most welcome laughs." *The New York Herald Tribune* applauded Booth as "superb."

The Sun: "Shirley Booth, an actress who brightens the lives and the plays of our dramatists, is terse and tough and endlessly amusing as the Congresswoman's secretary." *The New York Post* concluded, "If the heroine's sardonic secretary is of the familiar wisecracking school, at least her wisecracks are amusing and, as spoken by the beautifully incisive Shirley Booth, they even sound brilliant."

For her role in *Goodbye, My Fancy*, Booth received her first Antoinette Perry Award, or Tony Award, as Best Supporting or Featured Actress (Dramatic). Before it ended its run on Christmas Eve 1949, Booth opened in another show a month and a half earlier.

Booth had been honored previously for her performance in plays such as *Three Men on a Horse, Excursion, The Philadelphia Story, My Sister Eileen, Tomorrow, the World*, and *Hollywood Pinafore*. Nevertheless, *Goodbye, My Fancy* gave Booth the most prestigious award yet.

Rosalind Russell and Shirley Booth smile happily after winning Antoinette Perry Awards for their stage performances.

Shirley wins the Perry Award.

However, even greater recognition would come soon. Theatre Guild's Lawrence Langner told Booth of *Come Back, Little Sheba*. Booth: "He said it was a good play, but it needed warmth and humor. I didn't want to do it. That was a depressing time for me and I thought the play might have a morbid theme. But after reading it, I found that it was sad but not depressing. Mr. Langner asked me to try it out. 'Give a young author a chance to be seen,' he said. He thought I might weaken and he kept after me. I tried it out in Westport, Connecticut for a couple of weeks and the audience reaction was wonderful. I still wasn't sure about it though.

"He told me Fredric March and Florence Eldridge wanted to do it, but that he wanted me. I was scheduled to do a play for Brock Pemberton. Technically I could have gotten out of it because I hadn't really signed a contract, but I told Mr. Langner I had signed. He seemed to sense my excuse and since Pemberton's play only lasted two weeks, he got me after all. I guess it was fate. I'm a great fatalist."

While she appeared in *Goodbye, My Fancy* on Broadway, Booth played a New York working girl named Phyllis Hogan in the short-lived radio series called *Hogan's Daughter*. The show, sponsored by Philip Morris, ran on NBC on Tuesdays beginning June 21, 1949. It moved to Wednesdays on August 31 until the last episode broadcast on September 14, 1949. The writers, John Wheaton and Sam Moore, were responsible for the success of *The Great Gildersleeve*.

Several episodes of *Hogan's Daughter* are known to exist. In the episode entitled "New Television," broadcast July 12, 1949, jealousy gets the better of father and daughter. Phyllis' father, Tom Hogan (Howard Smith), is jealous that the next-door neighbors have a TV set. Phyllis is bothered by the attention her boyfriend Marvin (Everett Sloane) seems to give to the neighbor's daughter

Marie. As it turns out Tom learns about the emptiness of competing with the neighbors. Phyllis discovers that Marvin really finds Marie annoying and just tried to help set up the TV.

In "Gypsy's Predictions," an episode of *Hogan's Daughter* broadcast two weeks later (July 26, 1949), Phyllis learns from a gypsy at a tearoom that she will come into good fortune. She decides to give up an interview for a possible secretarial position and goes to a game show with her boyfriend Marvin (Everett Sloane). As a contestant, she gets the first question right about who sponsors the show. For the second question, Phyllis incorrectly attributes the Patrick Henry speech "Give me liberty or give me death" to George Washington instead. Of course, when she loses as a contestant, she blames her adversity on the fortuneteller. Phyllis complains to the tearoom and receives a refund of the money charged for her lunch.

Back on Broadway, *Love Me Long* followed up Booth's first award-winning success of *Goodbye, My Fancy*. This short-lived Brock Pemberton-produced domestic comedy proved disastrous. Pemberton had previously received acclaim for *Harvey*. In *Love Me Long*, Booth offered up the former "dizzy actress" Abby Quinn. However, this poor imitation of *Private Lives* presented a story by Doris Frankel that revolved around a housing shortage in New York City and two couples switching partners. George Keane, Russell Hardie, Anne Jackson, Harry Bannister, and Jennie Howard are among the cast.

The production had press coverage under the title of *The Time is Yes*, and before that as *Rondo in a Flat*. All told, *Love Me Long* received unanimous bad reviews.

Booth did her best, but to no avail since the boring characters lost the audience's interest early on. "Shirley Booth deserves high marks for gallantry, playing Abby for all she is worth, which is not

THE NEW PLAYS

Ike and Abby (left) discover that their fiancés, Margaret and Jim, are in love with each other.

November 7, 1949
Forty-Eighth Street Theatre

"LOVE ME LONG"

Produced by Brock Pemberton
Staged by Margaret Perry and Brock Pemberton
Setting by John Root
Costumes supervised by Margaret Pemberton

A comedy
by
DORIS FRANKEL

THE CAST

Abby Quinn	Shirley Booth
Mr. Sharp	Harry Bannister
Jim Kennedy	Russell Hardie
Moving Man	William Sharon
Ike Skinner	George Keane
Louis Ulmer	Jennifer Howard
Margaret Anderson	Anne Jackson
Phone Man	Heywood Hale Broun
Charles P. Anderson	Daniel Reed
A Caller	Carl Low

● "Love Me Long" played sixteen performances; fifteen more than decency dictated. The "plot" was infantile, the dialogue witless. Abby loved Ike, to whom she had been twice married and divorced; Abby was engaged to Jim; Margaret was engaged to Ike; Ike loved Abby. The conclusion surprised no one: at the end of three wearisome acts Abby got Ike and Margaret got Jim, a fate richly deserved by all concerned. Brock Pemberton, the producer, was also co-director, sharing the odious task with Margaret Perry. There were times when it seemed that Mr. Pemberton had assumed responsibility for one side of the stage and Miss Perry the other, leaving the actors to shuttle aimlessly between the two zones. Shirley Booth was badly miscast and quite noticeably embarrassed by the whole venture. The general ineptitude of the cast was best exemplified by George Keane, Jennifer Howard and Harry Bannister, all of whom exuded a quality of arrogant egotism. The only pleasant items were a quiet performance by Russell Hardie, in which he emerged as a real person and, as such, was out of place among the ridiculous, caricatured creations of the imprudent author; and a humorous setting by John Root.

On stage in *Love Me Long*.

a great deal," according to the *New York World-Telegram*. *The Sun* summed it up, thus: "Shirley Booth, who has brightened numerous plays with her deft and incisive playing, has no material and no chance in *Love Me Long*." *Theatre Arts* revealed, "Shirley Booth was badly miscast and quite noticeably embarrassed by the whole venture." The show closed at the 48th Street Theatre after a mere 16 performances, on November 19, 1949.

The day after the opening of *Love Me Long*, the *New York Journal American* reviewer commented: "Shirley Booth plays Abby Quinn as if she were preoccupied with Little Sheba on her mind." If that's true, maybe she realized that *Come Back, Little Sheba*, her next Broadway show, would be that quality role which could further advance her status as an actress beyond *Goodbye, My Fancy*.

Glowing with Success!
The 1950s

By now, Booth had performed in over 3,500 shows on stage. She endured the grind of featured and supporting roles, as well as being known primarily for her comedic talents on radio and stage. However, the watershed production for Booth had finally come.

Booth introduced *Come Back, Little Sheba* for a couple weeks at the Westport Country Playhouse in Connecticut. The Theatre Guild would use this playhouse to try-out new productions. The cast included Sidney Blackmer, Cloris Leachman, Lonny Chapman, John Randolph, Daniel A. Reed, Olga Fabian, Charles Hart, Wilson Books, and John Larson.

Come Back, Little Sheba, a two-act play produced by the Theatre Guild, directed by Daniel Mann, and written by William Inge (his first Broadway show), opened on Broadway at the Booth Theatre on February 15, 1950.

Booth played Lola, the slovenly and frumpy Midwestern homemaker. Sidney Blackmer played her husband, referred to as "Doc," a chiropractor kept sober for a full year by attending Alcoholic Anonymous meetings. Joan Lorring played Marie, a college student, who boards at Doc and Lola's untidy home. The monotony of Doc and Lola's dreary life is the focus of the first act. Nevertheless, it is the second act of *Come Back, Little Sheba*, in which the startling underside to this ordinary couple explodes onto the audience.

While trapped in their past failures, Doc and Lola live in a struggle to come to terms with their frustrations. The past folly has dominated their present life. Among the unresolved issues is the fact that Doc did not become a medical doctor because Lola's pregnancy forced him to quit school and marry, and then the baby died . . . The viewer must assume this triggered Doc's alcoholism, and henceforth allowed Lola to escape into laziness.

Apparently, after observing Marie's seeming promiscuity, and meeting one of her suitors, Turk (Lonny Chapman), Doc's bitter torment of past memories resurfaces. Doc fears that Marie and Turk will marry and repeat his mistake. With this, Doc relapses and goes on a bender, and then he attempts to kill the indolent Lola with a hatchet.

The title of the play, *Come Back, Little Sheba*, refers to Sheba, a white puppy that Lola loved and lost. Lola often dreams of searching and calling for Sheba. In the last scene after Doc returns home from his stay at the alcoholic ward of the city hospital, Lola concludes that she must not think of Sheba anymore; that the dog represents the past symbolically.

The final lines of *Come Back, Little Sheba* offer the wisdom gleaned from the experiences. Lola tells Doc of her dream she had of Sheba. However, this time she saw Sheba dead and all covered in mud with no one to help her.

Doc: Why couldn't you?

Lola: I wanted to, but you wouldn't let me. You kept saying, "We can't stay here, honey; we gotta go on. We gotta go on." (Pause) Now, isn't that strange?

Doc: Dreams are funny.

Lola: I don't think Little Sheba's ever coming back, Doc. I'm not going to call her anymore.

Doc: Not much point in it, Baby. I guess she's gone for good.

Lola: I'll fix your eggs. (She gets up, embraces Doc, and goes to stove. Doc remains at table sipping his fruit drink.)(The curtain comes slowly down.)

Lola's youth is gone. She seems to realize there's no point in trying to call the past back.

Booth: "I refused to put on 20 pounds because I felt that a good actress could make herself look any weight she chose. Mostly I stuck my stomach out and wore too-big dresses. But when I had to go to a doctor for something else, he told me I had curvature of the spine - something I had acquired in the eight months the play had run. I took remedial exercises all day to make up for my bad posture during the show at night."

When asked if people reacted with laughter in the wrong places, Booth answered: "The tragic element of the play caused embarrassment in many people. Laughter was an outlet for their embarrassment. Often the laughter would come with a very serious line. To avoid this, I began emphasizing lines before the serious ones, deliberately making them comedy lines so that the audiences would have laughed themselves out before the dramatic moments."

Kevin Minton: "She fought most fiercely and notably when she 'forced' playwright William Inge to transform Lola in *Sheba* from a well-educated, sharp-tongued nymphomaniac into a dumb, plaintive, doting, defenseless lump of pathos."

Booth told Morris Gelman in *The Theatre* (April 1960): "I fashioned Lola after three people. One was a frowsy woman I saw on 6th Avenue and 57th Street. She was looking wistfully into shop windows and with her was a saggy little dog. I felt a great deal of sympathy for her. I also used the mannerisms of an ex-mother-in-law, and the plaintive expressions of an aunt. A characterization is liable to become fuzzy in your mind, unless you have a real person to hang on to."

"Shirley Booth soars histrionically in a role that could dismay most actresses," said the *New York World-Telegram* and *The Sun*.

Some critics disagreed. "As Lola, Shirley Booth is required to make much out of a long and, owing to its nature, monotonous role," explained the *New York Journal American*. "She not only makes the most of it. She makes more of it than there is. Hers is a fine example of how to drive a man to drink with kindness." "She brings warmth and sympathy to her role which is rarely sustained by the script," agreed the *New York Herald Tribune*.

A photograph in *Theatre Arts* from April 1950 showed Lola in the kitchen holding a coffee pot with the caption: "SURPRISE PERFORMANCE . . . . Shirley Booth, usually cast for comedy, gives a heartbreakingly tender portrayal of Lola, the sloppy wife in *Come Back, Little Sheba*."

In his book *Broadway*, Brooks Atkinson observed: "Again Miss Booth is superb. She has the shuffle, the maddening garrulity and the rasping voice of the slattern, but withal she imparts to the role the warmth, generosity and valor of a loyal and affectionate woman." Further, "Until Shirley Booth played the slovenly housewife, she was invariably cast as an expert character actress of sardonic hussies . . . "

In a less adulatory review entitled "The Man, the Dog, and the Bottle," Richard Watts Jr., *New York Post*, concluded, "There is so much that is worthy about *Come Back, Little Sheba* that it seems a pity it isn't more skillful a drama, but Mr. Blackmer and Miss Booth are brilliant."

Booth paid close attention to detail. This is evident throughout her career. For instance, in *Come Back, Little Sheba*, Lola is sweeping; she finds a hairpin amidst the dirt and proceeds to put it in her hair. **Booth:** "Women gasped. But I am sure that many of them had unconsciously done the same thing." Critic Marjory Adams called this "those typical little Booth touches, that are so human they hit home, but which are homely, every-day gestures that most of us prefer to forget as being part of our lives."

Theatre Arts, July 1956: "Miss Booth's most effective creation was not in a vehicle but in a play, a genuine play that had something to say about human experience. Her naïve, slatternly, frightened and lonely woman in *Come Back, Little Sheba* was a complete, rounded work of art . . . When she got to work on Lola, Miss Booth was really able to use her good mind and her emotional resources, and she could harness her own élan vital to a character that already possessed robustness apart from her."

Booth: "I never tire of any role I like. That reminds me again of Rex Harrison. He says that he has never done one play that he hasn't been happy to see close. I don't understand how an actor can feel that way. In every performance of *Sheba* I found something new, some different interpretation of a line."

With the drama *Come Back, Little Sheba*, Booth won the coveted Tony Award for Best Actress (Dramatic), which catapulted her into worldwide recognition. Hollywood also came knocking with an offer to do the screen version of the play. Now, after nearly 40 years on the stage, Booth finally reached her long-awaited triumphant peak by garnering the most adulation and success in her entire career on the stage.

When she went to Sardi's, after her performance in *Come Back, Little Sheba*, people cheered. **Booth:** "How could you forget anything like that? It started a new trend. As I came in this couple stood up and then everybody in the restaurant stood up and I believe it was the first time it had happened and it was pretty thrilling."

Not only did Booth accept top honors as Best Actress in a Leading Dramatic Role at the Tony Awards, but she received other awards for her dramatic talent in *Come Back, Little Sheba*, including the Donaldson, the New York Drama Critics Award, and the Barter Theater Award for being the outstanding actress of the year. The latter award gave Booth the opportunity to name to the Barter Theatre Company two actors; she named 19-year-old Gaby Rogers and 23-year-old Jerry Lifkin.

Sidney Blackmer received recognition for his consummate acting skills by garnering the Tony for Best Actor. *Come Back, Little Sheba* closed on July 29, 1950 after 190 performances. The show did better than many of Booth's other Broadway efforts, but not as well as one might have expected based on the enormous attention it garnered. Booth went on to tour the show in other cities for six months more.

Booth would do a radio version of *Come Back, Little Sheba* in February of 1951. This *United States Steel Hour* production of *Theatre Guild on the Air* starred Gary Cooper in role of Doc. Later, Booth would do a production of *Ethan Frome* for the *United States Steel Hour* with Raymond Massey and Margaret Phillips, broadcast on May 20, 1951.

While doing *Sheba*, Booth revisited *Ford Theater* on CBS to co-star with Danny Kaye in "The Milky Way," broadcast March 26, 1950.

Peggy Cass, known for her regular appearance on *To Tell the*

Truth, had done stage work herself, such as playing Agnes Gooch in *Auntie Mame*. Cass told Kevin Minton: "I never knew her well, but knew her work tremendously well. We had met a few times at parties and in L.A. when we both had a series going. But, you know, she was shy, like me - not a great party gal. I remember, after seeing *Come Back, Little Sheba*, I did something I very seldom do, I went backstage to tell her what a talent she was, and how that performance touched my heart. She was so gracious, mild. No star pretense at all. I usually don't go backstage unless I know the actor well. I'm too shy!"

The award-winning actor and director Charles Nelson Reilly recalled to Kevin Minton: "Oh, my God! I first became aware of Shirley Booth when she was doing *Goodbye, My Fancy* on Broadway. I'd go with a friend for 90 cents - balcony standing room - 9:00 p.m. She was so very funny. I couldn't contain myself. I'd literally scream in laughter! After that I saw all her shows. When I saw her, I thought, 'My Lord, to be able to do that!' - make people laugh, cry, laugh again, cry again. And a roommate at the time said, 'Charles, you can do that.' Thank goodness, I believed him. When was *Goodbye, My Fancy*? Late Forties? Must have been. I was working in Miss [Uta] Hagen's class. It may have been later. I was first partner to Peggy Cass in a play called *Squaring the Circle*, and I knew I wanted to do what Shirley Booth did.

"Now, *Come Back, Little Sheba*, I caught the second act about 30 times. Never a dry eye in the house. If all the hankies in that theater had been wrung out at once, you could have filled the average Beverly Hills pool."

Booth had finally reached a supreme level of success, with a plethora of awards; this certainly boosted her spirits. To critic Jeff Stearn of the *Sunday News* Booth said she knew success arrived when she did not have to climb steps to the second or third floor to reach casting directors to get a job. "When they smile, and you don't have to climb those stairs, you know you're a success."

"In a way it's nicer to be appreciated as you get older. By that time you don't have the zip and vitality of youth, the resilience, and you have to fall back on creature comforts. When I was a small girl I would notice old people riding around in big limousines and wonder what they got out of life. I know now, of course, that these things are useful in buoying you up and giving you a sense of self-confidence. Not that I'm that old yet." Booth now was almost fifty-three years old, though the press reported her age as in her mid-40s.

Booth had a minimalist approach to her acting: "I'm economical. I hate waste motion and anything extravagant. When I start to study a part, I watch like a hawk to see just what can be left out. Maybe that's laziness - or maybe I'm just practical. The other thing I'm a crank about is honesty. I can't play a part I don't believe, and I don't think that audiences will accept what is phony."

In her own bylined article Booth stated: "For example, when I was first studying the role of Lola, the pathetic housewife in *Come Back, Little Sheba*, I remembered seeing a woman walking her dog on Sixth Avenue in New York. She was heavy, so heavy it seemed to go right into her spirit, and she shuffled somewhat. I used this ungainly walk to show insecurity in my characterization of Lola..."

As Booth's next project after the dramatic hit *Come Back, Little Sheba*, *A Tree Grows in Brooklyn* brought her tuneful talents to the forefront for the second time. Out of what would be Booth's darkest periods in her personal life came one of her brightest, most upbeat performances in her entire life. How Booth did this is most revealing of her ability as an actress and performer.

A Tree Grows in Brooklyn, arguably, is Booth's best musical among the five she did (*Hollywood Pinafore*, *By the Beautiful Sea*,

Juno, and *Look to the Lilies*). Though it ran on stage for merely eight months, besides losing money, *A Tree Grows in Brooklyn* nevertheless gave audiences a sensational follow-up to *Sheba*. It has the distinction of being Booth's longest-running musical.

During rehearsals, Booth told the *Philadelphia Inquirer*: "When I tried out a song from the Arthur Schwartz score, my range was this wide," indicating a space of an inch between fingers. "I don't want to sound like an opera singer. I'd just like my singing voice to sound as close to my speaking voice as possible so that I can move smoothly into song from dialogue. But I have a lot of rehearsing to do before I stop sounding like the end man in a minstrel show and start sounding like Aunt Cissy."

A Tree Grows in Brooklyn, co-written by Betty Smith, is based on Smith's best-selling novel published in 1943 about the Nolans, the turn-of-the-century family living and struggling in the tenements and slums of the seamier Williamsburg section of Brooklyn, New York. As a student attending the University of Michigan in 1930, Smith had written her story as a play called *Francie Nolan*. The story had a film adaptation in the 1945 Academy Award-winning version directed by Elia Kazan. It starred Dorothy McGuire as Katie Nolan, Joan Blondell as Aunt Sissy, James Dunn in his Oscar-winning portrayal of Johnny Nolan, and Peggy Ann Garner as Francie.

By 1951, the book had sold more than four million copies. Producer Robert Fryer had the idea to make *A Tree Grows in Brooklyn* into a musical for the stage. He told the versatile George Abbott about it. Abbott went on to produce (with Robert Fryer), direct, and collaborate on the more comedic, upbeat stage adaptation with author Betty Smith. Jo Mielziner created the settings, and Herbert Ross choreographed - including a Halloween delirium tremens ballet.

When Max Showalter left *My Sister Eileen* to go off to the U.S.

Army's Special Services during World War II, he met up with Lt. Robert Fryer from Shaker Heights, Cleveland, Ohio. Showalter talked of Fryer to Kevin Minton: "He possessed an intense love of theater, and once he discovered I had done *My Sister Eileen* with Shirley, he ordered me officially to accompany him to New York and to introduce him to her. 'She's one of the greatest actresses of our time,' he said, 'and I've got to meet her.' From that moment on, he kept in constant touch with her and when the war ended, he produced a number of shows starring her."

Originally, Irving Berlin, who had just completed *Call Me Madam*, intended to work on the show's musical score, but he found the creative juices barren. Thus, Arthur Schwartz and Dorothy Fields were brought together again. Previously they had collaborated on the 1939 production of *Stars in Your Eyes*, starring Ethel Merman and Jimmy Durante.

Schwartz did the tuneful music, and Fields contributed the energetic lyrics. "We found the script of *A Tree Grows in Brooklyn* so beautifully adapted by Betty Smith and George Abbott that it appeared to be a perfect vehicle for a thoroughly integrated score. All the flavor of Miss Smith's novel has been retained, as well as the warmth and realness of her people. It was a great pleasure for us to translate their emotions into words and music."

The rehearsals for *A Tree Grows in Brooklyn* began in February 1951. The show had two previews with a one-week trial run at the Shubert Theatre in New Haven, Connecticut beginning March 19, 1951. By the second preview at the Forrest Theatre in Philadelphia, the brothel scene was cut. Smith revealed that there were frequent revisions in the show, from adding and/or removing scenes and songs. The Broadway opening occurred on April 19, 1951 at the Alvin Theatre.

Smith had been initially reluctant to participate in writing a stage version. Earlier, when Hollywood came knocking, she did not wish to be involved in the film production. As in the past, she would give consent to an adaptation of her novel; this time, a Broadway musical, but had no interest in actually writing it. But as it turned out, she changed her mind and decided to collaborate with George Abbott.

To satisfy audience expectations and to stay faithful to the essence of the original story is a daunting task. It was also necessary to effectively capture the spirit of the original story in song. Indeed, Smith and Abbott overcame the difficulties in translating to the musical stage her best-selling work of fiction and Oscar-winning film.

"I think it was one of the most amiable collaboration in dramatic history," Smith said of her working with George Abbott. "We never disagreed on script. With no definite plan of procedure, we went to work. Sometimes I wrote the first draft of a scene and turned it over to George. He worked on it and turned it back to me. It went back and forth three or four times then we sat down and worked on it together. Sometimes George made the first draft. It was about fifty-fifty. We had one trait in common. Both of us were avid cutters. With something like delight, I cut his lines. In a matter of fact way he cut my lines. By accident I cut many of my own lines. With ruthlessness, he cut his own scenes and lines."

Smith continued, "After the fourth draft, we could no longer say, 'My lines,' or 'Your lines.' They were our lines. . . .Well, after ten months, we had what we called a working script. It was a thin little thing of ninety-four typed pages. All of a sudden the slight script became the center of intense activity. I answered no mail, resented outside phone calls."

Fans challenged any suggestion by those involved in the production that the title of the book and movie be changed to "Brooklyn Bridge Story," "Brooklyn Bridge," and even one staffer's title of "Kiss Me, Katie." It would remain *A Tree Grows in Brooklyn*.

Booth's beloved husband, William H. Baker, died of a heart attack reportedly in his sleep during the time *A Tree Grows in Brooklyn* was in rehearsals. He already suffered from a heart attack previously, which Booth helped him recover from. Booth sold the dairy farm soon after.

Over twenty years later Booth would recall to Penny P. Anderson, *TV Time and Channel:* "Being a farmer is the most underrated job in the world. It killed my husband, really, it did. There we were, two city slickers trying to work a farm. My husband had a history of heart problems and there were so many chores on the farm that were strenuous and foreign to him. It was too much. He died of a stroke."

Whether it was a heart attack as reports indicated at the time, or a stroke as Booth recalled, William Baker did encourage Booth out of retirement. Booth continued: "I tried so hard to take care of him and I think he pushed me back to work to get me off his neck."

She missed only two rehearsals before returning to work. Now widowed, it seemed that Booth's involvement in the musical gave her the strength to live through this shock. "It hardly gave me time to think of anything else and, of course, I tried not to." Years later Booth told *The Saturday Evening Post*: "He loved the farm. He'd seen so much devastation during the war that he wanted to make things grow. But he did too much. He always did the heavy work while his helper drove the tractor. He didn't know he had a heart condition."

Kevin Minton: "The loss of Mr. Baker hit her hard. Though neither fans nor critics would have guessed it, Miss Booth felt she sleepwalked her way through it."

A Tree Grows in Brooklyn presented the main characters of

Johnny Nolan (Johnny Johnston), Katie Nolan (Marcia Van Dyke), Harry (Nathaniel Frey), and Francie (Nomi Mitty). Both Johnston and Van Dyke were newcomers to the stage. The musical *A Tree Grows in Brooklyn* is the story of the troubles that lovers will endure. Unlike the movie version that had focused on their daughter Francie and her point of view, the musical shifted emphasis to the tumultuous courtship and marriage of Johnny and Katie.

Nightclub singer Johnny Johnston (1915-1996) had appeared in 1940s movie musicals, such as *Star Spangled Rhythm*, in which he sang "That Old Black Magic" to Vera Zorina's ballet performance. Marcia Van Dyke (1924-2002) had an established career as a concert violinist, but she had appeared as Louise Parkson in the 1949 movie *In the Good Old Summertime* with Judy Garland.

In contrast to the characters of Johnny and Katie, Booth offered audiences the very memorable and saucy lace-stockings-clad Aunt Cissy (spelled "Sissy" in the film and book). "Whoever was responsible for casting her as the frowzy, slatternly Cissy performed a stroke of genius," noted the newspaper critic from *Women's Wear Daily*.

Smith apparently developed the subplot character of the freewheeling Aunt Cissy with Shirley Booth in mind. Although Booth appeared in a secondary role in *A Tree Grows in Brooklyn*, audiences cheered and clamored for her comic portrayal of "Cissy," according to press reports at the time.

This stage adaptation offered Smith the chance to write with more freedom than in the novel, so scenes like one in the bordello were permitted. A scene that grabbed audiences occurred when Aunt Cissy fakes having a baby to fool her current paramour "Harry" into thinking he is a father. She married just the first "Harry," but calls the other four "common-law" husbands "Harry" too.

John Chapman, *Daily News*, credits Booth with "giving the

performance of her or almost any other comedienne's life. . . . Shirley Booth is truly something. I suspect she can do anything in the theatre and do it better than anybody else can."

Brooks Atkinson, *The New York Times*, observed how the show and Booth satisfied the audience. "For she has never had a part so ideally suited to her style of warm, magnetic comedy, and she has never given a more glowing performance." Even Smith found her performance to be astounding. Smith told *Collier's*: "She knows more about Cissy than I do."

"It is not exactly a secret these days that Miss Booth is one of the wonders of the American stage, a superb actress, a magnificent comedienne, and an all-around performer of seemingly endless versatility," remarked *New York Post* critic Richard Watts, Jr. "Furthermore, she can take a line of dialogue that is only passably funny and make it seem like a true masterpiece of hilarity. Combining humorous brilliance with a kind of rich humanity, her performance is a complete joy."

"I have rarely had more fun laughing, and never had more fun crying. This is an experience of real honesty, taste and ingenuity," observed William Hawkins, *New York World-Telegram*. "It is a salty, colorful, heart-wrenching salute to the nostalgic Nineties, which could be tragic as well as gay," stated Robert Coleman, *The Daily Mirror*.

Of eight major reviews, only two were unfavorable. John McClain, *New York Journal American*, thought the musical disappointed those familiar with the novel because he felt the script failed to bring the story to life. Otis L. Guernsey, Jr., the *New York Herald Tribune*, witnessed Booth's "grand performance" even though he recognized the deficiencies in story and direction. "Speaking in a thin nasal voice in the accent heard east of the Bridge, Miss Booth combines earthy expressions with the gestures of emphatic refinement in a delightful comedy turn . . . In tune or in fine sarcastic fettle, Miss Booth gives light and contour to a gloomy, flat piece of work."

Three or four songs written for the character of Francie had to be dropped from the show because Nomi Mitty could not sing. According to a friend, Mitty reportedly felt uncomfortable around Schwartz and Fields since she sensed that underneath their niceness they were disturbed because their songs for her were not being used. Abbott had insisted on selecting and keeping Mitty even though she could not sing.

Nonetheless, one of the highlights in *A Tree Grows in Brooklyn* is the Schwartz-Fields score, especially Cissy's inimitable singing to Harry all about love. "Cissy singing in a cracked lisp is a joy," according to William Hawkins, *New York World-Telegram*. Booth performs "Love is the Reason," the song critics considered a well-written number looking at the sharp side to love. With a fugue arrangement, Cissy's friends harmonize by interweaving comments and repeating Cissy's lines.

"He Had Refinement" is Booth's tongue-in-cheek solo in *A Tree Grows in Brooklyn*. She seems oblivious to the true nature of her first "Harry," since she considers everything about him as indicating his refinement.

Marcia Van Dyke and Company joined Booth in the bouncy and lively number "Look Who's Dancing." Booth and Albert Linville perform "Is That My Prince." Nathaniel Frey, Johnny Johnston, Marcia Van Dyke, and Booth reprise several of the numbers in the Finale, including Booth and Frey singing "Love Is the Reason" with additional lyrics, such as Cissy telling Harry, "Incidentally love is the quicksand and I'm sunk," and the suggestive "I would live in a barn, if you slept in my stall."

The investors included CBS, Leland Hayward, Joshua Logan, Betty Smith, and Johnny Johnston. And although the curtain dropped on the financially disappointing *A Tree Grows in Brooklyn* on December 8, 1951 after a moderately successful 267 performances, it seems it should have played much longer, especially given the superb Schwartz-Fields score.

Betty Smith's agent, Helen Strauss, attributed the weaknesses of *A Tree Grows in Brooklyn* to the fact that the show had been revised too many times. Others have noted that it had strong competition that season from *Call Me Madam*, *Guys and Dolls*, *The King and I*. Audiences may have found these shows to be considerably more pleasant and upbeat than Smith's slice of life.

Most importantly, perhaps, is the fact that the casting of charismatic Booth, a stage superstar, in a bright comedic supporting role noticeably unbalanced *A Tree Grows in Brooklyn*. This caused audiences to be distracted and to focus too much on the character part of Booth's Cissy. Not enough attention went to the darker main storyline of Johnny and Katie presented by the two leads.

With *A Tree Grows in Brooklyn*, Booth received the New York Drama Critics' Award for Best Actress in a Musical. Booth beat Vivian Blaine *(Guys and Dolls)*, Gertrude Lawrence *(The King and I)*, and Ethel Merman *(Call Me Madam)*. She also received the Billboard Donaldson Awards for Best Performance by an Actress of the 1951 Season.

Her commitment to go to Hollywood for the film version of *Come Back, Little Sheba* meant that she could not tour the show. However, Joan Blondell, who portrayed the character in the movie version, toured as Cissy. Yet, *A Tree Grows in Brooklyn* closed after just two months on the road.

Booth now returned to Hollywood for the second time. Earlier in 1938, Booth gave up her Broadway career for the sake of her first husband. "The next time I saw Hollywood was some years later. By this time Ed and I had been divorced and I had done quite a few Broadway shows. I was brought west by producer

Hal Wallis to make my motion picture debut in *Come Back, Little Sheba*, in the role I had created on the stage, that of Lola, the pathetic slovenly wife of an alcoholic."

Booth thought it was unfair that she received the opportunity to do the film role of Lola based on her Broadway part. She thus competed for the Oscar with other actresses who did not have such an advantage of the experience of playing the role on stage. However, Booth admitted she did have one disadvantage: "I had to get used to the camera."

She told Joe Hyams: " . . . the average movie star has only a few days to learn his part, whereas stage actors have months of experience in the role and also the tremendous advantage of having played it before an audience. By the time they get before the cameras in the part it's second nature to them.

"I had a lot of time to develop the character of Lola Delaney in *Sheba*. For three hours I had to prove to a stage audience that Lola was a colossal bore - without boring them. Transferring her to the screen after all that practice was not much of a problem."

Movies played some part in influencing Booth's life. **Booth:** "Yes, I'm a devoted moviegoer . . . have been for years. I can tell you the casts of pictures from away back. Deems Taylor has a book dealing with the history of films. A game I play during idle moments is to cover the names of the various players whose pictures are in the book and tell them myself. My score is almost one hundred."

Up until then, Booth refused Hollywood offers of big money. Hal Wallis, producer for Paramount Pictures, came calling for Booth to reprise her role of Lola in the screen adaptation of *Come Back, Little Sheba*. Wallis wanted some bankable names to help sell the picture to audiences, since this story seemed non-commercial. Sidney Blackmer was out since he had not appeared on the screen for a few years. As far as Lola Delaney's part, the story goes that

Glowing with Success 101

Shirley Booth smiles happily after winning the Best Actress Academy Award for her performance in "Come Back, Little Sheba." Presentation was made in N. Y.

Winning the Oscar.

Wallis had tried other actresses, but he liked Booth's screen test. This adaptation co-starred Burt Lancaster as Doc, Terry Moore as the roomer Marie Buckholder, Richard Jaeckel as Turk Fisher, and Walter Kelley as Bruce, Marie's boyfriend.

Booth: "Hal Wallis, who produced *Come Back, Little Sheba,* told me that if I would play Lola Delaney in the film as I did in the Theatre Guild production on the stage, I would have carte blanche - they wouldn't shoot until I approved the script."

Of course, Booth insisted on things done on her terms. A contract arranged by theatrical agent Audrey Wood outlined Booth's desire to act in the role as she understood it, her approval of the play, and terms of time management so as not to keep her from her Broadway acting.

The director of *Come Back, Little Sheba*, Daniel Mann, put the actors through an arduous three-week rehearsal period. This helped get the picture completed on schedule with only a day's worth of retakes needed. As a result, it took only a month to shoot the film.

Upon entering the gates to Paramount Studios to make *Come Back, Little Sheba*, Booth had rehearsed what she would say: "Miss Booth to see Mr. Hal Wallis, please." However, before she could say something, gatekeeper Tom Matson bowed: "Glad to see you, Miss Booth, and welcome to Hollywood." Booth quickly learned that Matson had seen every play of hers since *My Sister Eileen* because he vacationed in New York every year.

Again, the movie adaptation refers to a dog that never appears on screen at all. Backstage at the Empire Theatre, Booth told Peter Briggs, "Nobody knew what Sheba looked like, so to set our minds at rest, we let an animal painter decide its breed and do a portrait." The painter offered a portrait of an English sheep dog.

Hal Wallis: "It was a fine play, but it wasn't being frightened to death by Hollywood offers. Most companies were worried by the theme. What's interesting is that in the movie we did a lot more with the boy-and-girl affair than had been in the play and we had very little trouble with the Johnston office."

As for the scene between Marie and Turk, Wallis explained the issue with the censors: "It has to be obvious that he's trying to spend the night with her, but it can't be overcharged. We worked it out with them, cutting a line of dialogue in one place, and it was fine. I don't think the meaning is in doubt in the scene, but I don't think it's the kind of thing that will provoke giggles or smirks. "

"Brilliantly portrayed by the cast, the characters are completely real," observes *Redbook's* critic. "There's little more to say about Miss Booth other than that she has recently proved that she's a great actress in any form of production." "Rough on the emotions but rewarding, this is a story of youth - what it's like to live it and to lose it," according to *Photoplay*.

"In a skillfully contrived soap opera called *Come Back, Little Sheba*, Shirley Booth turns in one of the great movie performances of the year, of any year," said Al Hine, critic for *Holiday*.

Hine explains: "Miss Booth brings the role of Lola a rare kind of acting. There is one variety of great actor who leaves you breathless and admiring because you are conscious of his or her expert performance. There is another who seems, with even finer skill, to fall so effortlessly into the part that you see only the character and aren't aware of great acting until some time after you have left the theater. . . . Miss Booth partakes of the virtues of both, but winds up closer to the personal effacement of perfect character portrayal. She is so good she is embarrassing."

Burt Lancaster wrote to Kevin Minton: "In response to your letter re: Miss Shirley Booth and my acquaintance with her. Yes, I was aware that Hal Wallis brought me into the film as window dressing. Not one to brag, but I believe that as Doc I held my own. Not to say that another actor may have been more suited, namely Spencer Tracy or Gary Cooper, both wonderful actors who would have been wonderful as Doc Delaney.

"Of course, they were both considered; surprisingly, so were Ronald Reagan and Fred MacMurray. As for Shirley, of course she had played Lola hundreds of times, but a Hollywood actress with rare exception couldn't have brought the pathos to the character that Shirley did. Having not been reared in film, she did not have stilted, overly melodramatic tendencies. She played up to a camera exactly as she did to an audience."

Lancaster continued: "Yes, I know Bette Davis turned Lola down. Bette told me years later, around 1964 or so, that no matter what story I'd heard (and there had been many) that she felt strongly that only Shirley could do the role justice. She would have accepted only if Shirley had declined, so that she felt Wallis might give the role to Barbara Stanwyck. Davis wouldn't have liked that at all. But, I believe she was happy for Shirley. I had never worked with an actress so natural, so watchable."

Booth: "I've always loved audiences. In fact I think a good audience does half the player's work for it. But I also like an audience to stay in its place, which for me at least is the other side of the footlights. The camera, I've found, is no respecter of footlights or privacy. It goes anywhere. And where it goes, it tattles. I can't hide a thing from it. It's frightening. It's ghastly. It's awful in its privacy-destroying prying. It's the most shattering experience of my life. I hope I live through it."

Because of Booth's second trip to Hollywood, she had some very good fortune. However, Booth still did not absorb the Hollywood world: "Hollywood again existed as in a dream. I knew it was there, all right, but in the nerves and excitement of my first screen appearance I doubt if I could have felt Hollywood, had I reached out to touch it. I went to the studio each morning to play my part and home again to the hotel that night. That was my schedule and I stuck to it. I'm one of those people who can't seem to mix business with pleasure. When I work, I am awfully absorbed with it. Everything else has to wait. Then, too, I was on 'borrowed time,' for immediately after the picture version of *Come*

Back, Little Sheba, I was due back in New York to start rehearsals for a new play, Arthur Laurents' *The Time of the Cuckoo*."

Ten months after *A Tree Grows in Brooklyn* closed, Booth appeared on Broadway in another milestone in her career. The comedy *The Time of the Cuckoo* opened on October 15, 1952 at the Empire Theatre. This show previewed at the Walnut Street Theatre for a two-week engagement in Philadelphia.

Produced by Robert Whitehead and Walter Fried, written and directed by Harold Clurman, *The Time of the Cuckoo* takes place in Venice. *The Time of the Cuckoo* is Laurents' only success as a playwright. Laurents would later have success as the librettist for *West Side Story* and *Gypsy*.

Earlier, Laurents wrote the abortive *Heartsong* for Booth in 1947. *Heartsong* and *The Time of the Cuckoo* both offered Booth a hilarious scene in which her character is intoxicated. Critic Linton Martin found that the scene was funnier in *The Time of the Cuckoo*. Martin: "If they are canny, producers of future plays in which Miss Booth appears should insist upon having a clause in her contract requiring her to play a drunken scene."

The definition of "cuckoo" was offered in the program to the presentation: "The cuckoo is a summer visitant to the whole of Europe. It proclaims its arrival by a cry heralding the season of love." Booth played spinster Leona Samish, a single American secretary vacationing in Venice, Italy during the summertime. The action of *The Time of the Cuckoo* takes place in the garden of the Pensione Fioria. Leona's desire for affection leads her to a romance with the sophisticated Renata Di Rossi (Dino Di Luca), a married shopkeeper with a family. As a result, Leona, who calls everybody "Cookie," is disillusioned when she discovers that Renata is a philanderer; and consequently, she realizes the difference in moral standards of Europeans and Americans.

The co-stars included honeymooners June Yaeger (Geraldine Brooks) (succeeded after six months by Bethel Leslie) and artist Eddie Yaeger (Donald Murphy), a youngster named Mauro (Jose Perez), and the proprietress of the Pensione Signora Fioria (Lydia St. Clair). The secondary plot involves an affair between Eddie and Signora Fioria.

William Hawkins of the *New York World-Telegram*, on Booth's performance: "With a subtle vocal range and complete submission to the atmosphere, she creates an emotional dimension that is not in the words."

Hawkins explained: "When the jokes are weighty, she deftly mutters them under her breath or twists their inflection till they sound piquant."

The Daily News critic John Chapman noted how Booth "gave another of her seemingly artless and effortless performances, and again demonstrated her sure instinct and fine training for the theatre."

Brooks Atkinson: "Although Miss Booth never gives the impression of being dramatic, she gathers all the good-will, emotional turbulence and chagrin of the character in an immensely dramatic performance that is warm, easy-going and lovable."

"Shirley Booth has never been given a greater perimeter for her established talents: an ingenious entrance scene (funny), sympathetic interlude, love scene (schmaltz), drunken sequence (comedy-pathos) and finale," remarked John McClain of the *New York Journal American*.

Booth: "In *The Time of the Cuckoo*, I played a woman who was very sorry for herself. It was one of my most difficult roles. I kept telling the author that the minute a character is sorry for himself, the audience won't be." Later on, she remarked, "I had to fight myself to play her." It is difficult to determine whether it was

Booth's personal distaste for this type of self-pitying, self-indulgent woman, or whether her acting skill caused her difficulty.

Anyway, Booth made the show work. *The Daily Mirror's* Robert Coleman explained how *The Time of the Cuckoo* is "long on talk and short on action. It takes a couple of lengthy scenes to achieve anything resembling drama. The situations are weak, sketchily built, but some of the dialogue is quite amusing. Frankly, it would be an innocuous bore had not producers Robert Whitehead and Walter Fried landed Shirley Booth to star in it."

Arthur Laurents called Booth, "the most brilliant comedienne I have ever worked with." As far as stage direction, Laurents noted that during the rehearsals Booth "wasn't at all on the same wavelength as Mr. Clurman." Years later, in another incarnation of *The Time of the Cuckoo*, Laurents acknowledged Booth's acting limitations in the show. He said Booth could not satisfactorily do the second act party scene, which required what are called "the flips." These are the necessary rapid changes or shifts in Leona's character.

Unhappy with the part of Leona, Booth refused the offer to do the movie. **Booth:** "I loved my role as a drunk, and made Laurents promise that some day I could play another part like that. But I wasn't so enthusiastic about *Time of the Cuckoo* at first, because I thought there was no reason for my getting tight and disorderly. It didn't seem dramatically right. I wasn't surprised, therefore, when Katharine Hepburn eliminated the scene for *Summertime*, which is what they call the screen version."

While doing the show on Broadway, Hepburn asked that Booth visit her for cocktails. **Booth:** "So I went to see her, and she asked me if it was true that I had turned down the role of Leona in the movie. I said yes, it was true. Then she said, 'That's what I was told, but I wouldn't believe it until I heard it from you.' Well,

she went ahead and did the part in the film . . . and it was a great success." *Summertime* had David Lean directing and starred Hepburn and Rossano Brazzi.

Booth received Best Dramatic Actress of the year award in the Eleventh Annual Poll of the Foreign Language Film Critics' Circle. This award, known as the Golden Globe, resulted from hundreds of foreign-language newspaper reviewers being polled. The screenplay by Ketti Frings tied first place for Best Screenplay.

She received a Western Union, dated February 20, 1953 2:55 p.m., notifying her that she would be receiving the Golden Globe award. The telegram read:

"=MISS SHIRLEY BOOTH=
25 WEST 54 ST=

HAPPY TO INFORM YOU THAT YOU BEEN VOTED THE GOLDEN GLOBE AWARD FOR THE BEST DRAMATIC ACTRESS BY THE HOLLYWOOD FOREIGN CORRESPONDENCE ASSOCIATION Please keep it secret until presentation which will be Feb. 26TH Stop Knowing that you cannot be here in person kindly designate some other motion picture star to accept on your behalf stop PLEASE REPLY CARE OF 444 NORTH OAKHURST DRIVE BEVERLY HILLS CA 43476= BERT REISFELD PRESIDENT HOLLYWOOD FOREIGN CORRESPONDENTS ASSOC="

The movie version of *Come Back, Little Sheba* opened to rave reviews and tremendous box office sales. In the March 10, 1953 issue, *Look Magazine's* Annual Movie Awards selected *Sheba* and *The Greatest Show on Earth* as the Year's Best Pictures, Booth as Best Actress, and Hal Wallis as Producer of the Year for "tackling a story others feared to try and making it a compelling sensitive film."

Joan Crawford wrote to Booth on March 12 telling her she was glad to accept one award for Booth and how happy someone will be to accept the Oscar for her. Interestingly, Crawford was competing for the same Oscar.

Shirley Darling:
Thank you so much for the beautiful flowers. How happy I was to accept the Award for you - and I know how happy somebody's going to be in accepting the Award for you on the Oscar. I don't know who's going to do it yet, but it will be a pretty happy person.

Everybody knows you're going to win. There isn't a chance for anybody else, and you know something? We're all very happy for you. We believe you should win it.

Thank you, darling, for the flowers. Keep happy and keep well and if there's anything I can do for you, out in our town, just let me know.

Earl is going to arrive here Saturday and we'll be thinking of you. He's going to the Awards with me and we'll have the joy of hearing your name called off.

God bless you, darling. I hope to see you soon.
My love, as ever,

JOAN CRAWFORD

The next day Bette Davis wrote from New York Hospital on a notepad stamped "Merrill" (her husband Gary), part of which states: "...Wish I could be with you next Thursday. Am so sure you will win. My congratulations. You are so great. My sincere thanks for all. Bette D." Davis was competing for the Oscar that year as well.

The possibility of Booth winning an Academy Award for Best Actress upset her. Booth told Joe Hyams: "I hope I don't. I'm terrified of winning an Oscar. I'm afraid if I did I'd begin to take myself too seriously. It would make me self-conscious, always being aware that people expected something great from me."

Before the Academy Awards ceremony, Booth attended a pre-Oscar Pen and Pencil Restaurant party with the other nominees a few days earlier. Her friends were sure she would win. However, Booth reportedly had uncertainty that she would be victorious at the Academy Awards. After all, she endured many letdowns throughout the years. News reports stated: "Pen and Pencil host John Bruno gave Miss Booth a smiling *Sheba* caricature of an Oscar, aided by Kim Hunter, a 1951 Oscar winner for best supporting actress, and Jack Palance, a nominee this year for an Oscar."

On March 19, 1953, with a reported 15,000 fans enduring the drizzle outside the RKO Pantages Theater, and Bob Hope as the Master of Ceremonies, the 25th Annual Academy Oscars were first televised. Television paid $100,000 for the rights to broadcast the ninety-minute show.

A false air raid alarm did not dispel the energy.

The Motion Picture Academy awarded Gary Cooper the Best Actor Oscar (his second) for *High Noon*. The Best Picture Oscar surprisingly went to *The Greatest Show on Earth*. John Ford received the Oscar for Best Director for *The Quiet Man*. The Best Screenplay Oscar was awarded to *The Bad and the Beautiful*. Gloria Grahame (for *The Bad and the Beautiful*) and Anthony Quinn (for *Viva, Zapata!*) won Best Supporting Awards. Cooper and Quinn, both in Mexico, received their awards in absentia. John Wayne picked up Cooper's and Ford's Oscars.

Shirley Booth, as the odds-on favorite to win Best Actress, waited along with other nominated actors in New York at the time, including Jose Ferrer and Thelma Ritter. Booth left her Broadway stage show, *The Time of the Cuckoo*, so that she could get to the International Theater where the awards would be handed out in New York. The winners would pick up their award from Fredric March.

In the category of Best Actress, the nominees included Joan Crawford for *Sudden Fear*, Bette Davis for *The Star*, Julie Harris for *The Member of the Wedding*, and Susan Hayward for *With a Song in My Heart*. With 34 million television viewers watching, Ronald Colman announced in Hollywood the winner for Best Actress, Shirley Booth. In New York, the eager Booth tripped on her long gown upon going up the steps to the stage. She quickly picked herself up, smiled, and received the award from Fredric March along with a kiss.

The Hollywood audience at the theater watched on a big-screen TV as Booth received her award in New York. March told her that the New York coverage had been increased from one minute and fifteen seconds to about twenty-five minutes for her to make her speech. Booth stated: "I'm a very happy and a very lucky girl. My luck has many, many names. I won't attempt to list them all. All you have to do is look at the screen credits and you'll know what I mean. It's been a long, long climb. I guess this is the peak, but the view has been wonderful all the way. I want to thank my old friends for their faith, my new friends for their hope and everyone for their charity."

Not wanting to put anyone out, Booth attended with her press agent, "who had to be backstage, anyway. I didn't want to ask someone who'd have had to sit alone while I was performing on stage. It wouldn't have been nice."

Since she celebrated already, Booth did not party on the night she won. Shortly after winning the Oscar Booth told a reporter: "I'm just like a sponge, I guess. I just keep absorbing all the things that happen to me and the people I meet and I never seem to be filled up. I feel the way I felt on Thanksgiving Day when I was eight. We had just moved from Manhattan to Germantown, outside Philadelphia. The old neighborhood had been rather cold and aloof. But in Germantown all the neighbors came into our house to call and to bring little helpful things. I felt the new kids liked me. It was all so friendly and the whole house began to glow. And I began to glow."

A press report from early 1951 reported Booth's age as 45 years old. Actually, Booth was 52 years old. *The Daily Mirror*, in March of 1953, when Booth was 54 years old, stated, "This forty-two-year-old new screen sensation would be the first to admit that if her face or figure were her fortune she would be in the workhouse. BUT WHAT AN ACTRESS."

One interview Booth did at this time revealed much about her pursuit of stardom. **Booth**: "I was called 'the reluctant star' by one producer because he wanted to make me a star and I didn't think I was ready for it yet. It was probably that reluctance that made me put off going to Hollywood. I wanted to wait until I knew I was ready. Also I knew that if I waited until I was playing straight character parts, I would have no trouble. I didn't wait that long, but I waited long enough to gain one advantage."

Booth: "People in Hollywood were so pleasant to me. At a party Bette Davis came up, introduced herself to me and said she had seen my test and that no one else could possibly play the part. I didn't agree with her. But I loved hearing it."

She told Earl Wilson when asked why she never did a movie years earlier: "I didn't think my looks warranted the parts they offered me." And Booth did not think that her winning the Oscar would be a curse, as Academy Award nominee Terry Moore suggested. **Booth**: "You create your own jinx. It's like a man with a family. When he drives a car, he doesn't take the chances a single man takes. When you've won an Oscar, you might hesitate about accepting a certain type part, whereas if you hadn't won an Oscar, you wouldn't hesitate."

Booth: "I've heard that I am supposed to have refused Hollywood offers before because I was stubborn or afraid. That isn't so. I wanted to go with a feeling of security that I was doing the right thing. I had that and I went. I wasn't sure I wanted to win that Oscar for my first picture. I thought I should make a few and then be ready to win.

"For Hollywood, I have only humble thanks. I will never forget the crowning honor the men and women of the industry paid me by awarding me an Academy Oscar for my performance in *Come Back, Little Sheba*. It's here beside me in the den in a specially built cabinet." Booth had the honor of being one of the eight or so actors to win a Tony and an Oscar for the same role; the others were Jack Albertson (*The Subject Was Roses*), Anne Bancroft (*The Miracle Worker*), Yul Brynner (*The King and I*), Jose Ferrer (*Cyrano de Bergerac*), Joel Grey (*Cabaret*), Rex Harrison (*My Fair Lady*), and Paul Scofield (*A Man For All Seasons*).

Hollywood columnist Louella Parsons suggested that Booth's next project for Hal Wallis would be in the Erna Lazarus' romantic comedy, *Route 66*. Supposedly, Wallis wanted Booth in *The Solid Gold Cadillac*, but he could not work that. Wallis' long search yielded this story, according to Parsons, "about a shopworn show girl and a lazy, lovable, tinhorn sport who are thrown together on a cross-country trip." Parsons doubted Booth would be doing any more Broadway plays in the fall of 1953, when production was slated.

At the end of March in 1953, the American Theatre Wing awarded Booth their Best Actress Award for her performance in

The Time of the Cuckoo. She received the prestigious Antoinette Perry Award for "distinguished contributions to the current theatre season." This was Booth's third Tony Award; the previous were for *Goodbye, My Fancy* in 1949 (Supporting Actress), and for *Come Back, Little Sheba* in 1950 (Best Actress).

At a luncheon with the Drama Desk, Booth showed her modesty. "If I do anything wrong, please help me, tell me so."

After Booth won her Oscar, *Come Back, Little Sheba* continued to be the top-grossing movie of the year. The film critics of New York, Cleveland, Associated Press, and press and trade groups throughout the U.S., Canada, and Europe named Booth as the Year's Best Actress. The movie itself made the ten-best list all over the United States.

Congratulations came from everywhere. A letter from Gritti Palace-Hotel, Venezia, dated March 30, 1953, stated:

"Here am I, dear Shirley Booth, in your city. I last saw it in 1914. I read what you said in the *Ladies Home Journal*. I wish you hadn't read the serialized form of the novel. When I return to New York late in April, I'd like to send you a copy of *Giant*. Congratulations on the motion picture award. Every now and then they show genuine taste and judgment in a decision, don't they. Edna Ferber."

With all the attention focused on Booth, she appeared in a *Theater Guild on the Air* radio show broadcast April 11, 1953. This would be in *The Glass Menagerie*, the Tennessee Williams' role she would do for television viewers in 1966.

In addition to receiving the Academy Award, Booth earned on April 30, 1953 the Cannes International Film Festival Award for Best Actress of 1952. A mass interview of Booth by high school editors and writers occurred on May 7, 1953 in the Loew's Theatre Building in New York. The students questioned Booth on her notable career. The buzz at this time rumored that Booth would sing in her next movie role.

On the evening of May 24, 1953, a single performance offered the audience of 1,500 a chance to see the "Highlights of the Empire," a special farewell to the famed Empire Theatre, which would be demolished for a skyscraper. In 279 shows, the Empire Theatre hosted such top names as Sarah Bernhardt, Maude Adams, and the Barrymores. The farewell offered scenes from nine of the theatre's successful shows, including *The Time of the Cuckoo*.

Booth eulogized the closing of the Empire, after the final performance of *The Time of the Cuckoo*, on May 30, 1953. "I am sorry to have to tell you that this is the last performance to be given in this theatre. That is because there are not enough sentimental people in New York. But we here on stage are sentimental, and you in the audience are sentimental. That is why you are here. Will you join us in singing 'Auld Lang Syne'?" Afterwards, the curtain came down unhurriedly.

The Time of the Cuckoo lasted for 263 performances with Booth receiving at least five awards for her performance.

Booth told Louis Sheaffer, "I'm living in a sort of never-never world right now. There are a number of ifs on the horizon. If Vin Delmar's book shapes up, I'll be in that. If Edna Ferber's 'So Big,' adapted by Horton Foote, is right, I'll be doing that."

Booth and the entire *The Time of the Cuckoo* company would perform the show at the Central City Opera House in August of 1953.

She lived alone in an apartment located off Fifth Avenue on 54th Street in midtown Manhattan. It overlooked the Museum of Modern Art's Sculpture Garden. "I go away alone to lick my wounds when I'm hurt or feel defeated. Some people are terrified of being alone. But I love it. I find so many things to do, painting, watching TV and just puttering around the house." One of

Booth's favorite activities was remodeling her apartment.

Her animal companions at this time included a brown cocker spaniel named Candidate and a Siamese cat named Cissy. Apparently, the cat's name recalled the character she just portrayed in *A Tree Grows in Brooklyn*.

Booth: "Some of us are fortunate enough to get paid for acting. Most people don't. But they act all the time. People can't help it. All try to create an impression, to project as they would like to be. The man who delivers the mail is acting. So is the postman, and the preacher in the pulpit, and the salesman. Children start acting as soon as they become conscious of other people. Little girls act with their dolls. Boys make like cowboys. And none stop as long as there is breath.

"People act for various reasons, I think. Some just to project a front. Others, as autosuggestion, to boost their own morale. Life is drab for many, and it helps the ego and the courage to pretend it isn't. Part of it is just manners, 'what's expected,' an amiable social front which makes smoother the details and encounters of life.

"When the man who delivers my groceries asks how I am, he doesn't give a tinker's actually. He's just being Polite. At one time I tested that. I told him how I felt, figuring that if I told him often and fully enough, he would stop that nonsense and waste of time, going through the verbal gestures. So I detailed my symptoms. I figured wrong, though. He had asked, with that big smile, so long that he was stuck in the groove, he didn't know how to turn it off. But I will tell you something about myself. I became glad that he persisted. If he had just said 'good morning' and dumped my groceries, I would have worried - about him. A piece of the pattern would have been missing. It is necessary, a soothing balm, to pad life.

"However, one who makes acting one's trade, also gets paid for it. And now I even do the love scenes without inner agitation of embarrassment. It's expected, so I comply. On the stage, in my early teens, when the leading man kissed me I would duck my chin, so my impassioned lover had to plant his passion by a chaste smack on my forehead. That's no thrill to audiences. I hated myself for it, but it seemed wrong to be kissed in public. When I became conscious of myself as an actress, I got over that.

"I think the main thing is to be interested in people and studying them and seeing how they react. I think the most important thing is a sense of humor because I think a sense of humor is a sense of taste."

Time magazine selected a picture of a smiling Shirley Booth for the front cover of the August 10, 1953 issue. She received a five-page article detailing her career and her life's philosophy, along with plenty of pictures. The article stated that Booth "scored a complete and effortless conquest of the movie colony." *Time* called Booth "the hottest thing in show business" and "the first lady of the American stage and screen."

In 1953, Booth appeared as herself in an all-star musical comedy called *Main Street to Broadway*. The movie offers a who's who of Broadway with many stars in the cast portraying themselves, including Tallulah Bankhead, Ethel Barrymore, Lionel Barrymore, Vivian Blaine, Henry Fonda, Oscar Hammerstein II, Rex Harrison, Helen Hayes, Mary Martin, and Richard Rodgers. Agnes Moorehead, Rosemary DeCamp, Florence Bates, among others, were given character names.

Directed by Tay Garnett, *Main Street to Broadway* has a very thin and forgettable plot; which is merely an excuse to display the talents of these Broadway stars. The storyline is somewhat familiar: boy meets girl, boy loses girl, boy fails as a playwright, but boy gets girl again by the finale.

Main Street to Broadway even offers Oscar Hammerstein II singing the song he co-wrote with Richard Rodgers, "There's Music in You." Mary Martin offered a reprise.

In an article, entitled "I Didn't Get Around," Booth spoke concerning her stay in Hollywood, and how her lack of familiarity with Hollywood after three visits may have been due to her busyness. "I've just recently returned from my third trip to Hollywood. I went there for Mr. Wallis for my second Paramount film appearance in *About Mrs. Leslie*, a picturization of Vina Delmer's highly successful novel. In this I play a Beverly Hills rooming-house keeper who finds opportunity to look back into her life at the secret romance she shared with a Washington governmental figure, played by Robert Ryan.

"It's a very moving story of two lonely people who find a meaning for life in each other's company. Daniel Mann, who directed me in *Come Back, Little Sheba*, was assigned the direction of the new picture. I love working with Danny," concluded Booth.

Mann, in regards to *Sheba*, commented, "She doesn't act. She lives the part." Another source had Mann saying, Booth "lives on stage."

Booth had a very bad attack of bursitis beginning on the first day of shooting *About Mrs. Leslie*. Besides health problems, a bit in the papers stated, "Oscar has gone to Shirley Booth's head." It told how the set was closed to press and visitors on the first day and how the production is causing headaches for members of the company. The production "has driven more than one member of the company to the shelf where the headache powders are kept." The article pleaded, "Come back little Shirley, the way you were before movie fame struck you!"

With a screenplay by Ketti Frings and Hal Kanter, *About Mrs. Leslie* gave Booth another chance at screen drama. The cast included Robert Ryan as George Leslie, Marjie Millar as Nadine Ro-

land, Alex Nicol, Amanda Blake, Ellen Corby, Harry Morgan, and Jack Larson.

Hal Kanter: "One afternoon, Robert Ryan, Shirley's leading man, told me what a pleasure it was for him to play a role where he didn't have to knock somebody down or shoot somebody up. He appreciated the script and working with a leading lady of such stature."

A press report revealed that Booth "is getting the Hollywood glamour treatment for her new picture. She wears snappy clothes, fancy hairdos and even a bathing suit...."

About Mrs. Leslie offers a story via flashbacks of two people who find contentment by spending six weeks together every year at Mr. Leslie's California coast ocean house. Booth played Mrs. Vivien Leslie, "the other woman." Mrs. Leslie, a former nightclub singer, becomes a dress shop owner, and eventually runs a boarding house. Ryan played the wealthy manufacturer Mr. Leslie. Why she never married him is not revealed until the movie's ending.

This story of the yearly romantic rendezvous "is nothing more than soap opera," remarked Wanda Hale. "Miss Booth portrays this warm, friendly, kind-hearted woman with sustained brilliance, making you believe in her and by the force and elasticity of her performance she makes the sentimentality and the incredible story bearable." In short, the story and its incongruities of *About Mrs. Leslie* did not do justice to Booth's acting talent. However, some have considered Booth's role a good one as well as a welcome departure for her. She even sings in this movie.

In her bylined article Booth noted: "People have asked whether or not the shadow of my bright and shining Academy Award Oscar haunted me while making *About Mrs. Leslie*. I must be honest about a question like that. When I'm getting acquainted with a character, I get so engrossed that results are unthought of. I be-

About Mrs. Leslie. Photo courtesy of Thomas J. Watson.

About Mrs. Leslie. Photo courtesy of Thomas J. Watson.

About Mrs. Leslie. Photo courtesy of Thomas J. Watson.

Glowing with Success 125

About Mrs. Leslie. Photo courtesy of Thomas J. Watson.

come so absorbed I never think where it will lead. I concentrated on Mrs. Leslie. All my thoughts were of her . . .

"I love playing in pictures. Although it's hard work, I found it every bit as exacting and demanding as the stage, and I have the greatest admiration for those working behind the camera.

"Being a character actress and not having been born with the looks of a glamour girl, I was certain Hollywood wouldn't know what to do with me, and perhaps it would be best to mind my own business and stay where I was in the theater. Luckily that was not my final decision. I'm really surprised with my progress in Hollywood. They've all taken wonderful care of me, from producer Hal Wallis on down.

"While I was working on *About Mrs. Leslie,* Hollywood remained the shadowy location it had always been. I had an apartment in a quiet neighborhood. And from it I never stirred when I wasn't at Paramount Studios on the set. I told the publicity man on the picture, 'I'm afraid you will have a hard time getting any news from me.

"'Night after night I go home from the set, climb into bed, have my dinner there on a tray, where I relax watching television. Then I study my lines, and my light is out by ten. If you can find any excitement in that, you're a wonder.'"

Booth described her stay in Hollywood: "Geographically, I caught a glimpse of the Sunset Strip, the great street of cafes and agents' offices. And that's about all. As to parties, I got to none. Once on a Sunday, Danny Mann insisted I go to the circus with his wife because he said it would do me good to think of something else outside the picture. Nightclubs like Ciro's, the Mocambo, and the rest are still alluring names to me. I read about them in the columns."

As far as hobnobbing with the stars: "As to Hollywood stars, those I met at the studio - usually at the crack of dawn in the make-up department - I found to be cordial and friendly. I saw and met Bing Crosby, Danny Kaye, William Holden, Audrey Hepburn and Humphrey Bogart in the commissary at noon. Once, on the set, I looked out beyond the camera and there was Jerry Lewis looking at me. I met him a few minutes later and we had our pictures taken together with his arms around me.

"Barbara Stanwyck and Joan Crawford I have met a few times although, unfortunately, I saw little of them as all of us were too busy. When I was playing in the theatre in *Come Back, Little Sheba* Miss Stanwyck sent me flowers and a delightful note expressing her pleasure at my performance. Joan and I first met in New York and once at dinner in her Brentwood home."

"There will be other trips to Hollywood, I suppose, in the future," Booth anticipated, "as I am under contract to Mr. Wallis for two more pictures. Maybe then I'll get to do justice by this fabulous town. I'll be the tourist of all times, I'm sure."

After completing the shooting of *About Mrs. Leslie*, Booth returned to New York on Saturday, December 5, 1953. A press release indicated that Miss Booth will arrive by train on the *20th Century Limited*, compartment "H," car 2601, due at 9:30 a.m. at Grand Central in New York. She scheduled the return to begin rehearsals for her next Broadway show. According to reports, a doctor would be present in the theatre while Booth appeared.

Booth, in her bylined article, said, "I read scripts hoping to find just the right one. Meanwhile, I'd like to portray Mrs. Midget, the cockney charwoman in Sutton Vane's *Outward Bound*. This was played first by Beryl Mercer and then by Laurette Taylor. Both were magnificent. Maybe Hollywood will do *Outward Bound* once more. It was so beautiful.

"I'm certain I could never entirely give up the stage for motion pictures. I find it fascinating to do both. You never get a chance to become stale, lose enthusiasm or the eagerness to keep learning."

My Most Unforgettable Child offered Booth and other Hollywood luminaries the chance to assist the United Nations International Children's (UNICEF) fund. This radio program broadcasted nationally on the American Broadcasting Company network on February 14, 1954. Hosted by Bing Crosby, the show's well-known guests included Kirk Douglas, Greer Garson, Audrey Hepburn, Deborah Kerr and Brandon De Wilde. Booth and the other stars narrated true stories of children from throughout the world.

Booth's next Broadway show, *By the Beautiful Sea*, depicted turn-of-the-century Coney Island in the early 1900s. The nostalgic show included the excitement of Steeplechase Park's Tunnel of Love, the Old Mill boat ride, the Midway, and balloon parachuting.

Booth played the blonde-haired, vaudeville comedienne/performer Lottie Gibson. She runs a boarding house several blocks from the beach. Her love interest is an aging, divorced, and impoverished Shakespearean actor named Dennis Emery (Wilbur Evans).

How convenient is it that both Dennis' 17-year-old daughter "Baby Betsy" Busch (Carol Leigh) and Dennis' promiscuous ex-wife are boarders in Lottie's house? As the story goes, Lottie gives a check for a thousand dollars to Dennis. When she realizes that her father used the funds in the bank already, Lottie must make the check good. An opportunity arises when Lottie attempts to win the money by doing a parachute jump.

Baby Betsy's mother has kept her from dressing her age to keep her as a child star. With Lottie's assistance, Baby Betsy dresses as a woman, and then finds love. By the finale, Baby Betsy is no longer opposed to her father and Lottie marrying. This frees Lottie to wed Dennis.

Booth: "I'm romantic and looking for a knight on a white charger. He seems so educated. I brush up on Shakespeare, a couple of scenes from *Macbeth*, and set that playwright back a hundred years. I sing five songs, including 'Thirty Weeks on the Road,' a comic song about vaudeville. But I don't use a comedy voice as I did in *Tree Grows in Brooklyn*. And I dance a little. But not much. Everybody knows I'm not a dancer. I don't want people to think I'm saying - 'See how versatile I am.' I even go up in a balloon and come down in a parachute in this show. It's not a caricature of the period, it's a gentle satire."

By the Beautiful Sea gave Booth a third chance to perform musical comedy on Broadway. Robert Fryer and Lawrence Carr produced, Marshall Jamison directed (the show began with Charles Walters directing), scenic designer Jo Mielziner created the colorful settings, Irene Sharaff designed the period costumes, and Donald Saddler did the choreography.

The show previewed at Boston's Shubert Theatre beginning February 23, 1954 until March 13. From there, the show went on March 16 to the Forrest Theatre in Philadelphia for three weeks before its Broadway debut.

In an atypical manner for the Academy Awards, Booth announced the nominees and the winner for the 1954 Best Actor Oscar. She did this while backstage in Philadelphia. The actors up that year: Marlon Brando, Richard Burton, Montgomery Clift, William Holden and Burt Lancaster. The winner's name was whispered to her over a specially installed phone line as Donald opened the envelope onstage. The unlikely winner was William Holden that night.

On opening night in Boston, Booth wanted to wear a blush pink gown, but zipper trouble forced her wear a white dress. Many of the expensive clothes Booth was feted to wear would not be in keeping with the character.

Booth: "Most of those wonderful dresses I wear will have to go before the New York opening. I am supposed to be a vaudeville performer whose income will continue for a limited time. I am saving every cent I can afford for my theatrical boarding house. Lottie just wouldn't have been able to buy such a wardrobe. It is necessary for me to work too hard to overcome the handicap of all those expensive, exquisite costumes, in order to show how desperate I am to get hold of $1000. People can't believe that money means so much to me."

It has been said that Booth had to wear unflattering clothes over the years on stage due to the kind of roles she played, until her Boston premiere of *By the Beautiful Sea.*

When fitting for the costumes, Booth remarked to *Cue*: "This is the first show I've ever been pretty in." Later she explained: "Nothing but Mother Hubbard house dresses - and sloppy ones - for *Sheba*. In *Time of the Cuckoo* I had to wear the sort of conservative clothes a secretary would buy who had supported her family for years, and who was having her first trip to Italy, now that she didn't have to pay out for them any longer. You can imagine how much I enjoyed the Sharaff gowns I am now wearing. But I have to think my characters as well as act them. I must never be conscious of my clothes being too decorative for the kind of woman I play."

She did another radio production of *Stage Struck*, broadcast on January 1, 1954. This star-studded show, hosted by Mike Wallace, focused on the world of theater with interviews, musical numbers, and scenes from productions. This particular episode featured theatrical highlights of 1953.

Another episode of *Stage Struck*, broadcast on April 4, 1954, featured a preview of *By the Beautiful Sea*, which would open several days later. Lawrence Carr and Robert Fryer, the producers of the Broadway show, and Agnes Moorehead and Danny Kaye were among the cast.

Booth returned for the season finale of *Stage Struck*, broadcast on May 2, 1954. The show featured highlights from the 1953-54 theatrical season and had appearances by Ingrid Bergman, Katharine Cornell, Audrey Hepburn, and Deborah Kerr. Booth commented on the "death of the Empire Theater."

She had first appeared on the *Stage Struck* show of October 2, 1953. At that time, she mentioned the demise of the Empire Theater and introduced a recording of Basil Rathbone reciting Prospero's lines from *The Tempest*.

By the Beautiful Sea opened on Broadway on April 8, 1954 at the Majestic Theatre.

Wilbur Evans as Booth's love interest had experience on the stage already, unlike the leads in *A Tree Grows in Brooklyn*, Johnny Johnston and Marcia Van Dyke. Evans did the lead for *South Pacific* in London. However, a critic Saul Colin observed that not only did Evans fail, but there's "the familiar and ugly banality of the background," and songs which were "neither distinguished nor original." Nevertheless, Colin praised Booth for her "talent and grace and oozing a lovable quality seldom found on the stage."

Among the cast of *By the Beautiful Sea* were Cameron Prud'homme as Lottie's irresponsible father, blues and jazz legend Mae Barnes as Lottie's maid Ruby Monk, Richard France as juvenile Mickey Powers, Anne Francine as Flora Busch, and child actor Robert Jennings as Half-Note.

Once again, Arthur Schwartz and Dorothy Fields collaborated. Schwartz composed the music, Fields wrote the lyrics, and Herbert & Dorothy Fields (brother and sister) wrote the libretto.

In referring to Booth, *Theater Arts* (June 1954) noted: "She dances, hoisting her ample skirts to knee length on one occasion to run through a buck and a wing with little Robert Jennings that is elementary, old-hat and altogether captivating. And of course she acts with a range seldom seen on the musical stage, even though the content of this script would hardly tax the capacity of the Floradora girl."

New York Post critic Richard Watts, Jr. suggested that the book was at fault in that it interrupted the show; it should have been made "as a period vaudeville show without even the pretense of a libretto."

William Hawkins, *New York World Telegram*, saw Booth's outstanding performance: "She is adored because of her warm, personal quality, her contagious gaiety and the great good taste that keeps her from putting pressure on the audience . . . She is a million dollar value in show business."

Although the show is faulted for running out of steam by Act Two, "There is only one Shirley Booth and this is her show," exclaimed John McClain of the *New York Journal American*.

"Friendly, unassuming and good-natured, honest with the other performers as well as with the audience, she makes a Coney Island holiday out of her part," concludes Brooks Atkinson of *The New York Times*.

Walter F. Kerr of the *New York Herald Tribune* called it Shirley's show: "Miss Booth is the champ . . . There is such kindness in this nasal voice that no gag ever comes down hard. There is so much warmth behind the blowzy façade that the most routine musical-comedy love scene takes on a sudden defiant shine. Miss Booth may be the only performer in the world from whom a child cannot steal a scene."

Booth kept in one of her fourteen scrapbooks a letter (dated March 23, 1954) from a physician who saw the production in Philadelphia. Dr. Arthur First found the "Lottie Gibson Specialty" number upsetting and in poor taste as contrasted to the nostalgia of the rest of the show.

First: "My wife, who feels the same as I do, told me to mind my own business, but even though I have delivered thousands of newborn babies, I still get a thrill out of the next one and fail to see the humor in the sadistic implications of an unwanted little baby."

Booth sings "In the Good Old Summertime," as a countermelody to "Coney Island Boat," her optimistic view of being single, the witty lament "I'd Rather Wake Up By Myself," and "Lottie Gibson Specialty." Wilbur Evans sings "Alone Too Long," "More Love Than Your Love," while Mae Barnes sings two showstoppers on love: "Happy Habit" and "Hang Up."

Cast members would drop spare change into a water pump on the set. The funds were donated to the Damon Runyon Memorial Fund for Cancer Research. The full pump held $30.

The show had references to George C. Tilyou's Steeplechase Park at Coney Island, which was then opening its 58th year. A press report noted that the Tilyou family sent a telegram to Booth: "Good luck. We hope you run as long as Steeplechase has."

Booth appeared on a Cerebral Palsy Benefit radio show on May 15, 1954. This salute to Eugene O'Neill featured scenes from *Ah, Wilderness, Anna Christie, Desire Under the Elms,* and *Mourning Becomes Electra.* The cast included Joseph Cotten, Karl Malden, Roddy McDowall, and Geraldine Page.

The publication *Theatre World* selected Booth to be a presenter at their awards party on May 18, 1954. A letter from the editor Daniel Blum asked Booth to give out the awards. "I know they will get a big thrill receiving their award from one of the truly distinguished actresses of our theatre." The twelve winners included Orson Bean, Harry Belafonte, James Dean, Joan Diener, Ben Gazzara, Carol Haney, Jonathan Lucas, Kay Medford, Scott Merrill, Elizabeth Montgomery, Leo Penn, and Eva Marie Saint.

While Booth wooed audiences with *By the Beautiful Sea,* her latest movie, *About Mrs. Leslie,* opened. Actors Equity Association offered a gala premiere the day before the movie opened, to benefit the Actors' Fund at the Victoria Theatre on Sunday evening, June 27, 1954. Booth received a special award from the association. The award presenters included Billy De Wolfe, Barry Sullivan, John Hodiak, Paul Jones representing Equity, and Adolph Zukor. Radio and television announcer Ben Grauer offered his services as master of ceremonies.

By the Beautiful Sea ran until October 1, 1954 at the Majestic Theatre. The show continued at the Imperial Theatre, where it closed after 270 performances on November 27, 1954. Interestingly, *By the Beautiful Sea* reportedly had 178 financial backers, including Charlton Heston, Joshua/Nedda Logan, and Rosalind Russell.

Booth received an award for her performance that read as follows:

The Billboard
Eleventh Annual
Donaldson Awards
For Outstanding Achievement in the Theater
Season of 1953-1954
Presented by the People of the Theater to
Shirley Booth
Best Performance by an Actress
(Musical)
For
By the Beautiful Sea.

The signatures on the certificate represented the producers, critics, actors, actresses, Actors' Equity, Chorus Equity, stage managers, press agents and managers, dancers, stagehands, treasurers, scenic designers, and costume designers.

Booth also received the award for Best Feminine Performance in a Musical given by the *Variety* Drama Critics Poll of 1954. This is said to be Booth's twenty-fifth award.

On November 15, 1954, Booth received an award from the Finnish Film Journalists' Club (Elokuvajournalistit R.Y.). It said that they "have the pleasure to present you, Shirley Booth, this Honorary Award for your performance in the film *Come Back, Little Sheba* and declare you the best actress of the year in a foreign film shown in Finland for the season 1953-54."

Booth told *Cue*: "I have been lucky out there. I am picky, and they realize how much I care. I don't do anything I am not proud of; I don't want to leave any bad impressions. I have two more pictures to do, but I think they understand me now. Everything will be fine. They won't over-glamorize me."

To reporter Hal McClure Booth said: "I wish I hadn't won the Academy Award so soon . . . But, I felt it came much too quickly. It was my first motion picture, you know. I always think you should work up to something." She continued, "It's a funny thing when success arrives in your later years, no one is envious at all. Older people hope the same lightning might strike them; the younger folks aren't a bit jealous because they know you've been working for a long time . . . Now it's nice to just sit back and rest. Oh, not that you ever stop trying, but when you're a success your efforts don't have to be so strenuous."

In a newspaper article called "Shirley Booth Tells Why She Isn't Stage-Struck," the actress said, "As much as I enjoy acting, I could give up my career tomorrow and be very happy. I'm not like so many others of my profession who wither and die on the vine when they're not performing. For me, acting is not a compulsion.

I am able to stay at home and fill my life with many things that may not seem important in themselves but spell contentment and happiness."

Booth went on to say that she did not intend to give up her career, "I fully expect to act until I drop, if audiences will have me." This outlook, of not seeing her theater work as all life had to offer her, admittedly came with "maturity." Booth acknowledged she could not have said this earlier in her career.

Booth: "I love housework, picking up after myself. I'm a furniture rearranger. It's not safe having me around my friends' homes, let alone my own apartment. I'm always shoving rugs, chairs and sofas into different corners just to see . . . I enjoy sitting in front of the television screen for hours on end. I'm there every night, in fact, when I come back from a performance at the theater."

Jessyca Russell Gaver, in a piece entitled "Lady With a Light," remarked that although Booth was "beset by a great shyness offstage," she should have won a special Academy Award for her offstage acting. "The few people who knew of her heavy schedule of benefits, luncheons for fund-raising groups, visits to the sick or underprivileged, seldom realized that these are the things with which she fills a very lonely heart."

Gaver noted, "Just as other women buy themselves a new hat to get out of a bad mood, however, Shirley will tend to cut her hair or perhaps change its color." More telling is the observation that "Pain is something she will do anything to ease for others and which nobody can ease for her. She is the first to think up a trip or a treat to distract someone from grief, and those she visits are rewarded by the kinds of gifts that make department store owners happy and rich."

Gaver characterized Booth as not wishing to bother people so that she will cut short the few invitations she does accept. Her unassuming nature meant she did not seek to be the center of attention when offstage.

"There is something very genuine about Shirley Booth," observed Arthur Pollock (in an article entitled "Shirley Booth's Frankness Gets Her into Difficulties"). "You get the impression that she wouldn't be caught dead saying what she didn't believe or indulging in an affectation."

Booth appeared herself at the first ever Shirley Booth Festival. The Cape Playhouse in Dennis, Massachusetts offered a four-play festival. *My Sister Eileen, Time of the Cuckoo, The Vinegar Tree*, and *Come Back, Little Sheba* were presented for two weeks each. One of the highlights of the festival was when, at the last performance of *Come Back, Little Sheba*, Booth was given a gold medal of the patron saint of actors, St. Genesius.

Fan mail poured in for Booth from all over the world. Booth shared some from Japan with a columnist. Part of one letter said: "I would like very much to associate with you as my mother, sister or lover. Please become my guardian. I shall esteem you as my mother and make whole my sacrifices to you upon my honor." Another fan asked her to visit Japan; still another requested a loan of $10,000 for a business.

On August 21, Booth went back to New York for rehearsals for her next Broadway show, *The Desk Set*. To no avail, Booth tried to get the producers and playwright not to make her sing her favorite song, "Someone to Watch Over Me" during an office party scene.

Booth starred in *The Desk Set* on the Forrest stage in Philadelphia. The show opened on Broadway at the Broadhurst Theatre on October 24, 1955, where it quickly became a runaway hit. Produced by Robert Fryer and Lawrence Carr, directed at first by John Cromwell and later by Joseph Fields, and written by William Marchant, it is among Booth's longest-running shows with 296 performances. Interestingly, it was Marchant's second foray on Broadway. His first work was the short-lived *To Be Continued*, with the then-unknown Grace Kelly, who played "the young woman" in the show.

Marchant said he wrote *The Desk Set* for Booth. He remembered seeing her in a matinee performance of *The Philadelphia Story*. It was then that he was prepared to send her a valentine note when he realized she was married.

Marchant: "With the passage of time, cold though my suit might be, I continued to worship her, moving steadily all the while from the mezzanine to the more expensive seats, until one day last year when, with a musical comedy swirling about her... I decided then and there that I was her thrall and that it was high time I was getting that valentine into the mail." Marchant sent a script of one hundred pages.

Nevertheless, Marchant commented that he thought Booth would want "a vehicle manufactured expressly for her; this was precisely what she did not want." Marchant explained: "She felt that actresses were always asking for trouble when they appeared in tailor-made plays and, besides, there was no challenge to such an undertaking, nothing to keep a girl stimulated and interested night after night."

The Desk Set pitted woman against automation in this situation comedy that deals with job security. Booth played Bunny Watson, the head of a large radio-TV network's reference department in midtown Manhattan along with three female assistants. As a human encyclopedia, Booth humorously takes on EMMARAC, an efficiency expert machine installed in her department that is competing for her job. In one scene in the second act, Bunny is drunk at the office Christmas party, a scene reminiscent of Booth's earlier shows *Heartsong* and *The Time of the Cuckoo*.

Glowing with Success 139

FORREST • 2 WEEKS ONLY • Beg. Mon. Sept. 26

ROBERT FRYER and LAWRENCE CARR

present

SHIRLEY BOOTH

in

THE DESK SET

A New Comedy by WILLIAM MARCHANT

Directed by JOHN CROMWELL

with HARVEY STEPHENS and DOROTHY BLACKBURN

BYRON SANDERS • ELIZABETH WILSON • HARRY ELLERBE
MARY GILDEA • SALLY MOFFETT • JOYCE VAN PATTEN
LOUIS GOSSETT

—SEATS NOW ON SALE—

PRICES: All Evenings—Orch., $4.20; Mezz., $3.60; Balc., $3.00, 2.40, 1.80. Matinees Wed. & Sat.—Orch., $3.60; Mezz., $3.00; Balc., $2.40, 1.80, 1.20. All prices include tax. Please enclose self-addressed stamped envelope with order for return of tickets.

The cast included Frank Milan, Byron Sanders, Elizabeth Wilson, Harry Ellerbe, Mary Gildea, Louis Gossett, Sally Moffett, and Joyce Van Patten. Booth's research assistants, played by Clarice Blackburn, Dorothy Blackburn, and Anne Marie Gayer, are the desk set referred to in the show's title.

Over a dozen years earlier, Joyce Van Patten had appeared with Booth as a young girl in *Tomorrow, the World*. This time Van Patten played a sexy secretary named Elsa. Van Patten recalled that for some reason Booth could not really connect or relate with her in *The Desk Set*. Van Patten suggested that perhaps it was the fact that Booth remembered her as a young innocent child in *Tomorrow, The World*, and here in *The Desk Set* Van Patten played the office vamp. Whatever it may have been, Van Patten called Booth "that great actress who I so admired but never really got to know the way I would have liked."

Elizabeth Wilson, who played Mrs. Warriner in the show, remembered Shirley as "so great, so supportive, one of the funniest actresses and women ever . . . unbelievable." Wilson knew Shirley Booth for the year *The Desk Set* ran on Broadway.

"Booth needed to remain a star, she had to be in control," according to Wilson. During the show's pre-Broadway opening in Boston, Shirley got Glenda Farrell fired because she perceived her as a threat. Also, John Cromwell lost his job as director after he said to Shirley, "You are a great comedienne. Now I'm gonna teach you how to act." Joseph Fields took over direction.

Wilson recalled how she had spent so much time together with Booth during the show's run. They went to dinner after the show, benefits at the theaters; they even went to the movies together. Shirley and Elizabeth saw *Patterns*, in which Wilson acted alongside Van Heflin. Wilson: "Shirley was very natural, open and positive, very funny and relaxed; she had a great sense of humor. We would talk about mutual friends, about the business. But it never got unpleasant or too personal. They were really wonderful times!"

The friendship between the two came to a halt after one particular party over at Doris Roberts' house around the time *The Desk Set* was almost finished on Broadway. Wilson believes Joyce Van Patten was there as well, although Joyce does not recall. Wilson asked Booth a question that would sever the closeness totally. She casually remarked: "Shirley, I'd love to have a picture of you." Booth retorted: "Are you a friend or a fan?" After that evening, the friendship suddenly stopped. Wilson: "I remember being very upset at that." But there came from this incident a lesson that stayed with Wilson all her life: "Shirley taught me something - I never asked for a picture from anyone again!"

Why did Shirley react this way? Wilson concluded that Booth made a decision to stop the friendship because the question made Booth wonder whether she saw her as just a great actress. "She wanted to be treated as a human being; she didn't want to be treated as an actress."

Despite all her time with Booth, Wilson said Shirley never spoke about her personal turmoil with her father or her first husband. But Wilson surmised that she "did not have a happy personal life; she suffered through a lot of personal pain." Somehow, Shirley's need for privacy explained her own acknowledgement of herself as being an enigma. "Booth had to be this way; she had no choice. After that exchange at the party, I never got to know her anymore. And we never ran into each other ever again."

Wilson doesn't recall going on the road with the show. She left *The Desk Set* about six weeks before it closed on Broadway so that she could be in a prestigious Shakespearean production with Basil Rathbone.

Frank Milan played Abe Cutler, the vice president at the network that Booth weds by the finale. Booth had a good friendship with Milan that went back for years. Milan started on Broadway in 1925 with *Mama Loves Papa*, followed by *The Great Necker* (1928) and *Penal Law 2010* (1930). In *The Petrified Forest* (1935), he appeared with Humphrey Bogart and Leslie Howard. Milan's next show on Broadway came in *The Desk Set*. Milan's other credits included *Who Was That Lady I Saw You With?* (1958), *Once More, With Feeling* (1958), *The Highest Tree* (1959), and a short-lived revival of *Brigadoon* (1963).

Apparently, the chemistry between Booth and Milan was excellent. So much so that the press noted at the time that Booth's friends believed she "is expected to wed" Frank Milan before *The Desk Set* reached Los Angeles during its touring. A Las Vegas, Nevada wedding actually did not happen as the press reported it would. Elizabeth Wilson finds those press reports unbelievable since Shirley and Frank were just very good friends, and nothing romantic between them was likely.

The Daily Mirror critic said, "*The Desk Set* is a lightweight comedy" where "you will find Pixie Booth at her best, and that spells wonderful." Walter Winchell: "Shirley Booth is the Sun, the Moon, and the star of another laugh hit!" John McClain at the *New York Journal American* had his doubts: "The lovers of Miss Booth, who are obviously legion, will see her up to her old tricks, struggling manfully against a defiant script - but they'd better hurry. It is doubtful this play will last once the theatre parties fade."

As in the past, Booth remarked to a reporter of the difficulty of excelling at comedy. "When you have the audience using hankies, nothing can kill the effect. But anything - even a cough or a sneeze - can kill a carefully built laugh line. Building comedy is like building a house of cards. Push too hard and down it tumbles."

Brooks Atkinson: "As a deadpan comedian Miss Booth is

wonderful because her face is round and innocent and her voice is homey. She looks as if she were about to bake a batch of popovers."

Booth won the coveted Sarah Siddons Citation for *The Desk Set*.

The Boston Daily Record (October 1955) called Booth "that rare actress - gifted with humility as well as versatility." The paper repeated Booth's acting dictum: "An actress should make you forget everything she has done before."

Elizabeth Wilson told Kevin Minton: "Shirley Booth was that magical combination of laughter and tears. When you knew her as I did, you knew they were both real. Shirley didn't know how to fake in life or on stage or screen."

Wilson continued: "Shirley was not touched by any method of acting or any school of acting. In fact, she would have laughed at the idea. Her work was 'in the moment' all right, but it came from her, deep inside, that mix of laughter and tears.

"Her life had been hard. She had become, by the time I knew her, a bit of a loner. But she was not a loner with her audience. And, believe me, no other performer has ever worked with or even cared as much about connecting with those people out there. It was her life really.

"I was greatly privileged to play with her in 1955 in *The Desk Set* on Broadway. It was the first play to deal with computers - the very first. So that was a landmark. And while the play was slight, there was never anything but pure effort on Shirley's part to entertain, to touch, on the most human terms. You see her craft - art if you will - of acting. She really didn't know how to be dishonest, and her audience knew that. They trusted her. It was an amazing bond.

"I used to feel that when I was on stage with Shirley, she was surrounded with the light. There was a kind of light. I've only felt this one other time, and that was with Maureen Stapleton in her prime. It was as if their body energies gave out this special glow, and Shirley had that. We all used to talk about her timing. Now, you can't really talk about timing. It's too elusive.

"Shirley's timing changed with each performance, as it should. I mean, a good actor does that, but hers was different. She seemed to breathe with the audience. She knew just where she was taking them each night because she was very much in charge. But at the same time, she listened to them too and so hard that they were in charge too. It was a true collaboration."

Wilson concluded, "I think all the actors who worked with her adored and worshipped her. Really! All the time recognizing the pain, the bittersweet fragile soul that she was."

Martha Randall, wife of stage manager Wayne Carson, spent plenty of good times with Booth. Randall recalled how she had to forgo a honeymoon. *The Desk Set* had been scheduled to open on October 16, but then it was rescheduled for October 24. Wayne and Martha married on the 16th, with Wayne returning to rehearsals the following day after getting married.

It was a very close company. When there were benefit performances scheduled, the show's performers would get together for a brunch or something. Wayne and Martha would sort of "double date" with Booth and Milan.

Whenever they went to a club where Mabel Mercer performed, Booth would be so moved, as Mercer would pay tribute to Booth's late husband by singing "My Bill" when she walked in.

Randall said she remembered always respectfully addressing Shirley as "Miss Booth." After a considerable time of going out together, Randall asked Booth, "Miss Booth, may I call you Shirley?" To which Booth replied, "Yes, of course." Apparently, Wayne had been addressing Booth as Shirley for some time. But Randall just felt it was not appropriate without permission.

Randall: "I believed Shirley Booth was the greatest actress that ever lived. I loved her dearly! She could play any part given to her. Perhaps this crush was not right. Certainly, she may not have done well with something Shakespearean because she may not have had the elegant thing with her voice. But I felt she could do no wrong."

In a famous scene from *The Desk Set*, Booth is drunk, laughing up a storm. At one point, laughing, she smacks her leg, which always brought down the house. Randall asked Booth, "What gets you going? What are you thinking of in that scene?" Booth replied: "Tonight when I slapped my knee I looked down at my hand and thought I've never had an emerald. I think I'm going to get one." Randall found Booth's amusing response so revealing that she was not even thinking about doing that scene.

Broadway curtains closed for *The Desk Set* on July 5, 1956. Then the show toured for a season to cities that included Westport, Connecticut, where the press reported, "Shirley Booth cavorts through *The Desk Set*." Booth continued to receive excellent reviews for her perfect comic timing.

She finally managed to take a trip to Europe - something Booth had yearned for. Of course, it meant giving up *Long Day's Journey into Night*. Accordingly, Martha Randall took care of Prego, Booth's poodle. Randall fondly recalled that this was not the only time she took care of the adorable poodle. She recalls taking Prego for weekends to give the dog recovery time from Booth's other new poodle, Grazia. Randall: "Grazia was so jealous and mean to sweet little Prego." When they were in Coconut Grove, Florida Martha remembered Wayne took Prego to the veterinarian for an eye injury caused by Grazia. Booth told Randall that when she kept the dog for weekends not to worry about accommodating the spoiled Prego. Booth said that they could ignore the dog's habit of sleeping in the sheets with Booth. Instead, she recommended that Prego could sleep on a chair placed at the foot of the bed. Moreover, Wayne made it clear that he did not want to share his bed with the animal. Of course, Prego won out when he simply hopped in between the sheets as soon as the covers were turned down!

Booth next appeared on a live television production of *Playhouse 90*. In the episode, entitled "The Hostess with the Mostes'," she played the Washington, D.C. party-giver named Perle Mesta. The CBS-TV broadcast on March 21, 1957, offered a ninety-minute dramatization, which chronicled Perle's true story from her childhood to the current day.

As the story goes, Perle's husband, the manufacturer George Mesta, managed to get an advisory post in Washington. This gave Perle the opportunity to offer parties in which she could hobnob with bigwigs. In addition, Perle received from Senator Harry Truman - later President - the appointment of Minister to the Duchy of Luxembourg.

The cast of "The Hostess with the Mostes'," included Evelyn Rudie as young Perle, Shepherd Strudwick, Frank Milan, Hedda Hopper, Paul Millard, Joan Wetmore, Robert Lowery, Edgar Barrier, and Louise Beavers. Speed Lamkin wrote the play, which even has the appearance of the real Perle Mesta. The play is named after an Irving Berlin tune, "The Hostess with the Mostes' on the Ball," from the 1950 Broadway musical *Call Me Madam*. Ethel Merman played Perle in that show. In comparison to the stage hit, press reports promised that the television play would give "A more accurate picture . . . "

"When I did my first film," Booth told Jon Whitcomb, "I was aware, of course, that stage technique is considered much too broad for the screen. So I deliberately underplayed all my scenes. Then I saw the rushes. I was far too wooden and deadpan. From then on, I had to let things out a little out at the seams. After the Mesta TV show, Perle's sister, Mrs. Tyson, told me she was amazed at how closely I had captured Perle's mannerisms. She asked me how long I had spent boning up on Perle - and I told her frankly I hadn't done anything of the sort. I said I guessed Perle and I were rather similar people - simple, plain, and direct - and that I had try to play her that way.

"Naturally, Perle has gifts I could never touch - party-giving, for instance. I've seen her keep a party going at top speed with the most invisible pushes; a word here, a suggestion there. I can't imagine how she does it. In my business, of course, the whole problem is how to capture people's interest quickly. If an audience isn't fetched in the first ten minutes, it never will be."

During the broadcast of "The Hostess with the Mostes'," Booth injured herself. Booth gave a detailed account: "I was being young Perle Mesta, so I had to skip around. According to some directors, you can't be young standing still. You have to run around and whirl - like this - and kick one leg up at the back. (When I was a young girl I was a perfect stick!) Well, when I got to this door, I could feel my ankle swelling up. The camera moved in for a close-up, while down below I was moving my ankle this way and that, wondering whether I could walk on it. I never had time to find out."

Booth continued: "For the next eighty minutes I just ran through the action, leaping into my nineteen changes. The dressers could hardly keep up with me. So, what with one thing and another, my ankle never had a chance to get stiff."

"After the performance, I had three hours to go home and rest before the kinescope went on for West Coast audiences," Booth continued. "I sat watching myself, with my foot up on a cushion, and my ankle began to stiffen. Then I went out to Perle Mesta's party for the cast. I danced quite a lot, and I exercised the ankle all evening. The upshot was, it never did get really sore, and my sprain healed up in a hurry."

She used an especially uncomplicated method to selecting the parts she would play. "If the first page doesn't have it, I stop right there. For if the first page isn't interesting, neither will the second, third, middle or any of the other pages be."

Booth told William Glover: "It's stultifying to have a role you can play with your eyes shut. All the things I select are because I want a change of pace."

By now, Booth had owned her Cape Cod home for five years. A Hollywood report indicated that she lived in it for only five months. It further stated that she stayed at the apartment she leased in New York for less than an hour so far.

Back on Broadway, her next new play came almost a year and a half after *The Desk Set* closed. This is because Booth had to spend time in Hollywood completing her contractual obligations to make two more movies for Paramount Studios.

In Hollywood Booth made the final two movies of the four as promised. *Hot Spell* is a tragic tearjerker with a screenplay adapted by James Poe, based on the play and novel by Lonnie Coleman named *Beulah Land*. Daniel Mann directed Booth again (as in *Come Back, Little Sheba*). The second movie had Thornton Wilder's story providing Booth a chance at farce and romance in *The Matchmaker*. Thus, Booth had two movies circulating at the same time in 1958.

The title *Hot Spell* suggests a double meaning: the physical spell of hot weather and the fiery emotional/sexual spell. Booth played the pleading and at-first sympathy-evoking Alma Duval. Her uncaring Cajun husband John Henry or "Jack" (Anthony

Quinn) packs up to live with his mistress. Later, the affectionate middle-aged Alma is seen as holding so tightly to the past that she lives in denial. "If you keep calm, everything will turn out for the best" is her motto. By the tragic finale, Alma seems to come to terms with her misguided viewpoint.

Pa's nightly spree affects the three grown children, Buddy (Earl Holliman), Virginia (Shirley MacLaine), and Billy (Clint Kimbrough). MacLaine and Holliman did well enough with *Around the World in Eighty Days*, so producer Hal Wallis decided to use them again. Virginia (MacLaine) loses her boyfriend Wyatt (Warren Stevens) when she takes her mom's advice.

Eileen Heckart plays Alma's boorish friend who gives Alma lessons on how to alluringly smoke and drink. In studio publicity regarding *Hot Spell*, Booth observed: "There's no glamour to her, but she's real and that's what counts."

Heckart told Kevin Minton: "While working on *Hot Spell*, which was heavy drama, Shirley would lighten things up with this silvery laugh. A laugh such as I've never heard and probably never will again. She had been in this awful marriage to Ed Gardner, and then lost Bill Baker, a man she truly loved. I wondered out loud to her, 'How do you laugh like that?' How could she? 'Well,' she said, 'I bought a metronome, and I can laugh in eight octaves.' So, now I think, 'Okay, I'll try this.' And I go out, this is about 1957 or '58, and spent $16 on a metronome. Well, let me tell you, it didn't work. Silly me! That laugh, like everything else she did as an actress, was spontaneous! Wonderfully tragically, comically, naturally drop-dead spontaneity! And who can do today what she did yesterday! A true gem."

Booth's "extremely credible" performance and the overall drama received positive response from critics.

She characterized herself in the publicity as "only a character

The two Shirleys in *Hot Spell*.

actress." Booth continued to give a younger age; this time 48 - when she was actually 60 years old. "I haven't the slightest desire to return to my twenties. I wasn't really going places then. I didn't really start getting anywhere until after I was thirty."

A change from tragic to comic roles in her next movie role renewed Booth's spirit since she got the opportunity to play the type of role stage audiences knew she did well. The movie *The Matchmaker* (1958) also received positive reviews from the critics.

The film was produced by Don Hartman and Joseph Anthony directed (with screenplay by John Michael Hayes). Booth's first and only movie comedy is about the matchmaking widow, Dolly

"Gallagher" Levi. The latter tries to arrange a tête-à-tête with an attractive and youthful female for the wealthy Horace Vandergelder (Paul Ford) of Yonkers in 1884. Dolly could arrange for Vandergelder to meet either a milliner named Irene Malloy (Shirley MacLaine), or her imaginary rich friend Ernestina Simple. Instead, the matrimonial-minded Dolly opts to maneuver Vandergelder for herself.

Problems arise when Vandergelder's two young store clerks, Barnaby Tucker (Robert Morse) and Cornelius Hackl (Anthony Perkins), unbeknownst to Vandergelder, close his shop and take advantage of the holiday. They sneak off to find girls in Yonkers. Coincidentally, both Tucker and Hackl wind-up in the millinery shop, where their boss Vandergelder is. Matters become further complicated when Cornelius' develops a fondness for Irene.

The Matchmaker based its story by Thornton Wilder on his stage version from 1955. That Broadway version starred Ruth Gordon, with Joseph Anthony directing. Wilder had reworked his failed 1938 play, *The Merchant of Yonkers*. The latter got its origins from an 1835 Austrian comedy called *A Day Well Spent*. A musical version of *The Matchmaker*, called *Hello, Dolly!*, appeared on the stage in 1964.

As the feathered Dolly, Booth frolics throughout the sets whispering and commenting to the audience. These asides to the audience are remarks about what is happening in the show. They have their origins in the 19th-century theatre tradition.

"I recognize the audience as just one person and play for that one person," noted Booth in discussing her acting for stage and movies. "The important thing with acting is for the spectator not to be listening, but overhearing." As for her movie acting: "I always think of the camera as a person and talk to it as if it were a person."

Shirley backstage with Paul Ford. Photo courtesy of Thomas J. Watson.

Glowing with Success 153

Shirley informal singalong backstage. Photo courtesy of Thomas J. Watson.

Shirley with Joseph Anthony and producer Don Hartman.
Photo courtesy of Thomas J. Watson.

The Matchmaker. Photo courtesy of Thomas J. Watson.

The Matchmaker. **Photo courtesy of Thomas J. Watson.**

Booth insisted that the soliloquy scene remain in the finished movie. "To me it was the whole heart of all that the picture meant. I went to Hartman and he said, 'Well, if you want it, it stays.'"

"So far, all my pictures have been in black and white," Booth told Jon Whitcomb. "As for color, I've had at least one curious disillusionment: I used to be crazy about *Kukla, Fran and Ollie* on TV. During my husband's last illness we often enjoyed the show together. One night I leaned over to the screen and kissed Kukla on his little nose, and my husband mentioned it in a note to Burr Tillstrom. Burr sent me a picture of Kukla and invited me to watch him broadcast. When I went, there was Ollie looking sort of piebald with reddish fur on his head, and the sight of Kukla in resplendent color was a great shock to me. Somehow they weren't my friends anymore."

Upon completion of the shooting, Booth spent two months of quiet relaxing and resting at her Cape Cod home. Then she did some summer stock theatre before going back to New York to rehearse for her next Broadway show.

Miss Isobel, the original comedy-drama written by Michael Plant and Denis Webb, offered Booth a challenging and bizarre role. This show concerned an elderly woman whose mental state gradually deteriorates. Miss Isobel runs a rooming house in San Francisco that includes a blind Korean War veteran (Robert Duke), a young widow Ellen (Kathleen Maguire), and a Chinese woman (Edith King).

Produced by Leonard Sillman and John Roberts, directed by longtime actor Cedric Hardwicke, *Miss Isobel* opened in Philadelphia at the Forrest Theatre. It premiered on Broadway on December 26, 1957 at the Royale Theatre. As 70-year-old, white-haired Mrs. Ackroyd, Booth revealed her skill at playing a character that regresses and imagines herself to be younger. She is a sixteen-year-old Australian bride in Act II. The final act had her regressing to a second childhood, and even at one point thinking her spinster daughter (Nancy Marchand) is her mother. Only a 10-year-old boy (Peter Lazer) accepts Mrs. Ackroyd for who she thinks she is. The boy's mother, Ellen, loves the blind veteran.

Marchand may be better known now from her television roles. She played a magazine editor in *Lou Grant* and Livia Soprano on *The Sopranos*.

Booth: "I thought it was a wonderful play but the critics didn't. It was a voyage of discovery but I felt like I was on a boat-waving goodbye to the critics who were left on the pier. We just didn't reach them; they didn't understand."

Critical response ranged from finding Booth's performance as a child embarrassing instead of sympathetic to "Miss Booth can do no wrong. Her current vehicle can do almost nothing right," according to Frank Aston, *N.Y. World Telegram & The Sun*.

New York Journal American's John McClain: "There comes that horrible occasion when even the most gifted performer is defeated by an un-gifted script, and this happened to Shirley Booth at the Royale Theatre last night."

"But with all her brilliance, it is not simple to make the character she portrays engrossing," noted Thomas Dash of the *Women's Wear Daily*. Dash observed Booth's valiant attempts to work with a bad script. Mrs. Ackroyd's character is written in an unsympathetic light. *Theatre Arts* concluded: "Any sympathy probably should be directed at the long-suffering Miss Booth, though this is becoming an old story with her. The star's broad shoulders seem to be as vital at this stage of her career as her great talent."

Brooks Atkinson observed how since *The Time of the Cuckoo*, Booth has been "squandering her talents at random. Put 'Miss Isobel' at the bottom of the list. Conceivably it amuses Miss Booth. But it's tough on the noggin."

Time magazine acknowledged the subject matter's problematic nature. It's a story more fit for fiction than theater. Although Booth is credited for even drawing some laughter occasionally, the *Time* critic concluded: "With a look, a gesture, an intonation, she can be remarkably eloquent; but in the end the play, and even the part, is too much for her."

The New York Post critic Richard Watts Jr. contended: "But everyone has known for some years that she is one of the finest actresses in the world, and it didn't require so grueling a gamut of clumsy playwriting to demonstrate her brilliance. It merely seems a brutal waste of a beautiful skill."

Walter Kerr, critic for *New York Herald Tribune*, hailed Booth. "The text is impossible; the part is preposterous; but the actress is gloriously herself, believing in everything. Shirley, I love you. But these plays have got to get better."

The Daily Mirror and the *Daily News* were among many papers offering unenthusiastic responses to the show.

Booth concurred: "We knew the critics wouldn't like it. This is an audience play. Ladies like a good cry, and I can see them out in the orchestra, weeping and sniffling. Besides, we worked awfully hard on it, and I think we can take great satisfaction from a job well done. Of course, tonight we had a very bad audience. They laughed in all the wrong places. Well, I say let's make a run for it. The matinee tomorrow is sold out."

After 53 performances, *Miss Isobel* closed on February 8, 1958. Whether Booth had poor judgment in selecting this role as some critics noted does not matter. As in the past, her skill in playing the part brought praise nonetheless. As for the critical disdain for *Miss Isobel*, Booth expressed some restraint when discussing the critics to *World-Telegram's* William Peper: "They've always been wonderful to me personally, so I like them. But I do think it would be a good idea to rotate them. You know - the way the British did with soldiers in India. Send them home for a rest every five years."

Booth knew the importance of audience response. "Most of our young actors and actresses are acting within very small orbits and are not reaching their audiences. Therefore they are not benefiting from audience response."

In an article entitled "Neurotic? Be an Actor," *New York Journal-American*, July 28, 1958, Phyllis Battelle quotes from whom she calls "typical, off-beat stars": Shirley Booth, Sal Mineo, John Drew Barrymore (a.k.a. John Barrymore, Jr.), Anita Ekberg, Kirk Douglas, and Kim Novak. Booth said, "I was incredibly self-conscious of myself. The reason I act is because I had to act. The only way I could speak, really, was to take on the character of another, stronger person."

On another occasion Booth observed: "I think the thing that appeals is that sometimes actors have a feeling that they can step out of their own character. I feel sorry for people that don't have the pleasure of acting because I think it's a great release. And I don't think you hear of many actresses committing suicide because they can act out their fantasies." As regards Marilyn Monroe, Booth acknowledged she "had a history which was pretty tragic. She started off with quite a bit of poundage on her. I mean emotional poundage."

The movie releases of *The Matchmaker* and *Hot Spell* occurred very close together. Booth's own scrapbooks label *The Matchmaker* with the date of August 13, 1958 and *Hot Spell* with the date of September 17, 1958.

Booth performed in the stock theater production of *Nina* at the Westport Country Playhouse in Westport, Connecticut in 1959. Written by André Roussin, the play had a short-lived run on Broadway from December 5, 1951 to January 12, 1952. *Nina* had its setting in a bachelor apartment in Paris.

Booth next appeared on Broadway in *Juno*. She decided to do this show after reading the script a full year earlier, before she went to Hollywood to do her last two movies. This musical had the setting of the Dublin slums of 1921. Joseph Stein wrote the book based on Sean O'Casey's tragicomedy classic *Juno and the Paycock*. Marc Blitzstein wrote the words and music. As staged by Jose Ferrer, *Juno* premiered on March 9, 1959 at the Winter Garden Theatre.

Juno tells the somewhat tragic story of a poor family that believes they will be inheriting a fortune. They borrow money on that expectation. Booth played Juno Boyle, the long-suffering wife of a

Photo courtesy of Thomas J. Watson.

no-working Captain Jack Boyle. Juno holds the family together.

The musical concludes with the politically-motivated murder of Juno's son (who happens to be an informer) and the realization that the family will not inherit anything. In his first musical role, Melvyn Douglas played Captain Jack, the Paycock. Sara Allgood and Barry Fitzgerald had played the leads in the 1940 dramatic version.

Booth: "It is sort of opera. But that doesn't intimidate me. Labels don't mean anything. All you do is go by the strength of your convictions. You find something you love and then you make someone else love it too. And maybe understand it. That's all that entertainment is."

The cast in the musical included Tommy Rall as Juno's son, Monte Amundsen as Juno's daughter, Jack McGowran as Joxer, and playing one of the widows is Jean Stapleton, later known as Edith Bunker in television's *All in the Family*.

Brooks Atkinson: "As the sharp-tongued Juno, Miss Booth gives a performance that is warm and intimate, but less triumphant than most of her roles. The bitterness is lacking." John Chapman of the *New York Daily News* said Booth "gives a finely outlined characterization to Juno." Walter Kerr of the *New York Herald Tribune* concurred: "Shirley Booth is her handsome and delightful self when she is given a few seconds to spoon the Paycock's lunch onto his waiting plate; otherwise she seems a shade desolate."

Richard Watts, Jr., *New York Post*: "Everyone knows that there is no finer actress extant than Shirley Booth, and she is an admirable Juno, but the role somehow fails to be as dominating as usual." *The Sun* critic Frank Aston proclaimed, "Miss Booth still hasn't found a show to fit her genius." John McClain of the *New York Journal American* writes "of the incomparable Miss Booth. There she is, God bless her, with red hair and a fake Irish accent, and she even takes a pretty good belt at a song or two - but the material is lacking."

Generally, critics found the musical to be disappointing version of O'Casey's drama. Chapman: "All I wish is that O'Casey could have written the book, lyrics and music of *Juno*." *Theatre Arts* observed that "There are only a few occasions on which 'Juno' does come to life, and Agnes de Mille, the choreographer, is the person largely responsible for the vital moments." Examples of this are Act One's street ballet, and informer Johnny Boyle's dance of remorse in Act Two.

Atkinson concluded, "As a musical work, it does not have the drive, the scorn and the fury of the play."

In a review entitled *"Juno* Misses as Musical," the *Daily Mirror* indicates, "Blitzstein's score - he also supplied the lyrics - is more likely to appeal to musicians than the lay public. It's a first-rate job of its kind, though it's not calculated to make the jukeboxes' and disc jockeys' turntables burn out their bearings."

The songs Booth performed include "Song of the Ma," "Old Sayin's," "On a Day Like This," "Bird Upon the Tree," and "Where?"

After a meager 16 performances, *Juno* closed on March 21, 1959.

Booth bowed out of her next role before the show reached Broadway. She appeared in the two-week tryout of another William Inge play held in Washington. *A Loss of Roses* was the failed story of an abnormal relationship between a son and his mother. Warren Beatty debuted as the unbalanced son. Booth tried the role of mother, which she characterized as "a third-rate part." Betty Field replaced Booth when the show opened on Broadway, November 28, 1959, at the Eugene O'Neill Theatre. Booth's departure had a negative impact on the show, according to Inge. *A*

Loss of Roses closed after 25 performances. Another adaptation of *A Loss of Roses* appeared in 1963 called *The Stripper*.

Booth told *The Theatre's* Morris Gelman: "It has been consistently said about me that I have warmth and humor to offer. This play had no use for either. I'm convinced that no actress living can play every part equally well. I certainly can't. I was just wrong for the role. When I was doing it, I had to chastise myself mentally. I've always been determined to make the actual acting only a small part of the day. I shouldn't have to feel bad about doing it.

"I told Bill [Inge] and Danny [Daniel Mann, the director of *Roses*] that I wanted out. They called Betty Field on the Coast. She had already read the part. She was right for it. She has always played understated, drab, unemotional women. I didn't see the play after it opened in New York, but I'm sure I couldn't have done any better. Bill was very fair to me and I would certainly do any play for him if he wanted."

Although Booth managed to get generally good reviews of her last four Broadway shows, three failed to please the critics (*By the Beautiful Sea, Miss Isobel,* and *Juno*). Only *The Desk Set* seemed to be satisfying overall to critics and audiences.

On April 13, 1960, *A Second String* opened at the Eugene O'Neill Theatre. The dramatization was written by Lucienne Hill, adapted from the novel *The Other One* by Colette, co-produced by Leonard Sillman, Carroll Masterson and Harris Masterson.

The show concerns Farou, a womanizing playwright (Jean-Pierre Aumont), his loyal wife Fanny (Booth), and his secretary Jane (Nina Foch), among many conquests. By the finale, the two women resign themselves to the fact that they are the first and second strings, and that Farou will always be a philanderer.

New York Journal American critic John McClain noted that the story was not effective on this side of the Atlantic: "Most of us are unprepared for the situation in which a wife stands still while her husband carries on with not only the secretary and housekeeper in his own domain, but also a platoon of extra dramatis personae."

As far as Booth's performance, the reviews were mixed. Richard Watts Jr. of the *New York Post* said, "Shirley Booth gives another of her warmly human portrayals as the wife." McClain called Booth "merely magnificent, as always." *The New York Times*' Brooks Atkinson: "In skill at portraiture, in subtlety of perception, this is Miss Booth's finest acting since *The Time of the Cuckoo* in 1952. But that is all *A Second String* has to offer. The rest is trite and thin."

The Daily News critic John Chapman found the show "tiresome." Chapman observed: "And Miss Booth's attitude toward *A Second String* seems discouraged. This fine actress can light up a play when she puts her mind and skill to it, but she didn't appear to have much faith in what was going on last evening." *The New York Mirror* critic called the show second rate and, "Miss Booth struggles courageously . . . "

A Second String closed on May 7 after 29 performances.

Everyone's Favorite Maid
The 1960s

The 1950s ended with Booth receiving many awards and trophies. When asked would she move to a larger apartment to house them, Booth responded: "No indeed, but I'm having a bookcase made. I haven't got the courage to put them in my living room, but I sit and think about them and contemplate my novel."

Booth continued her stock production road tours. During the summer of 1960, Booth appeared in Sidney Howard's play, *The Late Christopher Bean*, at the Westport Country Playhouse in Connecticut. This is not the first time Booth appeared in Howard's play. She did it in Florida after she finished touring *The Desk Set* in Chicago.

The Late Christopher Bean is the comical story of how greed can overtake a respectable family. Before the story opens, a painter, Christopher Bean, had lodged with a financially strapped family, the Haggetts. They needed the extra income to help keep up appearances. Mr. Bean bequeathed to the cook named Abby (Booth), a painting of her that she wishes to keep as a sentimental memento of her love for him.

Greed takes hold as the family fights to wrest possession of the painting before Abby departs. Although they want to be seen as patrons of the arts, appreciating Bean's artistry, the Haggetts simply want the painting so they could sell it for $25,000. As it happens, Abby actually has 17 more pictures that were supposed to be destroyed in a fire. In addition, she secretly married the ailing Bean.

John Ross, the assistant designer, now Professor Emeritus of Theatre/Design at the University of Alabama, remembered Booth's very ordinary arrival: " . . . a middle-aged Chevrolet station wagon pulled in, driven by the arriving Miss Booth. Miss Booth was warm, spent time with the apprentices, and brought genuine life to a venerable warhorse of a play."

Ross noted, by contrast, Joan Fontaine booked the prior week for *Susan and God*, and came "in a chauffeured auto, with two additional cars carrying entourage, dogs, etc. While she was in no way rude, she remained aloof, distant and very much the 'diva,' as the term is used in 2004."

Of course, Booth liked to drive to work. One time Booth suffered a bruised shoulder and a demolished car as the result of a two-car crash with another driver in Hollywood on Valentine's Day. The press reported that she was driving to work. The driver, Paul Scheres, suffered a slight injury.

Booth appeared at the Tony Awards for 1961 held in the Grand Ballroom of the Waldorf-Astoria Hotel in New York City, broadcast on April 16. Phil Silvers introduced Booth by saying that "there's so much affection for this individual . . . a term I'm not crazy about it, an actor's actor, or actor's actress, which just means actors know you . . . just say the name and this big wave of affection speaks for itself. Miss Shirley Booth."

She announced the nominees for Director in the Musical category. The nominees were Peter Brook for *Irma La Douce*, Gower

Champion for *Bye Bye Birdie*, and Garson Kanin for *Do Re Me*. Booth opened the envelope, put it down, and with a sigh of relief, said "Personal gratification. The winner is Gower Champion." Kay Medford accepted on his behalf. Booth said, "I'm so happy for you." Medford said to Booth, "Aren't you glad he took dancing lessons?" To which Booth responded, "I wished he'd give them to me."

Booth asked Silvers to help her with the next two awards, one, a special award to the producer David Merrick, and the other to the Theatre Guild.

Her next appearance on television occurred in *The United States Steel Hour*, a series of live drama plays. On March 22, 1961, Booth played a housekeeper named Jenny in a rendition of N. Richard Nash's *Welcome Home*. In this Theatre Guild production directed by Don Richardson, Jenny is terminated from her position after 35 years of service for Charles & Laurie Austin (played by Henderson Forsythe and Flora Campbell).

Jenny, correctly sensing that her services may no longer be needed, applies in the name of her employers to adopt a girl named Amelia. She even collects a number of items for the orphan, including dolls and furniture. Upon the arrival of Mrs. Watson (Elizabeth Wilson) from "The Welcome Home for Foundling Children," the truth of the false application comes out.

Laurie tries to sell the orphanage on allowing Jenny to adopt the child since the latter helped raise Laurie's three children. However, the orphanage does not permit single people to adopt. To make matters worse, Jenny drinks some wine before Mrs. Watson's arrival, and clumsily drops a tray of cookies on her.

The final act opens with Jenny's supposed return from an employment agency. She explains how she did herself a disservice by revealing more than she needed to; such as that she sometimes takes a drink, she mumbles in the kitchen, and so forth.

Photo courtesy of Thomas J. Watson.

A melancholy mood pervades with Jenny sobbing at the kitchen table. But with the front bell ringing, Booth performs a dramatic tour de force. The mood quickly reverses when the Austin's daughter Linda returns from her Bermuda vacation to demand Jenny's services to help rear her own baby. The program concludes with Jenny's usefulness assured.

Welcome Home gave Booth an opportunity to display her portrayal of a "Hazel" type role in a more dramatic and sullen fashion, reminiscent of *Come Back, Little Sheba*.

On June 28, 1961, she returned to *The United States Steel Hour* in an episode written by Tad Mosel called "The Haven."

Booth next recorded an LP called *Dorothy Parker Stories*, directed by Howard Sackler. The album, released in 1962 by Caedmon Records, features her telling the stories of "Lady with a Lamp" and "The Waltz" on Side One. She reads the story of "Cousin Larry" and "A Telephone Call" on Side Two.

The cover notes explain: "Miss Parker gives her listener that grand feeling of special insight into character so skillfully that it is necessary to analyze carefully to see how she has done it. She has wit, compassion, understatement and a marvelous ear for straight talk, pared with the fine precision of her *New Yorker* writing style."

Booth had a five-room apartment now at the Osborne in New York City. This early luxury apartment building, located at 305 West 57th Street, is diagonally across the street opposite Carnegie Hall. The building's occupants included musicians and artists. The previous occupant in Booth's apartment had been Ethel Barrymore Colt. Martha Randall said that she visited this location, which was on the top floor with a balcony. It was small, having been a maid's quarters years ago, according to Randall. In a short time, the apartment would become vacant.

For over twenty years, Booth enjoyed the services of June Smith, a South Carolina maid. Smith apparently did not bear much similarity to the maid that Booth would soon be portraying. During the 1950s, her maid received press attention. In one interview Smith told reporters: "I can just wish a dress off her back easy," in regards to the dresses that Booth buys and gives away.

A new decade offered a fresh experience for Shirley Booth. The medium of television beckoned next. Booth had done some television already, but not on the scale of a weekly starring role. If Booth did something right in her life, something that would pay enormous dividends, then it was to develop her acting skill to such a zenith that her television acting would come across so effortlessly, so believable, and so natural. Her forthcoming show *Hazel* would quickly make her name and face familiar to millions of people every week.

Television viewers in the early 1960s loved *Hazel*. Many of the viewers growing up at the time the show was broadcast or rerun still love *Hazel*. It is not difficult to see why.

What must be clear from the outset is that Booth did not take to television stardom with the first opportunity. She had turned down offers, and made it clear she did not expect to do a regularly recurring role on television anytime soon. Industry people knew she would probably say "no" to any such offers.

The antics and memorable characteristics of the meddlesome maid that Booth played in *Hazel* exuded such humanity, warmth, and love that the viewer could believe that she is a real person. Booth engaged the viewers so much that the character became a mass-appealing phenomenon. She created for audiences such an indelible image of this feisty and outspoken home manager that, even today, you could just mention the word "maid" to most people, and the character of "Hazel" comes to mind.

Photo courtesy of Thomas J. Watson.

Hazel would be Shirley Booth's perfect culmination of her busy lifetime of experience from the worlds of stage, radio, and movie acting. It would truly demonstrate her superior comedic and dramatic skills.

The offer for Booth to have a star vehicle on television went against the expectations of friends and associates. The choice of going from the legitimate stage to television shocked many of Booth's professional associates. Among those disapproving was J. Walter Thompson, critic for *Variety*. Thompson belittled Booth's involvement in television as a "comedown."

Burt Lancaster allegedly said, "I'm ashamed of you, Shirley, lowering yourself with a thing like this *Hazel* series. I wish you'd get out of it." Lancaster said this at a party when Booth announced her intentions to do a television series. Shortly afterwards, Lancaster claimed he apologized to Booth.

Booth: "Burt Lancaster advised me against doing *Hazel*. 'Don't do television,' he warned. 'It'll ruin you!' Burt is a doll and a heck of an actor, but I'm glad I didn't follow his advice. Everybody under forty knows me better from *Hazel*, not from my movies!"

Lancaster explained to Kevin Minton: "When Shirley announced at a party at Jim Cagney's - I don't know, around 1960 - that she would do *Hazel* on TV, I admit I did lambaste her. I thought TV would cheapen her. It was the first time I saw her angered in a way. That night, before the party ended, I apologized. 'No need,' she said. 'Time will tell if it cheapens me, and if it does, I hope to be as cheapened as Lucy [Lucille Ball].' Point marked!

"That night at the same party, Judy Garland said to me, 'If Shirley Booth can be cheapened in any way, they haven't invented the medium to do it yet,' and they still haven't." Lancaster concluded: "God bless her, I say. The best actress I've ever worked with."

Booth told Richard Coe, *The Washington Post*: "So many people tell me they're embarrassed to find me playing a TV series. Why should they be? If there's one thing I am, it's an actress. I take the parts that come along, sometimes good, sometimes not so good. You never know. You can only hope. That's what makes all theater a gamble.

"Because of Lola in *Come Back, Little Sheba*, many think of me as a dramatic actress, but long before that I was considered a comedienne in *The Philadelphia Story, My Sister Eileen, Three Men on a Horse*. Then others think of me as a stage actress. Well, for years I was Mabel on radio's *Duffy's Tavern*. It kinda mixes people up. I guess, this switching around." Of course, Booth meant Miss Duffy, not Mabel.

"But that's what being an actress means and I'm delighted to have so rich a character to play before such a tremendous audience. It came about by chance. My agent gave me several stage scripts and also remarked that something had come along on 'Hazel' but it hadn't jellied for a TV series, he hadn't thought I'd be interested.

"Well several years earlier someone had tried a play on 'Hazel' but it hadn't jellied and I'd turned it down. This first script was good and so were the next half-dozen I saw. That's how I got into a TV series and judging by reactions, I'm anything but embarrassed. I'd had four stage flops in a row and it feels good to be in a hit again.

"Serial work is unlike anything I've ever done and can be tricky. For instance, scenes are often filmed for TV at the same time for different sequences. If there's a scene in front of a fireplace in many of a dozen or so scripts, we film those scenes at the same time while the lights are up before the given set. That means we skip around in episodes of several weeks at a time, parts of as many as six half-hour shows being done in one hectic day.

"All that, I don't need to tell you, requires a concentration tougher even than stage or screen. The result is I spend every night boning up on the next day's shooting schedule, trying to find the continuity that just isn't there on the set."

Back in 1952 Booth had said: "Hollywood is not my dish of tea. I must play to an audience, or I have no way of measuring my work." The same general problem seemed to worsen with television's "sequences from many episodes" shooting schedule, but that did not stop Booth from making *Hazel* a mammoth success.

Hazel had its beginnings as a cartoon strip by Ted Key. Key was born in Fresno, California on August 25, 1912. He attended the University of California at Berkeley. Key's cartoons appeared in many popular magazines, including *Collier's, Cosmopolitan, Good Housekeeping, Ladies' Home Journal, Look, McCall's, The New Yorker,* and *TV Guide.*

In 1943, the loveable maid debuted in *The Saturday Evening Post*. Millions of readers enjoyed the strip over the years until the demise of the publication in 1969. Since then, King Features Syndicate continued the series nationwide as a panel cartoon, published six times a week with syndication to 50 newspapers. Much of the story of *Hazel* that follows is told best from Ted Key's own words.

Key: "*Hazel* was a product of the labor shortage of World War II, when domestic help was hard to come by. I had been a weekly contributor to the *Post* and sold this cartoon to them."

Hazel did not start out the way we now know her. Key: "Physically she was thin, slope shouldered, round nosed and bleary eyed. This, to suggest stupidity, because almost all of the gags were one dimensional, based upon the themes of naiveté, ignorance and incompetence. Following the publication of this first drawing, the *Post* printed many more maid cartoons. Within a period of a year I had stepped up her IQ, sharpened her wits and cloaked her with independence. She was given a name and became the most popular feature in the magazine.

"Not until mid-1943 did she become a permanent feature in *The Saturday Evening Post*. She continued to appear on the last page of that magazine for over twenty-six years, then was distributed by King Features, to newspapers, for over thirty-three more."

Photo courtesy of Thomas J. Watson.

In reference to when the television series arrived, Key says, "Nineteen years had passed since *Hazel* first made her appearance in the pages of *The Saturday Evening Post*. A nameless maid then, she was one of fifteen cartoons I regularly submitted to magazines on a weekly basis, in hopes of a few freelance sales. When Curtis Publishing Company, the *Post's* parent, acquired the right to publish *Hazel* exclusively, *Hazel's* continued existence was assured."

For a while Curtis did not allow the character to be on television since it did not want any of its magazine features to tacitly endorse products. Eventually someone at the publishing company realized the massive value of the cartoon character becoming a television star.

Key: "Not until 1959 did Curtis permit the cartoon character to appear on television. One sponsor bought exclusive rights to advertising on the show - the Ford Motor Company. Their Mustang car was first introduced to the world on the *Hazel* show. Both received high ratings, pleasing Lee Iacocca, CEO of Ford. The Mustang was his brainchild.

"But only Screen Gems would commit itself to a total underwriting, not only of a pilot script but a pilot film, without any network investment. Networks underwrote most of the sitcoms in those days, assuming a fifty percent ownership position. We went with Screen Gems, a wise choice and a joyous journey, not only for me, but millions of others who went along for the ride. For five years and one hundred and fifty-five episodes, an incandescent star lit up our lives. Bigger than life. Incomparable. Named Shirley."

When it became apparent that the character could become a television show, the professionals went to work.

Eventually, nine more writers were added to the show. Ted

Key considered Louella MacFarlane to be the best writer from the staff of twelve.

"As the cartoonist who created *Hazel*, I had constantly tried to highlight her humanity. Hazel, to me, was not a cartoon, but a person. What approach would the show take? Any anxiety I had dissipated. Flesh and blood people, incredibly talented professional actors, were injecting real life not only into Hazel, but all my characters."

Before the cartoon could be a television show, the characters had to be fleshed out. The briefing that Key developed, a twenty-page-plus guide to the characters, was given to those individuals working on the production, such as writers, the director, the casting director, and so on. Referred to as the "Hazel Bible," this summarized the traits and attributes of the maid. Some excerpts from the edition revised for the final season include the following:

"She is a large person, physically, it's true, but her heart is the biggest part of her. The armor is there for good reason: her rightful and true role as a woman, that of marriage and bearing children, has been thwarted. Her instinctive creativeness seeks another outlet. And finds it by 'adopting' a whole family, a mother, a father, a seven-year-old son, and in the past two years, a six-year-old adoptee, Katie. Each of these people are handled with firmness, and in many cases, tenderness, but always as if each is her child and her responsibility. This suggests possessiveness, and it is. She runs this family, nurtures it, because she deserves to; Hazel is the most mature person in the group.

"Hazel is seldom topped. But to retain sympathy, she must always have moral or social justification to 'winning.' Otherwise, she would be insufferable. It is awfully difficult to put up with a know-it-all. Hazel is an outspoken, sharp-as-nails realist. What's due her is rightfully hers; what's just, is just.

"Hazel speaks directly, articulately, at length, and to the point only when that is the best way to handle things. Not all situations, or people, are best handled directly. In her case, there are times when silence, a gesture, a grimace, are more effective, and subtle weapons. She knows when to use them. Indirection, as a counterpoint, is part of her makeup. In her there are no lost emotions or words. She thinks clearly, walks and acts with a purpose, and quite often speaks like a truck driver with all this colorful language, but only when necessary.

"Always, she walks the fine line of propriety, never quite falling off the tightrope. She knows she's a maid. But she knows she's a human being first, entitled to dignity and the basic God-given human rights. Those who encroach on those do so at their own peril.

"I would say too that she is democratic with a small 'd,' and quite possibly with a big one. This is in contrast to her employers, who are marked conservatives. She has never been identified with the Democratic Party, nor her employers, with the Republicans. But it has been intimated and suggested. Her leanings are obviously with the 'little guy'; she's against the man who's pushing him around. Entrenched pride, power and greed are her natural enemies, and targets. In her present abode, located in staid, traditional lower upper class suburbia, she is surrounded with many examples of elegance and pomposity. Armistice is never declared. Stuffed shirtism sends her over the top.

"This woman is a baseball fan and a football and hockey nut. She could tell you, at the drop of a hat, just about every major leaguer's batting average, or a quarterback's completed passing average. And if she can't attend a game, she'll watch it on TV. Her great interest in sport isn't accidental. And if playing in a sport, she excels in it. Obviously, she was once a tomboy. And no man would dare accost her on a darkened street. He'd wind up flat on his back, a victim of Karate. On occasion, she has attempted to instruct the ladies of the garden club in this fine art, without success. When she has needed repose, she tried Yoga. She loves basketball, bicycles, bowling and billiards (home variety). Hazel's mind is open, attentive and young.

"How many children can identify themselves with a maid? Few have ever seen one. And yet Hazel is extremely popular with children. They instinctively recognize in her what is common to all of them, the rebellion against authority. She upsets apple carts, and the status quo; they're always trying to. But she compensates for them by succeeding. Almost all of us are 'losers' in the course of our daily lives. Hazel gives audiences, old and young, not only a winner, but someone to root for."

The character of Hazel definitely had a mouth. Unhesitatingly, she spoke her mind. She meddled in other people's business. Nevertheless, everyone loved Hazel!

Key: "Matrons who have had maids for years think Hazel is exactly like every maid they've ever had. Conversely, maids believe she speaks only for them. Women who work in offices, or who have hired babysitters, see in her a vociferous symbol of their sex, for centuries a muted minority. Any person who holds a job under a superior, views her as a fellow employee, the underdog, like themselves, saying or doing things they wish they could say, or do. The boss, in turn, has had to put up with people like her, independents, the unorganizational man, the non-conformist, almost every day in his life. Anyone who revolts against the pattern, the mold, or who has ever had the desire to (and this desire is in all of us) sees something of himself in this woman."

Booth best described the character: "Nobody gets hoity-toity with Hazel." She told *TV Guide*: "Hazel is a good part. She is a good human soul, honest and likable. The most important thing is that she's capable of honest anger - a good strong, purging emotion - without being nasty about it. Instead she substitutes a sense of humor - which is really a sense of good taste - and hence manages to get away with saying the things most of us wish we'd said."

As far as Hazel's "family," according to the "Hazel Bible":

"George Baxter, in his mid-thirties, comes from a 'name' family too, a wealthy one, but not one of extreme wealth. He's an 'arrived' executive now, a successful lawyer, who works hard for his money and appreciates its value. To the point of prudency. He's conservative in his tastes, his values and human relationships, has a restricted sense of humor and is a bit overbearing. He belongs to the 'best' and most conservative clubs, in the big city where he works, in the country where he lives. He is bright, alert, articulate, pig headed, often single-minded and persuasive. He is a proud man, moral and good, who moves in the company of men who are the 'decision makers'; in fact, he is one himself.

"He wears glasses, is fairly roundish; and is in a constant fight with the weight problem; and Hazel's attitude toward it. She is the one who dreams up diets for him, puts him on them and enforces them. And she is constantly one-up on him in matters of backyard golf (she often corrects his putting stance, as he seethes), fishing, badminton, ping-pong, horseshoes, barbeque chefing, etc. He takes himself quite seriously and it's Hazel who's apt to prick his little balloons. But she is considerate of his needs too, almost like a mother-hen.

"If he were to wake up at five in the morning for a trout fishing trip, he would be greeted in the kitchen by Hazel, not his wife, and the stimulating scent of percolating coffee. And she would have all of his paraphernalia in neat order for him; she'd double check his fishing flies and hand him the license he's forgotten. Then give him fishing tips. Certainly she rules him; but he couldn't do without her, because she is to him at home what his reliable, efficient secretary is to him at his office.

"And he always has a small bet with her, about some matter, whether it's a football game or a local election; he seldom wins, and when he does, the triumph means more to him than one in business. And it's usually of short duration; because she manages to top him in another fashion. Occasionally, with premeditation, she will let him win, if she feels his ego needs the bolstering. An active, busy man in the business world, he has to be dragged into his son's activities by Hazel; not that he doesn't love Harold or Katie, he does, intensely; but he simply doesn't have the time. Hazel makes him find the time. We may even see him, because of Hazel's influence, become a 'den father.' And a most unlikely den father he is, too.

"Dorothy Baxter (Mrs. 'B' or 'Cissy') is about thirty years old, and to sum her up, one might think of some of the characteristics of Nora in Ibsen's *A Doll House*: good natured, gay, flighty, bright but irresponsible, easy come, easy go, childish in many ways, mature in others. She was born and bred to wealth, and often bows to an articulate, nosey, dominating, wealthy, prestige-laden mother . . . George Baxter indulges her, and loves her. And she, him. She is a competent housewife and fair enough cook. But her biscuits can't match Hazel's. And the family knows the difference."

How did Booth come to be Hazel? Key said he always believed Booth would make a perfect Hazel.

Key: "Shirley almost WASN'T selected to play the role of Hazel. At an important meeting of those involved with the production, at Columbia Pictures in Hollywood (Harry Ackerman, Executive Producer; Bill Dozier, studio chief; me; the two writers who wrote the pilot; the casting director; the director; the producer and other Columbia execs meet to decide who would play Hazel). Time was running out."

Key, referring to several years earlier: "I told them how much Shirley wanted to be in the Hazel play that I had collaborated on, provided changes were made in the script. Those changes would have required that I commute to New York City three times a week to rewrite with my collaborator; he refused to commute to Pennsylvania, to be with me. I had been commuting for six months to N.Y.C. And refused to commute to him for the next six months. So I terminated the collaboration.

"There was no Broadway *Hazel* play, but Shirley never forgot the role. She was relatively 'unknown' then. All the others at that table suggested actresses to play the role, actresses they admired. Years later, when executives were casting the *Hazel* TV show in Hollywood. I told them of Booth's interest in that old *Hazel* play of mine. 'She'd make a great Hazel,' said Bill Dozier. He was studio chief. But his associates had their favorites, so screen tests were made of Agnes Moorehead, Bibi Osterwald, Betty Field and a fourth actress, not Shirley Booth. Her name escapes me. None of the 'four' were right for the role."

Key offered another account, published in the Foreword, in which three actresses were considered.

Hazel came about when Bill Dozier from Screen Gems spoke to Booth's agent. Booth received a call from her agent telling her about the television program. Though Booth did not want to do TV, she did agree to read the script for the show. According to one account, after Booth read it, she decided she wanted to do the show. Her acceptance meant she would be giving up her stage work for a while.

"Bill Dozier and I wanted Shirley, but others didn't. They went ahead with the testing, but none of those tested worked out.

Shirley Booth never tested. Still no agreement. 'It's Booth!' proclaimed Dozier.

"NBC gave Dozier a deadline: 'Get off your ass.' So he tossed my 'Bible' (of *Hazel*), a pilot script into his bag and flew to New York City, where he met Bill McCaffrey, Shirley's manager, in order to talk to Shirley. Art Carney, Mary Martin, and James Mason were McCaffrey's other clients.

"Dozier asked Bill to allow him to see Shirley; he had a great TV role for her. 'I have the perfect TV series for Miss Booth,' Dozier told McCaffrey.

"Bill said no, Shirley wasn't interested in any TV shows. None. 'Shirley doesn't do TV,' McCaffrey replied.

"'She'll do this one,' said Dozier.

"'She doesn't do any TV,' said McCaffrey. 'Any. Those were her instructions.'

"Dozier was persistent. He begged: 'I've come all the way across the country just to see her. 'Can I see her, Bill? I've flown three thousand miles just to make this presentation.' If she says no, I'll leave. At least phone her.'

"McCaffrey reluctantly got on the phone. McCaffrey dialed Shirley. 'Shirley? McCaffrey. Look, I've got Bill Dozier here from the Coast. He says he has a magnificent role for you in a TV project he thinks you'd like. I told him you don't do TV.'

"Booth told McCaffrey: 'Thank you, Bill, I don't. I'm not interested in TV projects,' she replied.

"'You want to tell him yourself?'

"'It's made for her,' Dozier insisted. 'It's made for you,' Bill McCaffrey told Shirley. McCaffrey glanced at Dozier.

"'What's the name of the series?' she asked.

"McCaffrey addressed Dozier. 'What's the name of your series?'

Photo courtesy of Thomas J. Watson.

"'*Hazel*,' said Dozier.
"'*Hazel*,' McCaffrey told Shirley.
"'I'll do it,' said Shirley."
Key concluded: "And that's how it happened. That fast. She had remembered my play. That's the way it really happened. Then she read the pilot script."

Finally, after nineteen years, the cartoon character would be depicted as a real person on television.

The show would run on Thursdays at 9:30 p.m. It ranked number seven nationally after two months. Episodes for the first season (1961-1962) were done in black & white, with the exception of one episode entitled "What'll We Watch Tonight? In the latter, Mr. Baxter buys Hazel a color television. Perhaps it would stimulate consumers to purchase the new receivers.

Starting with the second season, RCA and NBC-TV's head Dave Sarnoff paid several million dollars to have the episodes filmed in color. However, in retrospect, the color process used, namely Pathécolor, has been criticized for fading and not holding up with age.

In the beginning, the show received plenty of negative criticism. *Variety*: "*Hazel* is grossly unworthy of its star....The comedy in this Screen Gems opus is so banal and so shamelessly contrived that it can only be exasperating to the adult mind, particularly when the laughtrack finds hilarity in everything from the movement of an eye muscle to the merest complication of plot." *The New York Times*: "There'll be nothing but understanding for a grand trouper."

The success of *Hazel* with audiences would change things. After the first season, there were flattering articles. In a letter dated July 3, 1962, Associate Editor Thomas B. Congdon, Jr. of *The Saturday Evening Post* indicated his desire to do an interview, "... just

188 The Shirley Booth Story

SEE "HAZEL," STARRING SHIRLEY BOOTH, CO-STARRING DON DEFORE, ON RCA VICTOR "LIVING COLOR" TV

Now – a new and brighter Color TV – brighter than ever before! Unsurpassed Natural Color from RCA Victor!

The Performance-Proved Color TV for '64 is New Vista® by RCA Victor. Improved electronic circuits bring you clearer, sharper pictures than ever before in *unsurpassed natural color*. New Vista Color TV for '64 is definitely the finest color television ever designed by RCA—pioneer and developer of color television.

See the wide choice of styles and models, starting at a new low price of $449.95 — manufacturer's nationally advertised price, optional with dealer, for the Burbank, not shown. Prices, specifications subject to change. More people own RCA Victor than any other television — black and white or color! See Walt Disney's "Wonderful World of Color," Sundays, NBC-TV Network. Plan to see the RCA Color TV Center at the World's Fair.

THE SIENNA, ALL-WOOD
ITALIAN PROVINCIAL LOWBOY

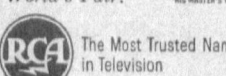

RCA The Most Trusted Name in Television

Tmk(s)®

An RCA ad.

to let you know that it won't be an ordeal. The *Post* article I'm going to write should be as happy and breezy as Hazel herself, and so should the interview."

Don Garrett, the Director of Publicity for Screen Gems, wrote Booth on July 11 suggesting a solution so that she would not have to interrupt her vacation to do the complimentary piece. Since the *Post* did not want to emphasize her TV production, they believed a visit to her Cape Cod home at the end of her vacation would provide a more personal portrait.

Garrett: "They are so anxious to do this story that they promise me a tremendous national advertising campaign on you and the story during the entire week preceding publication. This will mean an advertising budget in behalf of the Shirley Booth story of tens of thousands of dollars."

On July 19, Congdon thanked Booth for the interview and "the wonderfully sweet treatment." He acknowledged her maid and dogs: "Please give my regards to Mrs. Smith and 'the girls.'"

Congdon's interview appeared under the title of "At Home With Hazel." It began with the heading: "Shirley Booth is just as forthright and down-to-earth in real life as she is in her popular TV role as salty, snappy Hazel."

To those who criticized her and believed television offered lowbrow entertainment, Booth told Congdon: "I think you should do what you believe in and not worry about whether people are going to like it or not. I knew I'd be criticized. One actress went around saying, 'Oh, Shirley's going into a series,' as though that was the end of me!"

She acknowledged that fans felt she should not make such a long commitment of five years to a television role, away from the stage work she excelled at. She noted that people always connected her to the dramatic role in *Come Back, Little Sheba*, but they forgot that she had a wide range and excelled at "earthy comedy" as well.

Booth: "I think entertainment is entertainment. I'm not looking for depth in things. *Hazel* can do as much in its own way as some things that were much more pretentious. The show is everyday episodes which people have empathy for. There's no pressure when you're not a glamour girl. Nobody is envious of me. They just want to sit back and enjoy the character I play."

On another occasion, Booth explained the beloved character of Hazel: "I don't want her to be superhuman, infallible, gifted, above all people. She would be the life of the party, but she'd never take the party over."

Booth: "My mother told me that I had the soul of a maid, and here I am playing one. It worked out perfectly. I've had my own maid for 20 years. But I can't change. I'm one of those people who are always straightening things - ashtrays, everything. Nothing makes me happier than hammering nails or baking or gardening at my Cape Cod (Mass.) cottage." Indeed, Booth, just like Hazel, loved doing things around the house, whether it was cooking, cleaning, gardening, decorating, or whatever.

Part of the show's success had to be attributed to the casting choices. Key on Booth: "The artistry of a priceless actress was creating the maid as I drew her and saw her. She wasn't Shirley Booth. She was Hazel. I was moved and shaken."

In reference to the especially good casting of Don DeFore as Mr. Baxter, Key: "Don DeFore played Mr. George Baxter, a corporate lawyer for Butterworth, Hatch, Noll and Baxter. Hazel, in her peculiar shrill, referred to Mr. Baxter as 'Mr. B.' DeFore had co-authored a show that gave him his first Broadway appearance. He had plenty of supporting film credits as a rustic, including the starring role in *The Male Animal*. DeFore also played the neighbor in *The Adventures of Ozzie and Harriet* for six years before Hazel.

The pilot for *Hazel* had featured Edward Andrews in the part of George Baxter."

Key: "Don DeFore and I were good friends. When he came to visit once with his whole family (in a limousine his daughter had won for 24 hours in a contest), he asked for a copy of the 'Hazel Bible,' since he wasn't the original actor to play George Baxter. He replaced the first actor in the pilot at the request of Ford, the sponsor of *Hazel* for the first couple years."

Whitney Blake succeeded in the part of Mrs. Dorothy Baxter (or "Missy" to Hazel). Blake had received an Emmy nomination for *D.A.'s Man*. Back in 1957 she had starred in the first television episode of *Perry Mason*. In the space of a few years, Blake managed to star in over 100 television shows.

Bobby Buntrock played the Baxter's son, Harold. *Dennis the Menace* star Jay North told Kevin Minton: "The child stars on the Columbia Screen Gems lot went to school together, and we traveled to promote our series together, so I spent a lot of time (when allowed) with Bobby Buntrock. Once in awhile I'd sneak over to the *Hazel* set. God - she seemed to love that kid [Buntrock]. Though we [*Hazel* and *Dennis*] shared the same director, Bill Russell, where I found him an intolerable tyrant with kids, I'm sure Miss Booth would never have allowed Bobby to be mistreated."

North continued: "I envied him working with her. Even at my age, I knew talent when I saw it! I also remember she had two little dogs, poodles, I believe. She joined us (our cast) at the commissary one day, and those dogs were treated like kings. She'd lift them up to the table and feed them like babies. Bobby loved her - that's for sure!"

Hazel reportedly received 28 awards, including two Emmy Awards, the first awarded at the 14th Annual Emmy Awards on May 22, 1962.

Booth's second Emmy award came from the 15th Annual Emmy Awards, broadcast on May 26, 1963. She competed against Shirl Conway for *The Nurses*, Lucille Ball for *The Lucy Show*, Mary Tyler Moore for *The Dick Van Dyke Show*, and Irene Ryan for *The Beverly Hillbillies*.

Lorne Greene presented the 1963 Emmy Award for Outstanding Continued Lead Performance by an Actress in a Series. As Booth's second time in a row of winning an Emmy, she accepted the award, saying, "Boy I was in some category, you know. I had some wonderful gals in there." Then, looking at the statuette, Booth observed: "She looks as if she could bowl a good game too, don't she?" A very happy and smiling Booth continued, "You know there's an old saying that it's always the woman behind the man. In my instance, I'm afraid, it's the men behind the women. We have some wonderful men. My wonderful boss, Don DeFore, that I love. And our director, Bill Russell. Any day I expect him to walk on water. Harry Ackerman. Bill Dozier. It's just a wonderful, wonderful privilege to have. And I intend to share it with them. Thank you!"

For the 16th Annual Emmy Awards, broadcast May 25, 1964, Booth presented the award for Outstanding Directorial Achievement in Drama to Tom Gries for *East Side/West Side*. Booth received a nomination again for Outstanding Continued Performance by an Actress . . . Patty Duke, Mary Tyler Moore, Irene Ryan, and Inger Stevens were up for the award this time. However, the award went to Mary Tyler Moore from *The Dick Van Dyke Show*.

On one controversial note, the issue of race entered the picture when the NACCP threatened the sponsor Ford for the apparent lack of black actors in the show. Black actors were hired when the possibility of a boycott of Ford seemed likely.

"Ford has hit a bump with this show," concluded *Variety*. However, although critics found considerable fault with the show, the Nielsen ratings proved audiences were pleased with *Hazel*.

Booth lived in the Chateau Marmont, a Hollywood hotel, while shooting *Hazel*. The show's success meant that Booth would buy a house in Beverly Hills, as well as a house in Westwood Village for her sister at the start of the fourth season. She sub-let her New York apartment and shipped her valuable antiques to her new home in Beverly Hills.

The summer before the fifth season began had Booth being hospitalized for a "disabled heart." This last season of *Hazel* offered some changes, including a new cast and a new network (CBS) for the 1965-1966 season. George Baxter went to the Middle East, so Hazel and Harold stay with George's brother Steve Baxter (Ray Fulmer), a real-estate businessman. Of course, Hazel manages his household too.

Booth's role, as reported to *TV Guide*, would offer a more maternal involvement with the real estate agent Steve as compared to the fighting spirit she had for four years with attorney George Baxter.

Key: "Don DeFore and Whitney Blake were not used in the *Hazel* TV series during the fifth year of the series. Why, I never learned. A money problem? I don't know. But Mr. Baxter's younger brother (at a much lower salary level) became Shirley Booth's, Hazel's, new boss. His wife (also at a lower salary level) was played by Lynn Borden. I was called West to talk about the new 'storyline,' and the new characters. Hazel now lived in a 'new' home (befitting the younger Baxter's income). Hazel was there to care for Harold Baxter, the 'son' of the older Baxters.

"In the script, the old Baxter (Don DeFore) was sent on an important business trip to Cairo, Egypt. His wife went with him (for the whole year). From time to time, they called home to talk

The new *Hazel* cast. Photo courtesy of Thomas J. Watson.

to their son and Hazel. Naturally, you would only see Hazel and Harold on the phone, not Harold's father and mother in Egypt. That fifth year of *Hazel* shows was not as successful as the first four years of shows. The fifth year was the last year of the *Hazel* series."

Lynn Borden, a Miss America runner-up, played Barbara Baxter, the wife of Baxter's brother. Borden is the daughter of Bill Freyse, cartoonist of *Our Boarding House* with Major Hoople. After a two-year hiatus from acting when *Hazel* ended, Borden returned to be what she called "a working actress" by making television and movie appearances. Some of her credits include *Bob & Carol & Ted & Alice* (1969), her well-known part in the low-budget *Frogs* (1972), and *Black Mama, White Mama* (1972).

Borden told Kevin Minton that she was familiar with Shirley Booth from the time of *Come Back, Little Sheba*. " . . . I thought she was wonderful, a wonderful actress. When I saw her in *Sheba*, she was fantastic. I loved that woman. I mean, I really loved her, and I was so happy to work with her. . . . We had a couple of wonderful directors who directed most of the shows, and a couple of guys who came on the show that were older and a bit impatient with us new actors. This was my first show, and I wanted to make sure I was good.

"So, I'd go and talk to Shirley. She understood perfectly and would help me, and I wrote down the little notes. I was signed for 13 out of something like 36 shows, and I did every show, every episode. I loved it, every single minute of it. I'd do it all over again, a thousand times over."

Borden provided Kevin Minton with the following letter of tribute:

Dear Shirley,

How I miss you. You were a friend and private acting coach. I miss our fun times with hysterical laughter and our quiet times when you gave me painting and acting lessons, which I asked for and you graciously gave me. I still do the lunchtime naps with feet elevated for 15 to 20 minutes when I work so that by 4:00 or 5:00 I still have energy.

    I can remember the first time we met. The morning of our test there you were, ready to test with us. I couldn't believe it. But there you were, Shirley Booth, ready to go. You did so much to make me feel comfortable and at ease, as only you could do, my friend. I was living in San Francisco then, doing a play called *Take Her, She's Mine* with Walter Pidgeon. Every night I had a show to do in S.F., so I'd fly early in the morning, meet, then fly back home. The day we tested, I arrived the day before, a Monday, met with my character husband, Ray Fulmer. He and I rehearsed over coffee and sandwiches. That night and the next AM we tested with five other couples. I couldn't believe it. There you were, testing with all of us.

    After the show, I flew home to later find that Ray and I got the leads of Steve and Barbara Baxter. I was so happy I couldn't wait to get to work every day. You made it wonderful, Shirley. You taught me many things about acting and life. Whenever I had a question, I only had to ask, and off we would go to your dressing room, shut the door, and discuss it. Those are treasured moments.

    I can remember there was a while when Ray stuttered over certain words, one of them being 'Susie,' the name of our daughter in Hazel. One episode, the name 'Susie' seemed to come up hundreds of times. Apparently, after about 20 takes, I developed an uncontrollably nervous laughter, which, of course, made Ray worse and made for many more takes. It got so bad I had to leave the set. God, how I tried not to laugh. Unfortunately, the laughter became infectious and spread to the crew as well as to you. I remember we had to excuse ourselves so that we could go to your dressing room and bury our faces in the pillows so as not to be heard. We were so hysterical. Then you got serious and told me that I would have to find a way to contain myself, no matter what. Well, it worked, although it was hard at times.

I remember Monday mornings. Read and rehearse the new script. As I recall, we had three writers on the show. Two were great, in the way the words just flowed. But the third writer, who shall remain nameless, always left us tongue-tied with his stiff style. The words would just stick in your mouth. We would look at each other and say, 'Uh-oh, guess who again.' Then we would rewrite some of the script to make the words work for the characters.

E. W. Swackhamer was our director most of the time, and he was terrific. He really directed! The few shows Charlie Barton and Bill Russell did were awful for me as I was new and I wanted direction. I remember Charlie saying, 'It's OK, Lynn, just do what you're doing.' Oh brother! Shirley . . . help!

I didn't want to be OK. I wanted to be great! That's when our acting lessons began. I went to you for help. I wanted to learn everything I could from you; you never held back, you always answered my questions. I kept notes on what you taught me. I called them 'Notes from Shirley.' I remember that about the time your poor health finally ended our *Hazel* series, you were amazed that I had a 'Notes from Shirley' book. And why not? After all, I learned from the best.

You also know and admired my paintings and told me never to give up. Well, you will be glad to know that I didn't, and that

I have gallery showings, mostly on the East Coast. I'm sad that I had a showing in Nantucket just a month after you died. I so wanted you to see the show.

Shortly around the time that you were ill, shooting three hours a day, with a nurse administering to you what was needed to help keep you going, I recall the day came when you got Ray, me, and Julia together and told us you were ending the show because of your illness. How sad you were, as you'd expected us to go on for several more years. There were a lot of moist eyes that day, as we all loved you and wanted to stay together as the family we had become.

You influenced me greatly in my career, and in my life. I will never forget you. Thank you, Shirley, for all of your help and love. I truly miss you. I love you.

Lynn Borden

On her first day of shooting *Hazel*, Lynn told Kevin Minton: "I saw this man sitting off in the shadows. I went over and introduced myself. He said his name was Ted Key. Well, Ted is the man who's the cartoonist for *Hazel*. I said, 'Oh, that's very interesting. My father's a cartoonist.' And we talked. He said, 'Your father does 'Major Hoople?'' I nodded, and he said, 'Lynn, I wrote the script for the movie!'

"It was a movie called *Our Boarding House With Major Hoople*, with W. C. Fields playing Hoople. And Ted was the writer with my father! The movie wasn't done, though. W. C. Fields got on a drinking binge and died, so it never got done.

"Anyway, Ted saw that my father was happy doing what he loved, and he said, 'So, why can't I be a cartoonist?' And that's how he got started, and did *Hazel*. Now, little did he know, or I know, that we'd all be together doing *Hazel*. Since then we send

Christmas cards and all that. It's funny, I'd never met him before, and when I told my father, he couldn't believe it. It was a fluky thing!"

On that last season Julia Benjamin played Susie Baxter, the daughter of Baxter's brother. Benjamin later pursued work in commercials and changed her name to Racquel Thorne.

Some of guest stars and semi-regulars on *Hazel* included John Archer, Rosemary DeCamp, Virginia Gregg, Ann Jillian, Cathy Lewis, and Mala Powers.

Rosemary DeCamp told Kevin Minton: "I first met Shirley Booth in the 1930s. She was doing readings for the public by Dorothy Parker. I'd just arrived in New York. It was freezing out, and I stood in the back of this room in very worn shoes and a light coat, too light for New York winters. After the readings, I approached her. What a lady, what a star! She gave me bunches of advice and sent me a pair of shoes and a coat - I'm sure straight from her own wardrobe. Can you imagine? I've never forgotten her kindness. Years later I would play her cousin in a *Hazel* episode. I was having problems with the script. Shirley to the rescue. In a matter of hours she had me in stitches. Now to this day, I can laugh on cue."

Ann Jillian got the part of Steve Baxter's teenage secretary in the regular way. Jillian: "Your agent sends you in, you read for the part, and it is decided if they'll use you." What helped Jillian is that she had done some work with Don DeFore earlier in the series.

Jillian noted that Booth must have liked the fact that she was a quick study and she must have found her work to be satisfactory since she received the invitation to do more shows, and Booth did have control over those decisions. Sporting an English bob cut, Jillian remembers being self-conscious since she had braces and worried that the braces would shine on camera. But more than anything, she remembers a feeling of kindness associated with Booth. And Jillian believes that this is something that children will remember more than anything when it occurs.

Like many actors, Jillian admitted that she was shy, and benefited greatly from watching others. "The whole feeling on the set comes from the one at the top . . . that was Shirley Booth. The whole group was spearheaded by her."

Jillian remembered that Booth would at times give her a pat on the back, offer a complimentary remark, or offer a supportive wink when something went really well. Even an off-camera head nod from Booth indicated her approval. Although she did not appear in every episode of the last season, Jillian did find it to be a privilege to have been associated with Booth, even though for a limited time. At fifteen years old, Jillian did not associate with the other actors afterwards the way an adult would. Thus, she did not stay in touch with the cast members of Hazel.

Jillian: "Shirley was a lady, she was a pro. She had a sense of humility, and was a consummate professional."

Years passed since guesting on *Hazel* in 1965, and Jillian has achieved the distinction of being a three-time Emmy and Golden Globe Award-winning actress and singer. As stated in her website, "Since 1985, she has added motivational speaker to her impressive list of credits, addressing business, medical, professional, and women's groups with her own unique blend of humor and inspiration." However, most importantly, Ann's biggest personal project now is raising teenage son Andrew.

Unfortunately, Booth's chronic bursitis, a medical condition that required gold injections, caused Booth to stop *Hazel* after the fifth season. In all, *Hazel* played on network television for 154 episodes.

Booth suffered severe bouts with bursitis over the years. She once remarked: "I much prefer being a man. Women have to spend so much time pulling themselves together, and their shoes kill their feet." Certainly, the demands of acting took their toll on Booth's feet. Martha Randall once visited Booth's 54th Street apartment. Booth showed her one closet in which there were dozens of shoes in racks from top to bottom. Randall remarked to Booth about all those shoes. Booth replied: "Don't worry, honey, someday you'll have them!" To which Randall now says: "Not quite as many as she had."

Sylvia Field, who played Mrs. Wilson on *Dennis the Menace*, spoke to Kevin Minton about her years of knowing Booth: "Oh, I knew Shirley Booth forever. From stock theater way back. Perhaps 1917 or so. You know she really was a pretty thing, and always a step ahead of the rest of us. I never worked Broadway with her, but I think Ernie [Truex] did.

"We would meet many times through the years. We were doing *Dennis* and *Hazel* about the same time. I did *Hazel* and so did Ernie. We shared the same director on our shows, Bill Russell. Always a sprite, she could be a bit of a devil. But, I love her, just love her."

Before purchasing a house, Booth told Hollywood columnist Sheilah Graham: "I leave for the studio at 8 in the morning, get back to my apartment at 7:30 or 8, have dinner, go to bed and learn my 10 pages of dialogue before I go to sleep." She explained that it took her just five minutes to be made up with a wig, one costume of a maid's uniform (which saves time in fittings), and comfortable old shoes. "We made 39 a year for the first three years, 32 a year the last two years, the last four years in color. The one selling point in television is that it works for you while you are working on something else or merely sitting back counting your dividends."

Photo courtesy of Thomas J. Watson.

As regards to Hazel's wardrobe, Booth noted: "I wear those big, comfortable shoes of Hazel's. And instead of getting to the studio an hour earlier every morning to have my hair done, I wear a wig. Why, they even shoot lots of scenes of Hazel in bed. I've been known to fall asleep right there on the set while they shifted the cameras."

In one particular show, Booth remembered something unique about doing a television show. "The script had me serving smoked-oyster hors d'oeuvres to Mr. Baxter, then turning and sneaking one for myself. Well, every scene is shot at least four ways, from four different distances, and each of these four shots is repeated until the shot is right. I got so full of smoked oysters I couldn't speak. I just started laughing, and pretty soon we all were hysterical."

At home, Booth became involved in remodeling her Beverly Hills house. She still maintained her home in Cape Cod and her apartment in New York City as well.

Although it became more difficult to retain her privacy on the West Coast as compared to living on the East Coast, Booth still valued it. "I fight for privacy the way I would fight for air," she told *TV Guide*. "I can't always be acting. I have to let down, and it is impossible when I am in public."

Booth believed that the five-year contract she signed to do *Hazel* would not negatively affect her acting career. "An actress should be able to make you forget everything she's done before. Hazel is a strong character, but I don't think she'll leave an imprint so indelible that I can't shed it when I start doing plays again. Actually I'm reaching thousands of people through the show who might never have heard of me otherwise - like the little boy at the bean supper my church gave last week. When I arrived, he was waiting for me on the step, and he just wrapped his arms around me without saying a word. He'd identified himself with Harold Baxter, the little boy Hazel's so sweet to on the show.

"I'm working under the most favorable conditions. When I'm playing an emotional scene, our director, Bill Russell, sits there intently, and when I'm finished tears are streaming down his face. I don't miss having an audience, because Bill is it. And the cast is grand. As soon as we get in front of the camera, we enter another world, we become a family. It's a life we take on, and it takes us over. We get such pleasure from it that, if the audience gets pleasure, that's a bonus."

Those actors and technicians working on the set of Hazel for five days a week had an abundant share of laughs. Apparently, Booth had a way of enveloping all with her love and sense of humor. Yet underneath it all, there was a sense that she lived with pain and sadness.

In an article, "An Intimate Portrait of Shirley Booth: Her Laughing Days . . . Her Lonely Nights," published at the time of *Hazel*, Tricia Hurst took a revealing look at Shirley Booth's inner sadness when the performer's mask is off. Booth opened up about her deep love for her deceased husband and she revealed her compassionate personality to readers. "I miss my husband. Mourning for anyone or anything will not bring back the happiness. Life goes on, work goes on, you go on. . . ."

"Hazel Bible": "Hazel is basically a sympathetic, warm, compassionate woman, in great need of love, and giving it. Her wisecracks, her wit and the dominating, aggressive 'take charge' attitude are a defensive bastion. But she's an unfulfilled woman and knows it. And when the armor cracks, we are torn by the poignancy. She doesn't stay exposed long, though, because Hazel's best defense is an offense. And an overwhelming sense of humor.

"But still, in the late evening hours back in that nicely appointed, lived-in rear bedroom, its furniture decked with the photos of dear ones, and the walls with a few pin-ups of athletic heroes, we are confronted with a human being. A small phonograph plays Dixieland Jazz, her kind of music. There's a portable TV set, turned off; she prefers the one downstairs. This woman, like any other, has plans; she has hopes and dreams. Hazel lies in her bed, in her room, in her home. And in this home, she is alone."

Booth lived this aloneness that the character of Hazel shared with her own being. In a strange way, she considered it necessary to play this kind of character. As if it was therapeutic in some fashion.

She told Tricia Hurst: "There isn't anyone in this world who doesn't have his own private hurt, and that's the main reason why we must all be very gentle with one another . . . you don't get one thing out of this life if you try to add to those hurts, but you get a lot if you try to distract - both from others' hurts and your own. Understanding and love are always the answer . . . and, if you have the talent, make them laugh! I have the talent to make people laugh, and I've been told it's because I'm compassionate. I hope so."

When asked if her work fulfills her, Booth told Tricia Hurst: "Perhaps it would be better to say - it fills." As to whether her feelings for her deceased husband affect her work, Booth continued: "The answer is yes. I think I am more sympathetic to the characterization of Hazel than I would be, if he were alive. Hers is a more ribald and hearty sense of humor than mine, but I understand her not wanting people to feel sorry for her. She says and does things the rest of us wouldn't have the nerve to say or do - although we'd like to - but underneath is a kind woman who identifies with the Baxter family because it is the only one she has. Without them, she'd be alone.

"I'm alone, but I can also be alone without being lonely. There is always something in your past that sets your attitude towards people and situations in your present. My husband would have been pleased with *Hazel*. I think he, above all others, would have understood my need to play her. Every day, when I walk on the set, I have a family . . . I belong to a family, and it has become a very real world to me."

As to never seeming to lose her temper: "When someone blows his top or is rude for no apparent reason, I try to remember he probably has a good reason and something is eating at him inside. There isn't a person walking around who doesn't have troubles.

"Everyone blows off steam one way or another - and I find that, when I'm the most upset, I clown. The more disturbed I am, the sillier or funnier I become. That way, no one gets hurt, no feelings are bruised, no unkind words bantered about. Really, it's the best way, don't you think?"

In another magazine article, Booth said that Hazel "has warmth and a spirit that is touching. She is sad, too, and the shell of humor and hardness she wears is only to protect her."

Booth shared so much in common with the character of Hazel. Oftentimes the character of Hazel offers wisdom that reminds one of Shirley Booth's own personal experiences and view of life. Undoubtedly, she understood Hazel because she put so much of herself into the character. When simply questioned as to why she decided to do *Hazel*, Booth's reply was "Because I like her!"

The separation between the character of Hazel and the actress is truly blurred. Booth humorously told Thomas Congdon, *Saturday Evening Post*, "I'm starting to pick up Hazel's bad grammar. I keep catching myself saying 'ain't.'"

One thing is definitely the same. Shirley shared with Hazel the ability to cook well.

Booth explained: "There used to be a lot of Hazels. Today women seem to think they're lowering themselves to work in another woman's house. But domestic service can really be a noble way of life. There are so many lonely women who, if they could come into a home and take care of a family, would acquire a sense of being needed - which is what Hazel gets from the Baxter family.

"Hazel's so friendly that absolute strangers drop by here all the time, fully expecting to sit down and visit with me. Unfortunately, I can't see them. If I did, I'd have no time to myself, and I need to be alone . . . Once a woman walked around to my terrace and announced to me that she was a friend of Shirley Booth and wanted to see her. I told her Miss Booth couldn't be disturbed. That woman didn't know me from Adam."

James Fonda, producer of *Hazel*, said of Booth: "She isn't concerned with prestige. She's concerned with the job to be done that day. With most stars, there's a getting-to-know-you period, a sparring session or two. But not with Shirley. It's like working with someone I've always known."

While making *Hazel*, publications reported her age to be in her fifties, when in actuality she was in her sixties. One reporter wrote of wondering how Booth kept her skin wrinkle free - but hesitated to ask her.

Don DeFore told *The Saturday Evening Post*: "Shirley has succeeded in television where other stage actors have failed because, no matter how rushed she is, she still manages to bring subtleties into the performance. Half the shows end with Hazel and the Baxter family in the dining room, and the temptation is to play every dining-room scene the same. But Shirley doesn't pigeonhole her facial expressions. She thinks through every scene and makes each one unique."

Ron DeFore, Don's son, provided some excerpts from his father's transcripts. Don DeFore: "From the *Hazel* series' inception a warm, pleasant rapport between Shirley and myself had developed, both on the set and off. Her genteel manner and consideration to all immediately ignited reciprocal responses from cast and crew.

"At the time *Hazel* went into production I was the lessee owner-operator of a successful barbeque restaurant in Disneyland's Frontierland - Don Defore's Silver Banjo. On many weekends, Marion and I and our children took Shirley with us to the park. Along with partaking of the Banjo's barbeque goodies, always a must, our kids taught Miss Booth the shortcuts through Disneyland and eventually got her hooked on riding the fast toboggan ride through the Matterhorn."

DeFore described working with Shirley Booth as "a daily pleasure that guaranteed a lot of laughs. Many times while filming, she broke me up with her fabulous, plaintive delivery. This great asset of hers, coupled with the rarest of performing commodities - pathos - had lofted her to that high, rare plateau of special class amongst performers. A few silent stars like Chaplin, Stan Laurel, Larry Semon, Harold Lloyd, Buster Keaton, and Mary Pickford had it too. . . ."

Don DeFore went on to write a book, *With All My Love*. Key: "He wanted to produce another *Hazel* series several years after the first series had departed, but nothing came of that."

Whitney Blake did not strongly pursue acting after *Hazel*, but became a producer and writer. She made some TV appearances. More importantly, Blake co-created, with her husband Allan Manings, the groundbreaking television show *One Day at a Time*. This dealt with the world of the single-mother household. It ran from 1975 to 1984. The inspiration for *One Day at a Time* came from Blake's own experiences as a child and adult. Blake died of cancer in Edgartown, Massachusetts at the age of 76 on September 28, 2002.

Booth best summed up *Hazel* when she told *The Saturday Evening Post*: "Good situation comedy makes the audience feel that the things that happen in their daily lives are important. By dramatizing these things - actions as commonplace, perhaps, as cleaning out a closet or washing the dishes - a show can make their lives more interesting. There's no violence on *Hazel*, there's plenty of emphasis on the home, and it shows people how members of a healthy family behave toward one another."

She acknowledged the transparency between real person and actress: "I think there is a lot of me in Hazel.

"Well, the nicest impression and I don't know how much this is me and how much is part of the character I was playing. But I had the nicest thing said to me by a woman in the studio one time. Her husband asked her what she wanted for Christmas, so she said she would like to have a Hazel."

To *TV Graphic's* Erskine Johnson, Booth recounted that story: "Oh, Hazel, you know what I'm going to do - I'm going to ask my husband to give me a Hazel for a Christmas present. Not because I need a maid, but because I want to put my head on her shoulder so I can have a good cry."

"My experience with the *Hazel* series taught me a lot," Booth told Penny P. Anderson of *TV Time and Channel*. As part owner of the show, a 25% stake, Booth's problems with the *Hazel* series included the fact that she did not profit much financially because of the production costs. "I spent a fortune on attorneys and accountants to get the studio's books opened up just so I could have a look at them. The trouble was that every time someone in the sales department decided to take someone else to lunch, it was charged off against the show. And, being part owner, I paid for it." The show continued in re-runs, so Booth did, however, receive residual payments.

Key: "I wish I could name my favorite *Hazel* episode, or drawing, but I truly didn't have any. I still have a lot of the *Hazel* TV scripts lying in a dusty box somewhere in our basement, but I haven't reread any for years. The scripts were sent to me when the show was produced, during the early '60s.

"Recently, while mailing a letter at our local post office one of the workers, who I liked and knew, yelled, 'How's Hazel?!' "Great,' I replied, and he introduced me to some of his associates (3) who stopped serving their customers and started asking me questions.

"Years ago, Thelma Ritter wanted to play Hazel in a movie that John Foreman wanted to produce. MCA was putting the 'package' together. I asked the gathered executives (at a lunch in New York City which included Thelma Ritter) who would produce the TV *Hazel* series? 'Marilyn Monroe,' replied Ritter, seriously. Monroe was represented by MCA too. By 'producer,' they meant she would underwrite the show with her money. She was living in Connecticut. Then, unmarried, with a photographer and his wife, guy named Greene. She was attending the Actor's Studio and was about to marry the playwright who wrote *Death of a Salesman*, Arthur Miller.

"A *Hazel* movie was 'almost' produced in the past six years. Penny Marshall was under contract to Universal to produce, direct and act in movies for the studio. She wanted to produce *Hazel*. After five years of 'trying,' Universal released Marshall from the contract."

Key continued: "I've been receiving option payments during this time. No longer, of course. In collaboration with another writer, I wrote a *Hazel* script that wasn't used. Four more scripts, by four other writers, also were unacceptable. Penny Marshall wanted to direct AND play the lead. I'm not sure she was right for the role. Shirley Booth was. So now I'm free to wait for the next 'offer' to be made. If and when, CAA was, and is, my agent on this.

"I have no agent for the *Hazel* musical. I wrote it and Micki Grand, a talented singer, composer and lyricist, wrote the music and lyrics. Micki played the lead in an off-Broadway musical she wrote several years ago, and won an Award (Cleo?) for off-Broadway productions. *Don't Bother Me, I Can't Cope* was the name of her musical.

"Hazel didn't change much once she had developed into the Hazel we now know. Would Hazel ever retire? . . . Hazel found a man she loved. Who said he loved her. They made plans for a wedding. Had high hopes. She gave up her job for him. Act I ends as she's trying on a wedding gown, designed just for her - by a friend. A wedding celebration - a joyous dance - occurs on stage. As she dreams it. And wishes it to be. But never will be. Because . . . Act II will tell us what happens."

Key explained: "My *Hazel* musical deals with a period in Hazel's life she never expected to occur: she's engaged to be married. The time and place: Manhattan. Hazel's found the perfect mate. All her life, she has longed for this moment . . . and then . . . I don't know who would make a great 'Hazel' in a movie now. There aren't many out there who would obviously play the role.

"One of my biggest rooters in California was the Story Editor of Disney Studios, Frank Paris. In fact, he liked my work so much he quit his job and moved to Manhattan to raise money for, and produce, a musical based on Hazel. Sorry to state that it never happened: he was in New York just a few months when he died, suddenly. The *Hazel* musical still awaits a production."

After *Hazel* left the airwaves, Booth told *TV Guide*: "I wouldn't do another series right now. You get into the habit of thinking one character and it's not very challenging. But I enjoyed the people in *Hazel*. They did everything to make me happy. I like regimentation. I like being told what to do. It's so orderly."

The press reported that Booth wanted to make some more movies once the *Hazel* series was over. However, the few movies she would make would be television productions from now on.

Booth: "It would be lovely to retire again. Oh, I've done it twice, for both my husbands. I'm really very adaptable and lucky for it. Me, I'd enjoy myself cleaning out an old closet."

The character of Hazel would live on in the minds of millions. When the show made the airwaves Key told an interesting incident. "Hazel Bible": "Eleven *Hazel* books were published and three more will make their appearance in the next two years. But to me the greatest tribute to the character's influence and believability arrived in the mail three years ago. It was a small ad a fan had clipped from the classified section of a Boston newspaper. It read: WANTED: A HAZEL TO RAISE MY THREE MOTHERLESS CHILDREN. Almost coincidentally, the Aetna Insurance Company asked if it could issue a Hazel Insurance Policy. The Policy would have provided working fathers whose wives had died a Hazel-like woman to raise their children. I did not accept the proposal."

Before doing *Hazel*, Shirley Booth sued the publisher of the magazine *Holiday*, Curtis Publishing Company, and their advertising agency, Batten, Barton, Durstine & Osborn, for invasion of privacy. The lawsuit involved a color photograph depicting Booth in water up to her neck taken for a news story of Booth on vacation at Round Hill Hotel and Villas Resort, Jamaica (West Indies). The first publication of the photograph in February of 1959 did not matter. The re-publication in June of 1959 as advertisements for *Holiday* in two other magazines, *Advertising Age* and *The New*

Yorker, supposedly made commercial use of the photograph without Booth's approval.

In the suit, Shirley Booth vs. *Holiday*, Booth indicated that she did not like being "used commercially." A trial jury produced a verdict in favor of Booth, which awarded her a total of $17,500, composed of $5,000 in actual damages, and $12,500 in punitive damages. However, the Appellate Court Division in 1963 reversed the original verdict and set aside the award. The legal battle ended when the highest court in New York, the Court of Appeals, affirmed 5-2 the Appellate Division's decision.

The logic of the defendants' appeal and the final ruling involved two matters. The defendants' first point argued that Booth gave up her right to privacy as a public figure. Their second argument offered that the magazine had the right to advertise in order to provide the public with information. The Court concluded that although Booth did not give up her right to privacy, the republishing of the photograph served as just incidental advertising, which is a "vital necessity for preserving a strong and free press."

Variety noted: "The Court felt the privilege accorded the publisher of *Holiday* to use the Booth photograph in other periodicals, and at a later date, for the purpose of exploiting interest in and stimulating circulation of *Holiday* was a logical extension of this liberal rule favoring informational media."

Back in 1961, Booth told *TV Guide* that in regard to Tennessee Williams: "I think he writes beautifully. But I don't see myself in a Williams play." Her opinion changed when she decided to appear as Amanda Wingfield in the *CBS Playhouse* adaptation of Tennessee Williams' *The Glass Menagerie*, broadcast December 8, 1966. This two-hour television special, filmed at Rediffusion Television Ltd. in London, starred Hal Holbrook (Amanda's son Tom), Barbara Loden (Amanda's crippled daughter), and Pat Hingle (the gentleman caller). No stranger to the part of Amanda, Booth had done the radio version of *The Glass Menagerie* for *Theater Guild on the Air*, broadcast back on April 11, 1953.

Booth told Kay Gardella: "At first I wasn't enthusiastic about doing *The Glass Menagerie*. Frankly, I had misgivings about myself. I didn't think that anybody else could approximate the performance given by Laurette Taylor in the original Broadway version. Eventually, however, I let myself be talked into it." Producer David Susskind persuaded Booth to relent.

Booth explained: "Amanda is a challenging character to portray. She's a mother of many facets, more gallant than possessive. I was in perfect agreement with Laurette Taylor's interpretation of the role. I tried to make my own performance as clear as she did."

Booth acknowledged that the production had "less than perfect" scenes.

"I found the English people to be most gracious, accommodating and friendly. I'm sorry I didn't have more time to get around and see things. Sunday rides in the country were the best I could do this trip."

British director Michael Elliot did not receive satisfaction in the way Booth played Amanda. Booth gave her interpretation of Amanda. She did not play the character with the sizzle and energy that Eliot thought the Southern belle should have.

"Lionel Barrymore said you've got to be brave to be wrong," Booth told *TV Guide*. "I never give a complete characterization. I try to leave a little for the yeast of the audience's imagination and interest to work. I was never pretty, you know. I always had to catch an audience other ways. When they aren't interested in your beauty, you've got a better opportunity to make them interested in the person you are supposed to be."

The Glass Menagerie. Photo courtesy of Thomas J. Watson.

The Glass Menagerie. Photo courtesy of Thomas J. Watson.

Director Eliot did de-emphasize Booth's screen time, with the camera instead focused on Barbara Loden, who Booth called "a revelation." *The Glass Menagerie* used Booth's voice more, which explains why she told *TV Guide*: "I could have telephoned it in."

Though there were tensions in *The Glass Menagerie* between the director and Booth, the actress received an Emmy nomination for her portrayal of Amanda.

At home, as she did throughout her life, Booth enjoyed rearranging her furniture. She told *TV Guide* in 1966, "Small things occupy me, I can get as much fun rearranging a room as most people get from rearranging their lives. I don't think I'll ever marry again. I can be alone without being lonely."

In the role of a frustrated actress, Booth did a two-week revival of the Broadway hit, *The Torch Bearers* at a Cape Cod summer theater. Erskine Johnson acknowledged this as "the year's most improbable casting." Booth stated: "As an actress I have trepidations but no frustrations."

Booth told Johnson, "I fall in love with characters. I have to feel about them like I do about good friends."

Melvyn Douglas joined Booth in the *CBS-TV Playhouse* production *Do Not Go Gentle into That Good Night*, broadcast on October 17, 1967. Douglas had worked with Booth when he played Captain Jack in the unsuccessful Broadway musical *Juno*. This tele-movie takes its title from a poem by Dylan Thomas.

Do Not Go Gentle Into That Good Night depicts the story of an aging carpenter named Peter Schermann, who is sent to an institution for the elderly after losing his wife. Peter had been living in a house that he built himself, which his son, daughter-in-law and grandchildren now inhabit. Initially unwanted by his family, dejected and disturbed, Peter finds some peace away from his own children.

Booth makes her appearance as Heloise Michaud thirty-five

minutes into the ninety-minute program. Heloise asks Peter to dance with her in the home's entertainment room. He refuses. Nevertheless, in a short time, a friendship develops between the two. When his musician friend Slocum dies, Schermann realizes that the home is like a sealed box, unlike the real world where a person's absence is truly felt and mourned.

Schermann decides that he wants to leave the institution and return to his own house. Heloise begs him to stay at the home, explaining how he means something there, especially to her. She tells him how he gave her some meaning and some love. According to Heloise, this generation of children is independent, with no responsibility to parents. The production concludes with the unresolved conflict of an authoritarian Peter moving back home. Peter insists that he is the head of his house and he will not relinquish his authority over his son and daughter-in-law.

Booth's character of Heloise in *Do Not Go Gentle into That Good Night* attempted but failed to convince Peter that she had some insight. Her common-sense wisdom would be ignored. Clearly, this production made it certain that after many years as Hazel Burke, Booth was not typecast as the problem-solving woman whose good judgment wins out by the finale.

Booth made guest appearances on several television shows during the 1960's, including returning to *What's My Line* two times. She appeared on *The Perry Como Show*, *The Andy Williams Show* and *The Dick Van Dyke Show*.

She presented the 1968 Tony Awards at the Shubert Theatre in New York. Broadcast on April 21, Booth walked onstage with Art Carney as the tune of "I'll Buy You a Star" from *A Tree Grows in Brooklyn* played.

Carney asked Booth how it felt to be back onstage. Booth replied, "Oh just lovely. I'm here to present the award for Best Performance of an Actor in a Musical. I'm so excited." Carney asks, "Why?" Booth replies, "Why this is the most wonderful thing as good as a signed contract. Oh, it's fantastic." She told Carney that doesn't he realize Dick Van Dyke, Yul Brynner, Harry Belafonte all won this award. Booth reads the nominees: Scott Jacoby for *Golden Rainbow*, Nikos Kourkoulos for *Ilya Darling*, Michael Rupert for *The Happy Time*. Booth remarked to Art, "It don't sound like me . . . and Hiram Sherman for *How Now Dow Jones*. The winner is my old friend Hiram Sherman." When she realized nobody was coming up (and Carney whispered something to her), Booth said, "Well, that's a shame. Congratulations anyway, Hiram." Booth waved and left the stage.

In 1968, Booth returned to the Westport Country Playhouse to star in a revival of her 1955-56 hit *The Desk Set*. The cast included Paul McGrath, Ray Fulmer, Evelyn Page, Yolande Bavan, Alice Spivak, Liz Sheridan, Betty Linton, Peter Shawn, and Alan James.

Her next role occurred in the television movie *The Smugglers*, directed by Norman Lloyd. Booth played Mrs. Hudson, an American tourist traveling in Austria and Italy. Mrs. Hudson, with her stepdaughter/companion (Carol Lynley), becomes unintentionally mixed up with an international smuggling ring when they try to get through customs with some souvenirs.

Strangely broadcast on Christmas Eve, 1968, *The Smugglers* never played to its completion due to the interruption by a news broadcast of the *Apollo 8* space mission. It has been said that perhaps NBC intentionally scheduled this inferior and violent movie when they did, knowing that it probably would be pre-empted by the news coverage.

Later, Booth would tell *TV Guide*, "I entered my Gobi Desert period. Long and arid. For three years I did nothing, except putter." It seemed that Booth loved to putter around the house, especially as she got older. She told *TV Guide*: "I have the soul of a chambermaid. I'm a Virgo. We're perfectionists, overly critical about neatness. I'm a compulsive straightener, a compulsive ashtray emptier. We Virgos can't help it. We're sentenced. I count everything. When I wind my watch, I even count the number of times I wind the stem."

Charles Nelson Reilly told Kevin Minton: "Around 1967 or 1968 we did *The Ghost and Mrs. Muir* (the series) together. And she guested, played a medium. Well, my mother was around, and it was her birthday, and the cast and the crew threw a party for her, which Shirley so graciously attended. My mother looked very much like Shirley, it was uncanny. There the resemblance stopped! After meeting my mother, Shirley came over to me and said, 'Your mother is the worst woman I've ever met in my life!' (I had to agree. Mother was horrid, a nightmare, just a nasty creature.) So, what could I say to Shirley but, 'Yes, she is, but what a great part she'd be for you!' And Shirley goes, 'You know, you're right!' "

In an era when women's liberation took hold, Booth once remarked: "I think it's wonderful if they want it. But there are an awful lot of women that only do it because it's stylish now."

When the 1960s ended with all said and done, Booth would be best remembered for her television-starring role in *Hazel*. This character similarly gave Booth the fame and adulation that her stage role of Lola in *Come Back, Little Sheba* gave her in the 1950s.

Mrs. Claus' Spirit Till the End
The 1970s – 1990s

Booth's performance in *Three Men on a Horse* mesmerized and entertained one young future star, Dick Van Patten. Born in 1928, Van Patten was seven or eight when he saw Booth on stage. Some seventy years later, he still remembers her performance in that show "as being very funny."

Van Patten would work alongside Booth during the first two seasons of *Duffy's Tavern*. As Wilfred, the kid brother of Finnegan (played by Charlie Cantor), Van Patten played a character that spoke with a better command of language by using bigger words. Amusingly, the younger Wilfred had much more intelligence than older Finnegan.

He recalled how Booth's husband, Ed Gardner, used to treat Shirley coarse, such as yelling at her, and placing her in a subservient position.

He left *Duffy's Tavern* around the time Booth also departed. The one thing he credits Booth for at this time was that she taught him how to play gin rummy backstage. However, their paths would never cross again for almost 30 years.

Finally, Dick Van Patten met up with Booth again in 1970

when he was appearing in a show called *Adaptations Next*. Van Patten played in the Broadway show directed by and starring Elaine May for about a year.

Van Patten went to California to do the show there for about eight weeks. It was then that Booth came backstage to see Van Patten. She told him that she thought he was very good and that he deserved work out on the West Coast. Booth apparently told Van Patten that she would have Richard Wookie, a casting director from 20th Century-Fox, call him.

From that contact, Van Patten played in a series called *Arnie*, the Herschel Bernardi series on Mondays. Because of Booth's referral, Van Patten worked regularly in California from then on, doing some seven series.

In 1970, after a ten-year absence from Broadway, Booth made one more musical, called *Look to the Lilies*. Booth: "Well I've always loved the theater and I've been doing a lot of television lately. I've been doing about 6 years of it although I have sort of interspersed it with summer stock. And so in this way I have managed to keep a feeling for the audience which I think is very important."

During a break in rehearsals one day, Booth told columnist Leo Mishkin: "After all I was born in New York, and I played in New York, and this isn't my first musical, y'know. I did *A Tree Grows in Brooklyn* and *By the Beautiful Sea* and *Juno* long before I went to Hollywood . . . My last appearance here? That was in *A Second City*, just about 10 years ago." Of course, Booth was referring to *A Second String*, and she actually went to Hollywood for her first movie before *By the Beautiful Sea* and *Juno*.

Booth: "I think the pace, the tempo, is faster than when I was last here. Everybody seems so rushed, so busy. And, of course, there are all those new buildings that have gone up - Lincoln Center and along 6th Avenue, and the way they're expanding Rockefeller Center. But there are a lot of my old friends still around, and I'm busy fixing up a place to live, and - well, New York is New York, isn't it?"

Leonard Spigelgass adapted the book *Lilies of the Field* by William E. Barrett. Jule Styne wrote the music and Sammy Cahn the lyrics. A movie version called *Lilies of the Field* starred Sidney Poitier (who won an Oscar for Best Actor) and Lilia Skala in 1963. It tells the story of Homer Smith, a black handyman, who is caught up with a group of German nuns. They tell him that God wants him to build them a chapel in New Mexico.

On Broadway, Al Freeman, Jr. plays the handyman. In the role of Mother Maria, Clive Barnes observed, "Miss Booth, with her German accent you could strain sauerkraut through, is a delight as the totalitarian Mother Superior who is determined that God's way is her way and that He shall have it. There is a great depth and shading to this performance, which is never exaggerated but always sharply and comically expressed." Barnes does criticize the static story, poor staging, shortage of suspense, and the "deplorably frowsy settings." Booth and Freeman, Jr., offered "two very polished and enjoyable performances," observed Barnes.

With Joshua Logan directing, and Jo Mielziner offering lighting and scenic design, *Look to the Liles* previewed 31 times before the premiere opening on March 29, 1970 at the Lunt-Fontanne Theater. With only 25 performances, *Look to the Lilies* closed on April 18, 1970. Five days before the show closed, Booth made an appearance on *The Tonight Show Starring Johnny Carson*.

The summer of 1970 saw Booth return to Westport Country Playhouse for a British domestic comedy called *Best of Friends*, written by James Elward. The supposed death of an author in a plane crash creates problems for his wife and children, especially when it turns out he's alive and planning to marry a much younger woman. The production included Donald Woods, Patrick McVey, and Jennifer Warren.

It seems that Booth's chronic bursitis prevented her from appearing in the 1970 disaster movie *Airport*. Instead, Helen Hayes took the role of the old lady stowaway (and won an Oscar).

Over the years, Booth did turn down many roles for stage, movies and television. Her refusal was not always due to health reasons. For instance, Booth declined the lead role in the live TV drama *Trip to Bountiful* (Horton Foote). Back then in 1953, she said she did not want to play an old lady. She was 55 years old at the time.

In 1973 *TV Guide* revealed: "She refused to appear in the movie version of Nelson Algren's *Walk on the Wild Side*, because she disapproved of the gamy content. Tennessee Williams offered to write a play for her, as a brothel madam. She told him to forget it." Barbara Stanwyck would play the part of the lesbian madam in this 1962 picture.

Booth turned down the opportunity to do *A Pocketful of Miracles*. This 1961 remake would star Bette Davis. Booth allowed Davis to play the part because she felt she could not top May Robson from the original 1933 version, *Lady for a Day*. Frank Capra directed both versions of the Damon Runyon story.

Booth returned to the Broadway stage for the final time in a flawed revival of the Noel Coward comedy *Hay Fever* playing Judith Bliss. Produced by Leonard Sillman, directed by Arvin Brown, *Hay Fever* featured John Williams, Roberta Maxwell, Sam Waterston, and Booth as members of the eccentric Bliss family who ask some guests to spend the weekend with them in their country home only to frighten them with their emotionally-jarring conduct.

Rex Reed, in a review entitled "The Current Broadway - Less

Than Electrifying," blamed the producer and director, but he also observed the miscasting of most of the actors. Reed: "My admiration for Shirley Booth is boundless, but she doesn't have the timing or the attitude for *Hay Fever*. The egotistical loony she is supposed to be playing is there to be laughed at; Miss Booth is there to be loved."

Clive Barnes, in observing that the actors were miscast, said that Booth "plays the role as a series of muffled wisecracks. There is more to Judith than this, and more to acting the role than timing her jokes as if they were eggs." In short, "the whole play had a touch of frenzy more proper to farce than comedy."

Booth told *TV Guide*: "You need a Noel Coward to direct Noel Coward things. It's a meringue. It needs very light handling. We had a couple of very heavy Russian people in it."

There were 16 previews of *Hay Fever* before it opened at the Helen Hayes Theatre on November 9, 1970. The show closed on November 28, 1970 after 24 performances.

Perhaps Arthur Laurents offered an explanation: "She looked like a bargain-shopper, not an actress. I saw her when she came back to New York after *Hazel*. And the truth is that she could not act in the theater anymore. If you stay in television or in movies too long, the acting muscles atrophy."

Booth got involved in stock theatre productions again. She returned to the Cape Playhouse in Dennis, Massachusetts to play *Hay Fever*.

During February of 1971, she had a four-week engagement in *The Vinegar Tree* at the Paper Mill Playhouse, the famed regional theatre in Millburn, New Jersey. The play by Paul Osborn tells of the chaos caused by an empty-headed wife inviting guests to her home for a weekend. *The Vinegar Tree* first played on Broadway in 1930.

2-14-71

Here, Booth played Laura Merrick, opposite Staats Cotsworth, better known for his 1940s radio work, including *Casey Crime Photographer* and *Front Page Farrell*. Previously, Booth had done this show at the Cape Playhouse in the 1950s. She had appeared at least ten times at this playhouse between 1952 and 1972.

Later in 1971 Gig Young joined Booth in the revival of Mary Chase's *Harvey*. The Phoenix Theater offered *Harvey* with Moliére's *School for Wives* in a national tour running from September until Christmas in 1971. Founder and director of the Phoenix Theater organization, T. Edward Hambelton, noted: "We have a double purpose in sending out the two plays. It seemed to us that one of our important functions is to share fine theater with the rest of the country. Also, we hope to supplement the Phoenix income." The company touring offered productions in Central City (Colorado), Pittsburgh, San Francisco, Chicago, Cleveland, Wilmington, New Haven, Boston, Philadelphia, and Baltimore.

At this point Booth lived in the desert. Asked why, Booth replied: "Well I don't choose to live in the desert exclusively. I have a home in Cape Cod. And I stayed there for a year and a half, so I could see all the seasons. I wanted to feel a part of it. And it was not just a stopping place. I wanted to really feel it's my own and I put, oh, two whole seasons. I stayed through the winter."

In order to enjoy her desert home in La Quinta, California, Booth bought nearby land "just to insure quiet." She had a childhood that made her a peculiar person in terms of being introspective. "I'm very self-sufficient. I can be in the desert where I have a home and I have a dog and I have a wall around my home. In the first place, the wall was there because I was afraid of snakes. But I have a wall so ... I have privacy ... I'm a very private person. I enjoy doing things by myself and I don't have to have someone there every minute just so I won't be alone.

"Well I'm not an exuberant person, but I am a happy person. I think I'm one of the few happy people I know. I feel sorry for people that cannot be alone. I feel very sorry for people that cannot find things to do. I can be alone without being lonely.

"Nobody believes it, nobody believes that I can be happy. They think if you're on the stage that you have to have this whatever it is constantly fed, you know it doesn't with me.

"I enjoy refinishing furniture. I enjoy wallpapering. I enjoy needlepoint. I enjoy painting. I even enjoy cleaning out closets. So I'm never lost. I can always find something to do. As a matter of fact I don't know how the days go by."

Booth said she would have changed her nose if she could. "I'd take a pound and a half off each side. No, the point is, what's the use of having a perfect nose unless you have everything else perfect? And to ask for everything perfect is asking too much out of life."

As far as today's youth, Booth wondered, "Youth? Well I must say that some of them frighten the life out of me they know so definitely what they want. And I didn't know it at that age. I think they're the smartest we've had. I just hope they can handle it. I just wish they had a little more security and a little more love."

In regards to children, Booth revealed: "I couldn't have any. And I would have loved to have had them when I could have taken care of them, but now I'd be frightened to death."

It took Booth many years for her career in the theater to really develop. But she had no regrets. "I feel sorry for people for whom success comes too soon, before they've dug knife and fork in and discovered what they're eating, before they've developed an appetite and discovered what they want to do."

When asked about how it felt to be a star, Booth replied: "I just don't live up to it. I'm so average in appearance and I'm too old to get the Salk vaccine. I don't dress up to being a star. I don't entertain much. I don't go to the right places to be seen. I don't even have ulcers. On opening nights I take naps. I like everybody. I like audiences, critics and Hollywood."

Booth's chance for a comeback came in January of 1973. The 74-year-old Booth tried her hand at another television series, *A Touch of Grace*. The show's creator, Ted Bergmann, got the idea from his partner Herman Rush. Both *All in the Family* and *A Touch of Grace* came from British shows brought over by Rush. A British show called *For the Love of Ada*, created by Vince Powell and Harry Driver, inspired this series.

Producers Saul Turtletaub and Bernie Orenstein wrote the pilot to the show. Bergmann visited Booth when she appeared in the August 1972 summer stock production of Dody Goodman's comedy *Mourning in a Funny Hat*, while in Philadelphia. With Booth liking the script, this gave her another chance to work in a regular television series again, after not financially profiting much from the *Hazel* series.

Booth told Penny P. Anderson: "If I had a reason to retire, a husband to be with, I'd retire. Surely." Booth continued: "That's why this time I've hired a lawyer instead of an agent. You know, I was warned before I ever went into *Hazel* about what could happen to me. Ann Sothern, my good friend, is a very smart business woman. She gave me some suggestions and advice, but I decided I couldn't start out distrusting the people I was working with. I felt I would rather keep my disposition than my money. I don't believe you need to be wealthy, anyway. With money, there's always an obligation."

Before *Hazel* came along, Sothern had even offered Booth a TV series, which Booth turned down. Martha Randall recollected that Sothern suggested television to Booth in Chicago back in 1956 when they were on the road with *The Desk Set*.

J. Pat O'Malley and Shirley in *Touch of Grace*.

Anderson gave her impression of Booth: "Disarmingly friendly, open and charming. In some ways, she is very like the placid grey-haired grandma who was so much a part of my own growing up, witty, so wise and earthy she put the flippancy of my youthful friends to shame, so loveable I had to squelch the desire to hug her."

Booth: "I'm an oddity, you know. No one wears hats in Los Angeles - but I've noticed that the men take note of a woman in a hat, THAT's important."

The *TV Guide* promotion for *A Touch of Grace* read as follows: "You'll love Shirley Booth as the lively widow whose modern ideas shock her 'young fogey' family."

In this reversal of the generation gap, Booth played Grace Holliman (Grace Simpson, according to *TV Guide*), an Oakland, California widow with plenty of young ideas. She lives with her stifling daughter Myra (Marian Mercer) & son-in-law Walter (Warren Berlinger). Grace romantically dallies with her gravedigger friend Herbert (J. Pat O'Malley). Booth told *TV Guide*: "Grace is not a swinger. To play her as a swinger would be pandering."

Variety observed: "As characters, Miss Mercer and Berlinger are under-developed to the point of being little more than pivotal gimmicks. Miss Booth and O'Malley with expert performances manage to get a little more comedy out of the vehicle than there really is in the script."

"*A Touch of Grace* plays like run-of-the-tube sitcom with yock console support," concludes *Variety*. "There's little chance this one will be any threat to the ratings of CBS' Saturday night comedy block."

"I've waited a long time for a series to come along like this," Booth told Kay Gardella. It offers "gentle, romantic humor that older people can easily identify with. As you know, it was based on the English series, *For the Love of Ada*, created by Vince Powell and Harry Driver. I'm having the time of my life in it."

By comparison, Hazel "was more aggressive than Grace Holliman. Hazel was a frustrated mother who adopted her employer's family as her own. I'm playing a more gentle woman now. She needs companionship like a lot of people do today, which is the reason for late-blooming romances and marriages.

"Besides, we're living in the dungaree age. Everything is geared to young people. There is no tolerance and understanding of our older citizens. They're written off by the younger generation, who refuse to hold still for them. Unlike Europe, where the older folks are respected and integrated into family life, in America they are cast aside. The pace is so accelerated that young people are always in a hurry to do things. But it's the older people who bring real interest and experience to a project."

As with the *Hazel* series, Booth stayed at the Chateau Montmarte in Hollywood while appearing in the show. Booth: "I lived there when I did *Come Back, Little Sheba* and *Hazel*. It's a wonderful old hotel where a lot of actors and actresses stay, like Faye Dunaway, Keith Michell and Carol Lynley, I like the aura of the place."

With direction by Carl Reiner and Bill Hobin, the show taped twice on Tuesdays at 5:30 p.m. and at 8:00 p.m. before a live studio audience. It is known that Booth reworded some of the scripted lines to include her own malapropisms. Her perfectionism on the television set for *A Touch of Grace* led to one interesting story recounted to Penny P. Anderson. Once a local radio talk show was being used as background. Booth turned it off halfway through the scene. This angered the emcee present for the shooting that day.

Booth: "They wanted me to reshoot the segment, but I refused. Grace would not be listening to that kind of a show. I wanted to set the record straight at the beginning, to get things on the right track from the start. I'm a very strict disciplinarian. When I'm working, I never go out socially, I keep to myself and get plenty of rest. I must concentrate on my work so anything that HAS to be done, must be done on Sunday."

The show debuted midseason on Saturday, January 20, 1973, opposite NBC-TV's showing of Billy Wilder's 1960 Best Picture, *The Apartment*. The syndicated *Creature Features* series broadcasted the 1957 thriller *From Hell It Came* on local stations.

But probably more important is the fact that the show is "on the cusp of CBS' *All in the Family*," explained Booth to Kay Gardella. That is, *A Touch of Grace* competed against the follow-up show to *All in the Family*, that is, a show called *Bridget Loves Bernie*. The common wisdom is that latter benefits by following a successful show like *All in the Family*. It is generally more difficult to expect viewers to change channels and try another show.

"It's a shame," Booth told Gardella, "that in this business when something is good someone comes along and tries to knock it off. It's not enough to enjoy things, like I do *All in the Family*, but you have to be competitive with them."

She told Arnold Hano of *TV Guide*: "I always have high hopes when I go into something. When *Sheba* opened in Boston, the notices were less than we'd hoped for. I went out and bought a mink bolero cape and wore it to rehearsal that afternoon. 'This is what I think of the play,' I said. 'This is my flag I'm running up the mast.' And *Sheba* ran a year and a half on Broadway."

As far as *A Touch of Grace*, Booth explained," I wouldn't be here unless I liked it. It's a wholesome, wonderful show. I see it as an extension of *Hazel*, with the same pungent humor. That's my mission, to make people laugh with me."

Booth claimed that's 25% of why she acts. The other 75%: "I'm stage-struck. It's the closest I can come to playing God."

ABC-TV announced its fall schedule in April of 1973, and they did not schedule *A Touch of Grace*. So, after thirteen episodes (half a season), the final episode, was broadcast on April 21, 1973. This episode, entitled "The Engagement," had Grace accepting Herbert's marriage proposal.

Twelve years old at the time, Kevin Minton called Booth on the phone at her desert home in LaQuinta, California around the time Booth signed to do the ABC-TV series. Minton: "When asked about doing *A Touch of Grace* for ABC, she allowed that she looked forward to doing it and hoped it would keep her occupied for a few years. Asked if she had any film offers currently, her voice changed a bit, and she said, 'I feel no need to play anybody's demented grandmother, and I feel sorry that so many of my contemporaries get the same scripts. It's OK, I guess, if you really need the money, but luckily, I'm not in that position.'"

Booth graced the cover of *TV Guide* for the issue dated May 12 - 18, 1973. When asked by Gardella if she had some inkling for romance like the character she portrayed, Booth responded: "Suitors, I have none. I have no need for that kind of companionship. I'm too busy with what I'm doing. Acting takes up all of my time and energy. People who are not in a demanding profession feel a greater need for romantic companionship, but if your job fulfills you then that frequently is enough.

"Besides, being married twice is enough. It has been my experience that the older you get the more selfish you become, especially in the theatrical profession, where your business becomes your spouse. It takes up so much time and emotion that by necessity you must pander to yourself to conserve your energy. To make a marriage work in this business takes a lot of unselfishness."

"I love to watch TV," Booth told Gardella, "I do it while I brush the hair of my Maltese dog. It's wonderful therapy. As you brush, your nerves iron out. My favorites are documentaries, children's programs and Sunday night mystery movies - *Columbo, McCloud, McMillan & Wife.*"

Booth remarked to *TV Guide*, "People don't get old. They just get more tired-looking. I'd like to be 40 again. That would be a nice age. You've got a little mileage by then, a little tolerance, but you haven't started to sag." Booth was 74 years old, even though the publication reported her age as 65.

Next, Booth offered her voice to play Mrs. Santa Claus in her final project. She sang and told the story of *The Year Without a Santa Claus*, a Rankin-Bass stop-motion puppet special that appeared on ABC on December 10, 1974. Mickey Rooney reprised the voice of Santa Claus, which he did originally in *Santa Claus Is Coming to Town* (1970). The talents included Dick Shawn, George S. Irving, Robert McFadden, Rhoda Mann, Christine Winter, and The Wee Winter Singers.

The Year Without a Santa Claus tells of the year when Santa Claus is sick with a cold. Thanks to the dire advice from Santa's physician that nobody cares anymore about Christmas, Santa Claus decides he will not deliver presents. However, his elves, Jingle Bells and Jangle Bells, think that if they could convince Santa otherwise, he might change his mind.

In order to accomplish this, the elves have to get to Southtown, U.S.A. to find children who care. However, there is Heat Miser and Snow Miser to contend with who have a problem deciding on whether it should snow or not in Southtown. Mrs. Claus intervenes by going to Heat Miser and Snow Miser's mother. By the conclusion, Santa realizes the error of his thinking and decides to deliver presents after all.

This television program could have been more aptly titled, "Almost the Year Without a Santa Claus." There are several songs, including the title track and "I Could Be Santa Claus," both with Booth singing. Rooney sang "I Believe in Santa Claus." The mayor and townspeople offered "It's Gonna Snow in Dixie." The Snow Miser and Heat Miser both provide a song. In addition, the little girl sang "I'll Have a Blue Christmas Without You." The children all joined in the finale with "Here Comes Santa Claus."

In 1974, Bobby Buntrock (Harold Baxter) died in a car crash at the age of 21 years old on the same bridge where his mother was killed a year earlier. He apparently drowned in a creek. Whether Buntrock's mysterious death resulted from suicide could not be determined for sure.

According to a later article in *The Enquirer*, entitled "Whatever Happened to Cast of Hazel?," other cast members of the show were not informed at the time, so they were surprised to learn of this tragedy. Bobby's father: "Bobby's car turned over and he drowned in a creak. It was a freak accident. He was only 21. I was so shook up that I never informed anyone in the cast about Bobby's death."

Julia Benjamin (Susie Baxter) responded to the newspaper informing her. "I'm shocked. I can't believe it. When we were doing the show, we were like brother and sister. I had no idea this had happened."

Health problems would seriously dictate Booth's activity in her final years. *The Enquirer* reported that Booth had been losing her vision due to an incurable condition of degeneration of the retinas. Alone with her two cats named Cash and Carry, Booth indicated she could not sew, read, write, drive, or pursue her hobbies of painting, needlework, or refinishing furniture. Her hearing also failed her. Aging had taken its toll. Martha Randall remembered seeing a photo of Booth and was surprised that it looked nothing like her.

Despite the limitations imposed on her by these conditions, Booth still chose to be happy, cheerful and thankful to be alive. Her aide Eleanor Mutose assisted her. A friend of hers told the tabloid: "She's the most courageous person I've ever met... She's high on life, whatever her handicaps. She doesn't let anyone feel sorry for her."

However, Booth's description to *The Enquirer* reporter seemed poignant: "But I can see TV if I sit up close to it. I can only see the faces, and then if a new character comes in I zoom up real close with a magnifying glass. It is just like trying to see through several chiffon veils."

Lynn Borden told Kevin Minton: "I sent her a card at Christmas every year to tell her the news. Sometimes I wrote her during the year and always at Christmas. I think she got them but her eyes were bad, and I didn't really expect her to write back. I think probably about five years ago was the last time I heard from her [1991]. DeFore kept in touch with her too."

On November 7, 1979, Variety reported a Theatre Hall of Fame reception on November 18 at the Uris Theatre Building in New York to honor 48 theatre people, including Shirley Booth. Drama critics chose the honorees, including theatre producers, writers, directors, and actors. Among those honored with Booth: Tennessee Williams, Jerome Robbins, Ray Bolger, Hume Cronyn, Henry Fonda, Lillian Gish, Laurence Olivier, Ralph Richardson, and Jessica Tandy.

Max Showalter told Kevin Minton he last saw Booth at her Cape Cod home in 1981. "I wrote to her but never received answers, so I resorted to phoning her periodically to keep in touch... I was touring as VanderGelder in *Hello, Dolly* with Carol Channing, and we had a free day while we were in Hyannis. I called Shirley and asked if Patric Quinn (our Cornelius) and I could visit. 'You sure can,' she quickly said. 'Come for lunch, but,' she laughed that Shirley Booth laugh, 'don't be surprised when you see me. I look like a sumo wrestler.' 'I don't give a damn what you look like,' I retorted. 'I just want to see you again, I've missed you.' 'Come ahead,' she answered. 'I'll be waiting.'"

Showalter continued: "When I arrived at a charming unpretentious fenced in New England saltbox, there she was in her rose garden. Her hair was white, and she had gained considerable weight but was still, unmistakably, Shirley Booth. I hugged her and kissed her, and she held my face in her hands. 'I don't see so well anymore,' she said. 'But I certainly see well enough to tell you haven't changed at all. You must have some kind of secret. Now come on in. You're 30 minutes late, but it doesn't matter. We're having a cold lunch anyway.' In spite of time, the Booth energy and vitality still remained.

"After lunch she gave us a tour of the house. 'Here are the three miniature paintings you gave me. I've treasured them all my life. And here is the portrait you painted of me as Hazel, which was given to me at some award ceremony. I didn't think you'd done me justice, so I tried to redo my face a bit.' She laughed and continued, 'Lord knows I should have left it as you painted it. You saw me more beautiful than I ever saw myself.' 'You're happy here, aren't you, Shirley?' I asked. 'Oh yes, I love it here. I have a wonderful woman who looks after me, and I visit with Charles Nelson Reilly and Don DeFore by phone. Now, come outside. I want to show you my roses. I'm so proud of them myself. They're about the only things I can take care of.'

"She thanked us profusely for coming to see her. I kissed her goodbye, and she cut the most beautiful rose she could find and gave it to me. 'Don't ever forget me, dear Max,' she said. 'How could I ever forget you, Shirley?' I assured her she was always a part of me from the time I just met her. We drove away, and there she stood among her roses, waving to us until we turned the bend, and she was no longer in sight. I knew somehow that I'd never see her again, but every month I called her until there was no answer. I had never considered age with Shirley. I had no idea she was 20 years my senior. It was unbelievable. God bless you, dear Shirley. My life was so rich, by knowing, loving, and working with you."

When asked if she believed in God, Booth replied: "Indeed I do. I used to be a choir singer in the Episcopal Church. I was baptized in Trinity Church in New York. And my father was a choir singer when he was a boy, phenomenal voice. For a time I was very much in rebellion because I had to go to church three times on Sunday. And I think children get fed up a little bit and it takes a little while for them to come back to the fold. But I have been religious. I've not always been a dutiful Christian but I've always been a believing Christian."

Booth noted that she did not fear growing old. "No, and as a matter of fact, these people that vainly go around, not vainly because sometimes it's very effective. But the thing is so many people are having their faces lifted and their noses bobbed and a tuck taken here and they think it's great, but then immediately people say, but do you know how old she is? This is defeating themselves. You can't get away from that."

Booth: "Well I have a poem that I found that I liked once. It said, Give me a good digestion, Lord and also something to digest. Give me a healthy body, Lord and the sense to keep it at its best. Give me a healthy mind, Lord, and keep the good and pure in sight. When seeing sin be not appalled, but find a way to set it right. Give me a mind that is not bored, that does not whimper, whine, or sigh. Don't let me worry overmuch about this fussy thing called I. Give me a sense of you, my Lord, give me the grace to see a joke. To find some happiness in life and pass it on to other folks."

Finally, contrary to years of understating her real age, a press report actually added a year to her age. A *New York Times* article, dated August 31, 1984, indicated that Booth celebrated her 87th birthday. Actually, she reached 86 years on August 30, 1984. Thanks to a poison ivy rash she got from gardening, the article reported, "She looked like a leper." However, "her spotty appearance had not affected her spirits or her future digging and weeding plans."

Charles Nelson Reilly, as told to Kevin Minton, remembered his friendship with Booth: "For some reason, Shirley and I hit it off and became great friends. We stayed in touch all through the late Sixties up until her death. In the late Seventies and Eighties and so on, it was mainly by phone. Starting around 1988, she would call, leave a message on my answering machine. 'This is Shirley. Call me. I have a joke to tell you.' And I'd call, and it would go something like this:

Shirley: 'A young girl went to confession and said, 'Father, I've been very bad! I was taken by a man!' 'Against your will?' said the Father. 'No,' she said, 'against the china cabinet. And you should have heard those dishes.'

"The way she would tell it, I'd be on the floor in stitches!"

NBC's 60th Anniversary Special, broadcast on May 27, 1986, offered a clip of Booth as Hazel appearing on the *Dean Martin Show*. Martin: "I believe I first met Shirley at a party in the mid-Fifties. Funny, I don't remember for whom or what the party was for. But there was an odd assortment of characters there. By 'odd,' I mean people not associated together ... Irene Dunne, Donna Reed and Judy Canova did some routine with that Disney kid actor Bobby Driscoll. Shirley had won her Oscar by then for that great film with Lancaster (*Come Back, Little Sheba*). We were introduced by Judy Garland, just mutual exchanges of admiration.

"Years later she guested on my show. A real cute routine in a bar. You know how much time she needed to rehearse? Zero! Which was great for me. I never cared for over rehearsal. So what can I say that really matters, other than in a town like this ... she was a real lady! And anyone in this business long enough knows that says a lot."

In March of 1990, someone sent a letter to *The Globe* asking if Shirley Booth was still alive. The paper's response offered the age discrepancy: "Booth is alive and alert at 83 and spends most of her time on Cape Cod." Of course, Booth had reached 91 years old at the time. *The Globe* mentioned some of her credits, and the column concluded by noting: "Fans who remember Booth can tell her by writing to her at P.O. Box 103, North Chatham, MA 02650."

Charles Nelson Reilly reminisced about Booth's friendship with Julie Harris: "Some time around -- oh, the date escapes me - I was in West Chatham at Julie Harris' home with Leonard Frey. We were rehearsing the play that is the current film with Jonathan Price. 'Carrington' is based on . . . about the bond between the painter Dora Carrington and the Bloomsbury giant Lytton Strachey. Anyway, Shirley lived near Julie, and Miss Harris visited her often. They adored each other. Well, every time I saw Shirley in Massachusetts, we'd have to go to this restaurant. So, after dinner we all went back to Julie's house to rehearse. Shirley got up - mind you, she must have been mid- to late 80s - and improvised this character she used to do years ago. About a lonely charming lady who ends up cleaning an office in a high rise, where years before her husband had committed suicide after the stock market crash in the Great Depression . . . sort of like the character

Carol Burnett used to do. I tell you, Leonard and I sat there utterly charmed, with tears pouring from our eyes. She still had it. She never missed a beat."

Reilly continued: "You see Shirley was never propelled for self-gratification. She never edited herself; she just did it. She had her little cottage, her cats. Her small garden. She had the money to live like a queen, but that wasn't Shirley. Do you remember around 1990 or 1991 when she broke her hip and may have had it replaced? I believe she was in Hyannisport Hospital, and I called. Before the nurse put me through, she said, 'My goodness, you can't keep her down. She's so high-spirited!' Boy, did I know. So I got Shirley on the phone. We talked awhile, and before we hung up, she said to me, 'Charles,' 'Yes?' 'I'm still a hot ticket!' There was magic in that statement, that voice, and I go 'Shirley, you always were and you always will be!'"

Booth spent her final years secluded among the dunes alone at a small single-story Cape Cod cottage in Chatham, Massachusetts, overlooking the Atlantic Ocean. Although Booth once referred to the home as pre-Revolutionary, it actually dated after the Revolutionary War to 1810. She had purchased this saltbox years earlier. It had white shutters, gray shingles, driftwood beams, broad-plank floors, walls covered with picture frames and plenty of fireplaces. Booth had antiques sprinkled throughout her home.

As Booth told *The Saturday Evening Post*: "I'm alone a lot, but I'm never lonely. I find hundreds and millions of things to do. I'm very sorry for people who can't be happy alone. Up here there are lots of widows, and many of them had never in their lives prepared to be alone. They're going to pieces, and it's just too bad. They start to drink, and they go up and lock themselves in their rooms for weeks at a time." Booth, referring to her character of Hazel, observed: "She knows that you build your own prison walls and that people can't confine you if you won't let them."

Over ninety-four years had now passed. Shirley Booth had performed in thousands of shows on stage, entertained countless millions of people via her radio and television shows. Critics adored her. She had won every possible award and honor.

With the exception of her maid Eleanor and pets, Shirley lived alone. She no longer had any audiences to applaud her. Nevertheless, she had plenty of wonderful memories and the spiritual maturity to know that being alone does not necessitate loneliness.

On the scenic coastline of Cape Cod, Marjory Ford, known the world over as Shirley Booth, gave up her last breath on October 16, 1992. She reportedly died of natural causes. One report stated that she died after a brief illness.

Variety's obituary disclosed her true age: "While reference books listed Booth's age as 85, a spokesman at the Nickerson Funeral Home in Orleans, Massachusetts, gave her age as 94." After cremation, her remains were returned to New Jersey where they were buried on December 14, 1992 in Mount Hebron Cemetery in Upper Montclair, New Jersey.

Shirley Booth is interred with her second husband, William H. Baker, Jr., in the Catherine E. Baker lot, Plane Lawn lot #8. In her final resting place, a simple stone reads "Baker."

Thus, some fifteen years ago the last curtain fell on the beloved Shirley Booth. As a dazzling performer and extraordinary human being, she proved how wonderful life can really be! Indeed, love is the reason for it all.

Postscript:

A press report dated November 9, 2000 headlined: "Shirley Booth Wins Hollywood Park Feature." Yes, Booth had a four-year-old Kentucky-bred horse named after her. The horse won the $42,785 feature race at Hollywood Park, beating Radha by 11/2 lengths. The horse had Alex Solis as the rider, and paid $3.60 to win. At that time, the total career earnings reached $85,080.

Booth's Oscar and Emmy Awards were donated to the Cape Playhouse archives in Dennis, Massachusetts, by her sister Jean Coe. Booth had appeared ten times at the Playhouse. A *Special Tribute to Shirley Booth* was held in her honor on August 22, 1993. Gavin MacLeod emceed. Patricia Neal, Elizabeth Wilson, Burt Lancaster, and Julie Harris were among the participants. Messages from her associates were read aloud. The tribute also included a screening of *Come Back, Little Sheba.*

Unfortunately, health problems precluded actress Julie Harris from contributing more than the following statement in 2006: "We were neighbors and best friends for a long time. She was funny, bright, and a lovely person. I loved her very much."

Undoubtedly, everyone loved Shirley Booth so very much!

References

Atkinson, Brooks. *Broadway. Revised edition.* New York: Macmillan Publishing Co., Inc., 1974.

Bordman, Gerald. *The Concise Oxford Companion to American Theatre.* New York: Oxford University Press, 1987.

Botto, Louis. *At This Theatre: 100 Years of Broadway Shows, Stories and Stars.* New York: Applause Theatre & Cinema Books, 2002.

Geisinger, Marion. *Plays, Players & Playwrights: An Illustrated History of the Theatre.* New York: Hart Publishing Company, Inc., Revised ed. 1975.

Kanter, Hal. *So Far, So Funny.* McFarland & Co., 1998.

Lackmann, Ron. *The Encyclopedia of American Radio: An A-Z Guide to Radio from Jack Benny to Howard Stern.* New York: Checkman Books. Updated edition, 2000.

Newspaper and magazine articles, Theater Programs and Related Clippings on Shirley Booth (1925 – 1992). Obtained from the New York Public Library, Shubert Archives, and other sources.

Phone and in person interview with Martha Carson

Phone Interview with Ann Jillian

Phone Interviews with Dick Van Patten

Phone Interviews with Joyce Van Patten

Phone Interviews with Elizabeth Wilson

Credits

The following is a listing of all known appearances of Shirley Booth. There are probably many other appearances, especially regarding stock theater.

Broadway
January 26, 1925 -?   *Hell's Bells*
November 2, 1925 - January 2, 1926   *Laff That Off*
October 7, 1926 -?   *Buy, Buy, Baby*
October 6, 1927 -?   *High Gear*
September 24, 1928 - December 1, 1928   *The War Song*
April 21, 1931 -?   *School for Virtue*
October 2, 1931 -?   *The Camels Are Coming*
November 30, 1931 -?   *Coastwise*
May 8, 1933 -?   *The Mask and the Face*, (also credited as May 6, 1933
1934   *Sunday Nights at Nine*
February 7, 1934 -?   *After Such Pleasure*
January 30, 1935 - January 9, 1937 *Three Men on a Horse*
April 9, 1937 -?   *Excursion*
November 15, 1937 -?   *Too Many Heroes*
March 28, 1939 - March 30, 1940   *The Philadelphia Story*
December 26, 1940 - January 16, 1943   *My Sister Eileen*

April 14, 1943 - June 17, 1944 *Tomorrow, the World*
May 31, 1945 - July 14, 1945 *Hollywood Pinafore*
December 11, 1946 - December 14, 1946 *Land's End*
January 16, 1948 - January 17, 1948 *The Men We Marry*
November 17, 1948 - December 24, 1949 *Goodbye, My Fancy*
November 7, 1949 - November 19, 1949 *Love Me Long*
February 15, 1950 - July 29, 1950 *Come Back, Little Sheba*
April 19, 1951 - December 8, 1951 *A Tree Grows in Brooklyn*
October 15, 1952 - May 30, 1953 *The Time of the Cuckoo*
April 8, 1954 - November 27, 1954 *By the Beautiful Sea*
October 24, 1955 - July 5, 1956 *The Desk Set*
December 26, 1957 - February 8, 1958 *Miss Isobel*
March 9, 1959 - March 21, 1959 *Juno*
April 13, 1960 - May 7, 1960 *A Second String*
March 29, 1970 - April 18, 1970 *Look to the Lilies*
November 9, 1970 - November 28, 1970 *Hay Fever*

Stock Theater

Booth did many hundreds of shows throughout the country. Below are a select few:

1912?	*Mother Carey's Chickens* (Hartford, Connecticut)
1929	*Claire Adams*
1947	*Heartsong*
1959	*The Loss of Roses* (2-week tryout in Washington)
1949	*Come Back, Little Sheba* (Westport Country Playhouse)
1956	*The Late Christopher Bean* (Florida)
1959	*Nina* (Westport Country Playhouse)
1960	*The Late Christopher Bean* (Westport Country Playhouse)
1968	*The Desk Set* (Westport Country Playhouse)
1970	*Best of Friends* (Westport Country Playhouse)

Sept. - Dec. 1971   *Harvey* (Phoenix Theater production, touring from Central, City, Colorado to Pittsburgh)

August 13-19, 1972   *Mourning in a Funny Hat* (Mountainhome, PA)

Films
1952 *Come Back, Little Sheba* (Lola Delaney)
1953 *Main Street to Broadway* (herself)
1954 *About Mrs. Leslie* (Mrs. Vivian Leslie)
1958 *Hot Spell* (Alma Duval) (some list 1957)
1958 *The Matchmaker* (Dolly "Gallagher" Levi) (some list 1959)

Television
Regular Appearances
1961 - 1965   *Hazel* (Hazel Burke) (NBC) 9/28/61 - 3/25/65
1965 - 1966   *Hazel* (Hazel Burke) (CBS) 9/13/65 - 4/11/66
1973   A Touch of Grace (Grace Sherwood) (ABC) 13 episodes 1/20/73 - 4/21/73

Guest Appearances
January 22, 1949	The March of Dimes Benefit Show
August 28, 1949	Celebrity Time (ABC) (herself)
January 1, 1950	Celebrity Time (ABC) (herself)
April 29, 1951	This Is Show Business (CBS) (herself)
December 2, 1951	Celebrity Time (CBS) (herself)
December 19, 1952	The Kate Smith Show
March 19, 1953	25th Annual Academy Awards, (Winner of Best Actress Award)
March 22, 1953	*Toast of the Town (CBS), Ed Sullivan hosting

---
*Not confirmed.

March 25, 1954	26th Annual Academy Awards (Presenter of Best Actor Award)
May 3, 1953	What's My Line (mystery guest), Episode #153
March 16, 1954	**The United States Steel Hour, "Welcome Home" (Jenny)
May 11, 1954	***The Kate Smith Show
November 13, 1955	The Ed Sullivan Show (formerly Toast of the Town prior to 9/25/55) (herself)
March 21, 1957	Playhouse 90, "The Hostess with the Mostes'" (Perle Mesta)
October 11, 1958	The Perry Como Show (herself)
November 30, 1958	The Dinah Shore Chevy Show (NBC) (herself)
February 16, 1960	The Garry Moore Show (CBS) (herself)
[date uncertain] 1961	Here's Hollywood (NBC) (herself)
March 22, 1961	The United States Steel House, "Welcome Home" (Jenny)
April 16, 1961	The 1961 Tony Awards (Presenter)
June 28, 1961	The United States Steel Hour, "The Haven" (Eunice)
October 5, 1961	Art Linkletter's House Party (CBS) (herself)
November 1, 1961	Perry Como's Kraft Music Hall (herself)
January 12, 1962	Here's Hollywood (NBC) (herself)
May 27, 1962	What's My Line (mystery guest), Episode #615

**Note: Conflicting information on this entry. Booth's appearance on this live telecast could not be confirmed. She might have been a last minute replacement. TV Guide listed Helen Hayes as Jenny.
*** Not confirmed.

March 10, 1963	What's My Line (mystery guest), Episode #654
March 15, 1963	The Merv Griffin Show (NBC) (herself)
May 26, 1963	The 15th Annual Emmy Awards (Recipient)
January 10, 1964	The Jack Paar Program (NBC) (herself)
May 25, 1964	The 16th Annual Emmy Awards (also reported as May 24)
November 16, 1964	The Andy Williams Show (herself), Episode #44
December 8, 1966	****CBS Playhouse, "The Glass Menagerie" (Amanda Wingfield)
October 17, 1967	CBS Playhouse: Do Not Go Gentle Into That Good Night (Heloise Michaud)
April 21, 1968	22nd Annual Tony Awards (Presenter)
December 24, 1968	NBC Tuesday Night at the Movies: The Smugglers (Mrs. Hudson)
April 21, 1968	The 1968 Tony Awards - Presenter
November 6, 1969	The Ghost and Mrs. Muir (ABC) "Medium Well-Done" (as spiritualist Madame Tibaldi)
March 12, 1970	The Dean Martin Show (NBC) (herself)
April 13, 1970	The Tonight Show Starring Johnny Carson (herself)
December 10, 1974	The Year Without a Santa Claus (ABC) (Special) (Booth provided voice of Mrs. Claus)
September 13, 1981	33rd Annual Emmy Awards
May 12, 1986	NBC 60th Anniversary Show

****TV Guide does not use CBS Playhouse tag

Discography
Albums
1962   *Dorothy Parker Stories* (Narrator) (Caedmon) ("Lady with a Lamp -12 min. 25 sec., "The Waltz - 8 min., "Cousin Larry" - 8 min. 30 sec., "A Telephone Call" -10 min.)
1968   *Story Hour with Shirley Booth* (Leo the Lion Records)

Cassettes/CDs
1997   *Dorothy Parker Stories* (Narrator) (Caedmon)
?   *This American Life*, "Teen Getaway"

Voice
December 10, 1974   *The Year Without a Santa Claus* (Mrs. Claus) ABC

Awards
-1949 Antoinette Perry (Tony) Award, Best Supporting or Featured Actress, *Goodbye, My Fancy*
-1950 Antoinette Perry (Tony) Award, Best Actress in a Leading Role, *Come Back, Little Sheba*
-1950 New York Drama Critics Award
-1950 The Billboard Donaldson Award for Best Performance by an Actress of 1950 Season - *Come Back, Little Sheba*
-1951 New York Drama Critics Award, Best Actress in a Musical, *A Tree Grows in Brooklyn*
Newspaper Guild Award
-The Billboard Donaldson Awards for Best Performance by an Actress of 1951 Season- *A Tree Grows in Brooklyn*
Received a dozen new honors with film career, including:
- 1952 The Barter Theater Award, *Come Back, Little Sheba*
-1952 The Billboard Award, *Come Back, Little Sheba*

- 1952 New York Film Critics Circle Award, Best Actress *Come Back, Little Sheba* (film)
- 1952 Academy Award Oscar, Best Actress, *Come Back, Little Sheba* (film)
- 1952 Golden Globe Award, Best Dramatic Actress, *Come Back, Little Sheba* (film)
- 1952 National Board of Review Award, Best Foreign Film, *Come Back, Little Sheba* (film)
- 1953 Antoinette Perry (Tony) Award, Best Actress, *The Time of the Cuckoo*
- 1953 Cannes International Film Festival Award, Special Mention, Best Actress, *Come Back, Little Sheba*
- 1954 Best Feminine Performance in a Musical, Variety Drama Critics, *By the Beautiful Sea*
- The Billboard Donaldson Awards for Best Performance by an Actress of Season 1953-54, *By the Beautiful Sea*
- 1956 Sarah Siddons Citation, *The Desk Set*
- 1958 Nominated for New York Film Critics Circle, Best Actress, *Hot Spell*
- 1958 Nominated for New York Film Critics Circle, Best Actress, *The Matchmaker*
- 1961 Emmy, Outstanding Continued Lead Performance in a Series, *Hazel*, presented 5.22.62
- 1962 Emmy, Outstanding Continued Lead Performance in a Series, *Hazel*, presented 5.26.63
- 1963 Nominated for Emmy, *Hazel*
- 1963 Nominated for Golden Globe, *Hazel*

Radio

June 1, 1936 - May 27, 1938 *Betty and Bob*. Sponsored by General Mills. Started off as part of the *Gold Medal Hour*. CBS

August 6, 1936 - September 28, 1939 *The Royal Gelatin Hour* (a.k.a. *The Rudy Vallee Program*). Booth provided female voices for supporting roles for skits in numerous episodes of this series. Exact number of episodes she appeared on remains unknown. She did appear in the December 17, 1936 broadcast which featured the radio premiere of Edgar Bergen and Charlie McCarthy.

October 24, 1937 *The Columbia Workshop*. "I've Got The Tune" Composed by Marc Blitzen. Norman Lloyd was among the cast. CBS.

January 8, 1938 *This is New York*. CBS. With George Jessel, Ted Peckham, and Hiram Sherman.

May 30, 1938 - March 15, 1940 *Betty and Bob*. Sponsored by General Mills. NBC. Series was syndicated after March 15, but Booth was not among the cast for the syndicated series.

Circa 1939 - May 12, 1939 *Guess Where?* Mutual Network. Sponsored by Philip Morris. Stars June Walker and Budd Hulick.

July 1939 *The Goldbergs*. CBS

May 31, 1940 - August 23, 1940 *Strictly Business*. Drama about press agent. Stars Lawson Zerbe and Booth. Blue Network.

March 1, 1941 - June 14, 1941 *Duffy's Tavern*. Booth played the role of Miss Duffy during the entire season.

September 18, 1941 - June 30, 1942 *Duffy's Tavern*. Booth played the role of Miss Duffy during the entire season.

October 1, 1941 - February 25, 1942 *Texaco Star Theater.* Starring Fred Allen. Booth played the recurring character of Dottie Mahoney in a number of broadcasts. Exact number of episodes remains unknown. CBS, Wednesday night.

March 8, 1942 - June 28, 1942 *Texaco Star Theater.* Starring Fred Allen. Booth played the recurring character of Dottie Mahoney in a number of broadcasts. Exact number of episodes remains unknown. CBS, Sunday night.

May 2, 1942 *The Adventures of Ellery Queen.* "The Living Corpse" (East Coast only) Booth was guest armchair detective with Ed Gardner. The West Coast broadcast was on April 30, with two different guests.

October 6, 1942 - June 29, 1943 *Duffy's Tavern.* Booth played the role of Miss Duffy during the entire season.

November 15, 1942 *Radio Reader's Digest.* Shirley Booth appeared in the cast. This half-hour presentation offered two, fifteen-minute dramas. "The Clock Strikes" and "They Called Her Mouse." Sponsored by Campbell Soups. CBS.

December 11, 1942 *The Kate Smith Show.* "The Waltz"

March or April of 1943 *Stage Door Canteen.* Booth appeared in an episode with Yehudi Menuhin.

Transcribed on July 19, 1943 *Treasury Star Parade.* Programs #229 in a series sponsored by the Treasury Department. This syndicated series was broadcast on various days and times across the country. Booth appeared in the cast of "I Am An Army Nurse."

December 13, 1943 *The Cavalcade of America.* "Check Your Heart at Home" NBC

April 30, 1944 *Freedom Never Dies.* Booth appears in a drama entitled "Freedom House," with guest Burgess Meredith and Elsa Maxwell.

May 10, 1944 *Arthur Hopkins Presents.* "The Philadelphia Story" with Katherine Hepburn

July 9, 1944 *The Silver Theater.* "Adventure for Two"

July 23, 1944 *The Silver Theater.* "The Long Engagement"

August 14, 1944 *The Cavalcade of America.* "The Gals They Left Behind" NBC

November 3, 1944 *It Pays to be Ignorant.* Booth is guest on this CBS quiz program/farce.

November 21, 1944 *Theater of Romance.* "Bachelor Mother" CBS

January 25, 1945 *Theater of Romance.* "Ball of Fire" CBS

January 28, 1945 - May 27, 1945 *The Eddie Bracken Show.* Booth played the role of Betty Mahoney. NBC.

Total of 44 shows broadcast between 1945 and 1947 (see season two listed below).

September 17, 1944 - June 10, 1945 *The Kate Smith Show.* Booth appeared in a number of episodes during this season. On February 18, she sang "When Irish Eyes Are Smiling." She also reprised her 'Mahoney' role. In this show she was called 'Dottie Mahoney' in a number of episodes. CBS.

August 7, 1945 *Theater of Romance*. "My Sister Eileen"   CBS. With guest Judy Holliday.

September 9, 1945 *The RCA Show*. "Hamlet"   NBC

October 2, 1945 *The Raleigh Room*. Starring Stu Erwin. Booth and Erwin do a spoof of *To Have and Have Not*.

November 25, 1945 *The Fred Allen Show*

November 25, 1945 *Theater Guild on the Air*. "Mornings at Seven" with Aline MacMahon and Frank Lovejoy.

December 9, 1945 *Theater Guild on the Air*. "Ned McCobb's Daughter" with Alfred Lunt.

December 14, 1945 *Pabst Blue Ribbon Town* Starring Danny Kaye. CBS

circa 1946 *The Adventures of the Red-Feathered Man*. Sponsored by Community Chests, this short-run series of 13 episodes was syndicated across the country from 1946 to 1947.

July 4, 1946 - September 26, 1946 *The Vaughn Monroe Show*. Booth reprised her "Dottie Mahoney" character in a number of broadcasts.

January 6, 1946 *Theater Guild on the Air*. "Three Men on a Horse" with Stu Erwin and Sam Levene. This episode originated from the Vanderbilt Theater in New York.

January 18, 1946 *Pabst Blue Ribbon Town*. Starring Danny Kaye. CBS

February 16, 1946 *Celebrity Club*. With Art Carney, Jackie Kelk and John Daly.   CBS

September 29, 1946 - March 23, 1947 *The Eddie Bracken Show.* Booth played the role of Betty Mahoney. CBS

Total of 44 shows broadcast between 1945 and 1947 (see season one listed below).

December 29, 1946 *Theater Guild On The Air.* "Broadway" with James Dunn.

circa 1947 - ??? *Here's to Veterans.* Sponsored by the Veterans Administration, starring Vaughn Monroe, this series ran over 1,500 episodes and was broadcast at various days and times. Booth appeared in a number of episodes beginning in late 1947 through 1948.

January 6, 1947 *The Cavalcade of America.* "The Woman on Line Rock" Booth played the lead of Ida Lewis with guest Les Tremayne.

February 9, 1947 *The Fred Allen Show.* Sponsored by Tenderleaf Tea. NBC

May 8, 1947 *Radio Reader's Digest.* "Uncle By's Two Wives" with guests Everett Sloane and Karl Swenson

June 1, 1947 *Theater Guild On The Air.* "Three Men on a Horse" with David Wayne and Sam Levene.

October 5, 1947 - December 28, 1947 *The Fred Allen Show.* Sponsored by Tenderleaf Tea. NBC. Booth appeared in a number of episodes during this time.

October 23, 1947 *Radio Reader's Digest.* "The Bradlock Chest" CBS

January 4, 1948 - June 27, 1948 *The Fred Allen Show*. Sponsored by Ford Motors. NBC. Booth appeared in a number of episodes during this time.

February 26, 1948 *Radio Reader's Digest*. "The Woman Detective and the Stolen Jewels" CBS

Recorded April 9, 1948 *Our Miss Brooks*. Audition recording, not broadcast on radio. Booth was intended to play Miss Connie Brooks, but while the audition was successful, Booth was not. Eve Arden got the role.

April 12, 1948 *The Cavalcade of America*. "The Man Who Took the Freedom Train" with Eddie Albert. NBC

June 13, 1948 *The Ford Theatre*. "My Sister Eileen" with guests Ted de Corsia and Arthur Q. Bryan.

October 3, 1948 - June 26, 1949 *The Fred Allen Show*. Sponsored by Ford Motors. NBC. Booth appeared in a number of episodes during this time.

April 21, 1949 *Theater Guild On The Air*. "Hamlet"

June 21, 1949 - September 14, 1949 *Hogan's Daughter*. Booth stars in this short-run summer series. NBC

October 29, 1949 *Kate Smith Calls*. ABC Network. Short-run series starring Kate Smith.

December 11, 1949 *The Theatre Guild on the Air* (a.k.a. *The U.S. Steel Hour*). "Street Scene" with Karl Malden and Thelma Ritter CBS

March 26, 1950 *The Theatre Guild on the Air* (a.k.a. *The U.S. Steel Hour*). "The Milky Way" with Danny Kaye

February 4, 1951 *The Theatre Guild on the Air* *(a.k.a. The U.S. Steel Hour)*. "Come Back, Little Sheba" with Gary Cooper

May 20, 1951 *The Theatre Guild on the Air* *(a.k.a. The U.S. Steel Hour)*. "Ethan Frome" with Raymond Massey

October 2, 1953 *Stage Struck*. "Behind the Scenes of Broadway" Host: Mike Wallace. CBS.

April 12, 1953 *The Theatre Guild on the Air* *(a.k.a. The U.S. Steel Hour)*. "The Glass Menagerie"

January 1, 1954 *Stage Struck*. "The Theatrical Highlights of 1953" with Basil Rathbone and Burgess Meredith. CBS

February 14, 1954 *My Most Unforgettable Child.* United Nations Radio Syndication with Bing Crosby, Kirk Douglas and Audrey Hepburn.

March 16, 1954 *The Theatre Guild on the Air* *(a.k.a. The U.S. Steel Hour)*. "Welcome Home"

April 4, 1954 *Stage Struck*. "The Story of Spring On Broadway" with Danny Kaye and Agnes Moorehead.

May 2, 1954 *Stage Struck*. "The Theatrical Highlights of the 1953-54 Season" with Ezio Pinza and Claude Rains.

May 15, 1954 *Salute to Eugene O'Neill*. With Helen Hayes, Roddy McDowall and Karl Malden.

November 14, 1965 *The Chase and Sanborn 101st Anniversary Show.* With Oscar Levant, Fred Allen and Milton Berle.

Booth appears by recordings of previously-broadcast Fred Allen programs.

October 7, 1973 *Same Time, Same Station.* "A Tribute to Fred Allen, Part 3" Rebroadcast of The Chase and Sanborn 101st Anniversary Show above.

QUOTES
Some of the quotes attributed to Booth include the following found at www.creativequotations.com:

In *The Matchmaker*, Booth's character says, "Life's never quite interesting enough, somehow. You people who come to the movies know that."

"There is an audience for every play; it's just that sometimes it can't wait long enough to find it."

"Why is it that men who can go through severe accidents, air raids, and any other major crisis always seems to think that they are at death's door when they have a simple head cold?"

"I much prefer being a man. Women have to spend so much time pulling themselves together, and their shoes kill your feet."

Hazel Episode Guide
First Season
These episodes are currently available on DVD from Sony Entertainment. All are in black and white, except for episode number 6.

NBC Thursdays 9:30 p.m.

1. Hazel and the Playground
2. Hazel Makes a Will
3. Hazel Plays Nurse

4. A Matter of Principle
5. Dorothy's New Client
6. What'll We Watch Tonight? (Color)
7. A Dog for Harold
8. George's Niece
9. Everybody's Thankful But Us Turkeys
10. Winter Wonderland
11. Hazel's Winning Personality
12. Hazel's Christmas Shopping
13. Dorothy's Obsession
14. Hazel's Dog Days
15. A Replacement for Phoebe
16. Hazel's Famous Recipes
17. Hazel's Tough Customer
18. Hazel's Secret Wish
19. Hazel, The Tryst-Buster
20. The Investment Club
21. Hazel's Mona Lisa Grin
22. Hazel and The Gardener
23. Dorothy's Birthday
24. Number, Please
25. Them New Neighbors Is Nice
26. Hazel's Pajama Party
27. Three Little Cubs
28. Bringing Out the Johnsons
29. Hazel Quits
30. Hazel the Matchmaker
31. Rock-A-Bye Baby
32. The Burglar in Mr. B's PJ's
33. Heat Wave
34. George's Assistant

35. Hazel's Day

Second Season
Starting with this season on all episodes are in color.
NBC Thursdays 9:30 p.m.

36. Hazel's Cousin
37. Rosie's Contract
38. We've Been So Happy Till Now
39. How to Lure an Epicure
40. Barney Hatfield, Where Are You?
41. A Four-Bit Word to Chew On
42. Hazel's Tax Deduction
43. Mr. B on the Beach
44. License to Wed
45. Genie With the Light Brown Lamp
46. The Natural Athlete
47. New Man in Town
48. Herbert for Hire
49. Hazel and The Lovebirds
50. Top Secret
51. The Sunshine Girls Quartette
52. A Good Example for Harold
53. Hazel's Highland Fling
54. Ain't Walter Nice?
55. Mr. Griffin Throws a Wedding
56. Hazel and the Stockholder's Meeting
57. Hazel's Day Off
58. I've Been Singing All My Life
59. The Fire's Never Dead While the Ashes Are Red
60. Hazel's Navy Blue Tugboats

61. The Hazel Walk
62. Hazel Digs a Hole for Herself
63. Hazel Sounds Her "A"
64. Hazel's Luck
65. Oh, My Aching Back
66. Maid of the Month
67. So Long, Brown Eyes

Third Season
NBC Thursdays 9:30 p.m.

68. Pot Luck a La Mode
69. An Example for Hazel
70. Dorothy Takes a Trip
71. You Ain't Fully Dressed Without a Smile
72. Cheering Up Mr. B
73. Piccolo Mondo
74. Hazel Scores a Touchdown
75. George's 32ND Cousin
76. The Baby Came C.O.D.
77. All Hazel is Divided into Three Parts
78. The Vanishing Hero
79. Call Me Harve
80. The Retiring Milkman
81. Hazel's Nest Egg
82. Hazel and the Halfback
83. Hazel and the Model "T"
84. Hot Potato a La Hazel
85. Scheherazade and Her Frying Pan, Part 1
86. Scheherazade and Her Frying Pan, Part 2
87. The Fashion Show

88. George's Ordeal
89. The Reluctant Witness
90. Democracy at Work
91. The Countess
92. Hazel's Midas Touch
93. Everybody's a Comedian
94. All Mixed Up
95. Arrivederci, Mr. B
96. Such a Nice Little Man
97. Campaign Manager
98. Let's Get Away From It All
99. Maid for a Day

Fourth Season
NBC Thursdays 9:30 p.m.

100. Never Trouble Trouble
101. Luncheon with the Governor
102. Ain't That a Knee Slapper?
103. The Marriage Trap
104. The Flagpole
105. Welcome Back, Kevin
106. Mind Your Own Business
107. High Finance Hits a New Low
108. Just Me, Harold and the Universe
109. Mix-Up On Marshall Road
110. Lesson in Diplomacy
111. To Build Or Not to Build
112. Hazel Squares the Triangle
113. Better to Have Loved and Lost
114. Just 86 Shopping Minutes to Christmas

115. Champagne Tony
116. It's a Dog's Life
117. Love 'Em and Leave 'Em
118. Temper! Temper!
119. Bonnie Boy
120. Stop Rocking Our Reception
121. What's Bugging Hazel?
122. Hazel's Day in Court
123. Hazel's Inquisitive Mind
124. George's Man Friday
125. The Investor

Fifth Season
CBS Mondays 9:30 p.m.

126. Who's in Charge Here?
127. Hazel's Second Week
128. How to Lose 30 Pounds in 30 Minutes
129. Do Not Disturb Occupants
130. The Hold Out
131. A-Haunting We Will Go
132. Hazel Needs a Car
133. Hazel Sits It Out
134. A "Lot" To Remember
135. A Bull's-eye for Cupid
136. The Crush
137. Kindly Advise
138. Noblesse Oblige
139. Hazel's Enduring Young Charms
140. A Car Named Chrysanthemum
141. Once an Actor

142. $285 By Saturday
143. Boom Or Bust!
144. Harold's Gift Horses
145. How to Find Work Without Really Trying
146. My Son, The Sheepdog
147. Please Don't Shout
148. But Is It Art?
149. Who Can Afford a Bargain
150. Hazel's Free Enterprise
151. Bee in Her Bonnet
152. The Perfect Boss
153. A Little Bit of Genius
154. A Question of Ethics

Copy of birth certificate of SHIRLEY BOOTH,
born MARJORY FORD, August 30th, 1898

(donated by Warren G. Harris)

Index

A

About Mrs. Leslie, 35, 119-127, 134
Abbott, George, 18, 38, 40, 91, 93, 94
Ackerman, Harry, 9, 183, 192
Adventures of Ellery Queen, The, 57
After Such Pleasures, 38
Allen, Fred, 57, 67, 70
Andy Williams Show, The, 218
Arthur Hopkins Presents, 65

B

Bachelor Mother, 66-67
Baker, Jr., Corporal William Hogg (Shirley's 2nd husband Bill), 58, 59, 60, 95, 144, 148, 149, 243
Ball, Lucille, 174, 192
Ball of Fire, 67
Benchley, Robert, 38, 40
Benjamin, Julia, 194, 199, 236
Best of Friends, 223
Birth Certificate, 27, 268
Blackmer, Sidney, 83, 87, 88, 100
Blake, Whitney, 9, 191, 193, 208
Bogart, Humphrey, 32, 37, 127, 142
Booth, Shirley & Various Topics:
    On Acting, 19, 20, 29, 30, 60, 61, 87, 90, 117-118, 135-136, 159-160, 233, 234

On Audiences, 63
On Average Woman Appeal, 21
On Aversion to Alcohol, 59
On Being Alone, 116, 206, 217, 228, 242, 243
On Being a 'Reluctant Star', 113
On Being a Star, 228-229
On Being Happy & Sad, 68-69, 204, 228
On Belief in God, 239-240
On Black & White vs. Color, 156
On Building Prison Walls, 243
On Burglary of Mink Coat, 47
On Camera and Movie Acting, 104, 151
On Car Accident, 168
On Cats, 236
On Children and Youth, 24, 228
On Comedy, 53, 142
On Confusing Personality with Character, 63
On Criticism of Doing TV, 189
On Divorce, 58, 99
On Dogs, 40-41, 60, 117, 145-146, 234-235
On Drinking, 242
On Easing Other People's Pain, 136, 205

On Failure, 21
On Fan Appreciation, 88, 207, 209
On Farming, 59, 95
On Growing Old, 239
On Having A Perfect Nose, 228
On *Hazel*'s Characterization, 181-182, 203-204, 205, 207, 209
On *Hazel* Series, Problems with, 187-189, 209-210
On *Hazel* Series, Shooting, 175, 204
On Hazel Transparency with Booth, 206, 209
On Hazel's Wardrobe, 203
On Health Problems, 85, 200-201, 224, 236-237, 242
On Her First Public Performance, 22
On Her Lawsuit
  212-213
On Her Own Character Traits, 18
On Hollywood, 47, 60, 99, 104, 113-114, 119, 126-127, 175
On Homes
  New England Cottage, (Cape Cod, MA), 148, 157, 189, 190, 203, 227, 238, 240, 241, 242, 243
  Flatbush Apt. (Brooklyn, NY), 22
  Dairy Farm (Bucks County, PA), 59, 95
  Desert Home (La Quinta, CA), 227
  Germantown, PA House, 113
  Philadelphia, PA hotel, 22, 24
  New York City apts., 47, 58, 116-117, 148, 171, 201, 203
  E. 61st townhouse, 58
  5th Avenue & 54th St., 116-117, 201
  Osborne (305 W. 57th St.), 171
On How Miss Duffy Voice Developed, 54
On Housework, 136, 190, 212, 220, 228
On Hurts, 205
On Husband Bill Baker, 17, 58, 95, 144, 149, 204, 205
On Husband Ed Gardner, 35, 43, 50, 51, 56, 57, 58, 99
On Interior Design/Redecorating, 24, 58, 117, 217, 228

On Jewels and Possessions, 21
On Laughter, 85
On Losing Temper & Clowning, 206
On Marriage, 51, 57, 217, 234
On Minimalist Approach to Acting, 90
On Money, 64
On Movie Acting vs. Stage Acting, 100, 135-136, 159-160
On Movies, 100
On Name Change, 26-27
On Nervous Breakdown, 58
On Never Being Nervous At Openings, 48-49, 229
On Never Having Stage Fright, 61
On New York, 222-223
On Not Being Stagestruck, 135-136
On Noel Coward, 225
On Old People, 232, 235
On Painting, 59-60, 116, 228
On Perfectionism in *A Touch Of Grace*, 232
On Privacy, 227
On Quitting School, 25, 27
On Quoting Lionel Barrymore, 214
On Quoting Oscar Wilde, 74
On Retiring, 212
On Selecting A Role, 60-61, 148
On Situation Comedy, 209
On Stock Theater, 41
On Success, 135, 228
On Theater- Feeling for Audience, 222
On *Touch of Grace* vs. *Hazel*, 232
On Wardrobe, 130
On Watching Television, 116, 136, 234-235
On Wearing Hats, 231
On Winning Academy Award, 111, 113-114, 135
On Work, 104, 205, 233
Winning Speech, Academy Award, 112
Winning Speech, 2nd Emmy, 192
Borden, Lynn, 193-197, 237
Broadway, 71

Buntrock, Bobby, 191, 194, 236
Burnett, Carol, 242
By the Beautiful Sea, 19, 22, 90, 128-135, 164, 222
Buy, Buy Baby, 33

C

Cahn, Sammy, 223
Camels Are Coming, The, 35-36
Cantor, Charley, 45, 221
Carney, Art, 71, 185, 218-219
Carson, Wayne, 144-146
Cass, Peggy, 88-89
Cat and the Canary, The, 29, 38
Cavalcade of America, The, 65-66, 75
Celebrity Club, 71
Champion, Gower, 168-169
Chantler, Peggy, 9
Claire Adams, 35
Coastwise, 36-37
Columbia Workshop, The, 56
*Come Back, Little Sh*eba (film), 6, 12, 99-105, 109, 111, 114, 115, 119, 130, 135, 148, 171, 174, 189, 195, 232, 241, 244
Come Back, Little Sheba (play), 6, 18, 78, 81, 83-90, 127, 130, 137, 161, 171, 174, 189, 220, 233
Come Back, Little Sheba (radio), 88
Cooper, Gary, 67, 103, 111
Cotsworth, Staats, 227
Coward, Noel, 224, 225
Cowley, Bill, 9
Crawford, Joan, 110, 112, 127
Crosby, Bing, 46, 127, 128
Curtis, Billy, 42

D

Davis, Bette, 104, 110, 112, 113, 224
Dean Martin Show, The, 240
Death Takes A Holiday, 37
DeCamp, Rosemary, 199
DeFore, Don, 8, 188, 190-191, 192, 193, 199, 207-208, 237, 238

Dennis the Menace, 191, 201
Desk Set, The, 137-145, 148, 164, 167, 219, 229
Dick Van Dyke Show, The, 192, 218
Do Not Go Gentle Into That Good Night, 217-218
Dorfman, Nat, 25, 27, 52
Dorothy Parker Stories, 171
Dottie Mahoney character, 67, 68, 70
Douglas, Melvyn, 162, 217
Dozier, Bill, 6, 7, 183, 184-185, 187, 192
Duffy's Tavern, 19, 44, 45, 50, 53-56, 63, 64, 175, 221

E

Eddie Bracken Show, The, 67
Ethan Frome, 88
Excursion, 42, 76

F

Ferber, Edna, 115, 116
Field, Sylvia, 201
Fields, Dorothy, 93, 98, 131
Fields, W.C., 198
Fonda, James, 9, 207
Ford, Albert James (Shirley's Father), 17, 22, 23, 25, 26
Ford, Jean Valentine, aka Jean F. Coe, (Shirley's Sister), 23, 24, 244
Ford, Marjory (Shirley Booth's Original Name), 21-22, 26, 27, 243
Ford Theater, 75, 88
Fred Allen Show, The, 70
Fulmer, Ray, 193-194, 196, 219

G

Gardner, Ed (Shirley's 1st Husband), 35, 36, 38, 43, 44, 45, 50, 51, 54, 56, 57-58, 65, 99, 221
Garland, Judy, 174, 241
Ghost and Mrs. Muir, The, 220
Glass Menagerie, The, 115, 213-217
Goldbergs, The, 56, 57

Goodbye, My Fancy, 75-78, 79, 81, 89, 115
Guess Where?, 45

H

Hallmark Reader's Digest Radio, 57, 73-75
Hamlet, 70, 71
Harris, Julie, 14, 112, 241, 244
Harvey, 227
Hazel, 2, 5-6, 7, 10, 11, 12, 17, 19, 21, 172-212, 220, 225, 229, 232, 233, 240, 242
Hay Fever, 224-225
Heartsong, 72, 105, 138
Heckart, Eileen, 149
Hell's Bells, 31-32, 46
Hepburn, Audrey, 127
Hepburn, Katherine, 45-46, 107, 109
Here's To Veterans, 71
High Gear, 33-34
Hildegarde's Radio Room, 70
Hogan's Daughter, 78-79
Holbrook, Hal, 213, 216
Holden, William, 127, 129
Hollywood Pinafore, 69-70, 76, 90
Hostess with the Mostes', 146-148
Hot Spell, 148-149, 160

I

It Pays To Be Ignorant, 66
Inge, William, 83, 163, 164

J

Jessel, George, 34
Jillian, Ann, 14, 199-200
Juno, 91, 160, 162-163, 164, 217. 222

K

Kanin, Garson, 41, 42, 169
Kanter, Hal, 35, 118, 121
Kate Smith Show, The, 68
Kaufman, George S., 49, 68
Kaye, Danny, 88, 127, 131

Key, Ted, 5, 14, 176, 178-185, 187, 190, 191, 193, 198, 204, 205, 208, 210, 211, 212
Kollmar, Richard, 73-74

L

La La Lucille, 28
Laff That Off, 32-33, 38
Lancaster, Burt, 101, 103-104, 129, 174, 241, 244
Land's End, 71-72
Late Christopher Bean, The, 167-168
Laurents, Arthur, 72, 105, 107, 225
Lion and the Mouse, The, 26
Little Old New York, 28
Lloyd, Norman, 219
Look to the Lilies, 91, 222-223
Loss of Roses, A, 163-164
"Love Is the Reason For It All" (song), 18, 98
Love Me Long, 79-81
Lux Toilet Soap, 39
Lynley, Carol, 219, 232

M

MacFarlane, Louella, 179
MacLaine, Shirley, 149, 150, 151
McCaffrey, Bill, 6, 7, 185, 187
Main Street to Broadway, 118-119
Marshall, Penny, 210-211
Martin, Dean, 240-241
Mask and the Face, The, 37-38
Matchmaker, The, 148, 150-156, 160, 261
Maugham, W. Somerset, 37
May, Elaine, 222
Men We Marry, The, 74
Mercer, Mabel, 144
Milan, Frank, 140, 141-142, 144, 146
Minton, Kevin, 13-14, 24, 49, 59, 85, 89, 93, 95, 103, 143, 149, 174, 191, 195, 198, 199, 201, 220, 234, 237, 240
Miss Isobel, 157-159, 164
Monroe, Marilyn, 10, 160, 210
Mother Carey's Chickens, 28

Index

Mourning in a Funny Hat, 229
My Most Unforgettable Child, 128
My Sister Eileen, 6, 47-50, 52, 54, 59, 64, 70, 73, 75, 76, 91, 93, 102, 137, 175

N

NBC 60th Anniversary Special, 240
Nina, 160
North, Jay, 191

O

Our Miss Brooks, 75
Outward Bound, 127
O'Malley, J. Pat, 230, 231

P

Parker, Dorothy, 38, 49, 199
Patterns, 140
Perkins, Anthony, 151
Perle Mesta, 146, 147, 148
Perry Como Show, The, 218
Philadelphia Story, The, 45-46, 56, 65, 73, 76, 138, 175
Pitter Patter, 25
Poli's Stock Theater Company, Sylvester, 24-25, 27, 28
Praise House, 65
Private Lives, 79

Q

Quinn, Anthony, 148-149

R

Radio Reader's Digest, 57, 73-75
Raleigh Room, The, 70
Randall, Martha, 14, 144-145, 171, 201, 229, 236
RCA Show, The, 70
Reilly, Charles Nelson, 89, 220, 240, 241, 242
Reiner, Carl, 232

Ritter, Thelma, 10, 210
Rooney, Mickey, 235
Royal Gelatin Hour, 56
Russell, Bill, 9, 191, 192, 197, 201, 204
Russell, Rosalind, 52, 77
Ryan, Robert, 119-121

S

Sarnoff, David, 187
Scandal, 28
School for Virtue, 35
Schwartz, Arthur, 93, 98, 131
Second String, A, 164-165, 222
Showalter, Max, 49-51, 59, 91-92, 93, 237-239
Silver Theater, The, 65
Smith, Betty, 91, 93, 94
Smith, Kate, 68
Smugglers, The, 219
Sothern, Ann, 229
Stage Struck, 130-131
Stagedoor Canteen, 59
Stagedoor Canteen (radio show), 57
Stanwyck, Barbara, 67, 103, 127, 224
Street Scene, 71
Styne, Jule, 223
Sunday Nights At Nine, 38

T

Texaco Star Theater, 57
Theater Guild On The Air, 70-71, 77, 88, 115
Theater of Romance, 66, 67, 70
This Is New York, 43
Three Men On A Horse, 39-41, 42, 56, 64, 71, 76, 175, 221
Time of the Cuckoo, The, 6, 105-107, 112, 115, 116, 137, 138, 158, 165
To Have And To Have Not, 70
Tommy Dorsey Show, The, 70
Tomorrow, the World, 61-65, 73, 76, 140
Tonite Show Starring Johnny Carson, The, 223
Torch Bearers, The, 217

Touch of Grace, A, 229-234
Too Many Heroes, 42-43
Treasury Star Parade, 65
Tree Grows in Brooklyn, A, 12, 90-99, 105, 117, 129, 131, 218, 222
Tristan and Isolde, 71, 72

U
United States Steel Hour, The, 88, 169, 171

V
Van Heflin, 45, 46
Van Patten, Dick, 14, 221-222
Van Patten, Joyce, 14, 62-63, 140, 141
Vaughn Monroe Show, The, 71

Vinegar Tree, The, 137, 225-227

W
War Song, The, 34
Welcome Home, 169, 171
What's My Line, 218
Wilder, Thornton, 148, 151
Williams, Tennessee, 115, 213, 224
Wilson, Elizabeth, 14, 140-143, 169, 244
Wright, Virginia (Shirley's mother), 22, 28, 29

Y
Year Without A Santa Claus, The, 235-236

www.ingramcontent.com/pod-product-compliance
Lightning Source LLC
Chambersburg PA
CBHW021805220426
43662CB00006B/191